IMAGES
of America

NAHANT REVISITED

I0805758

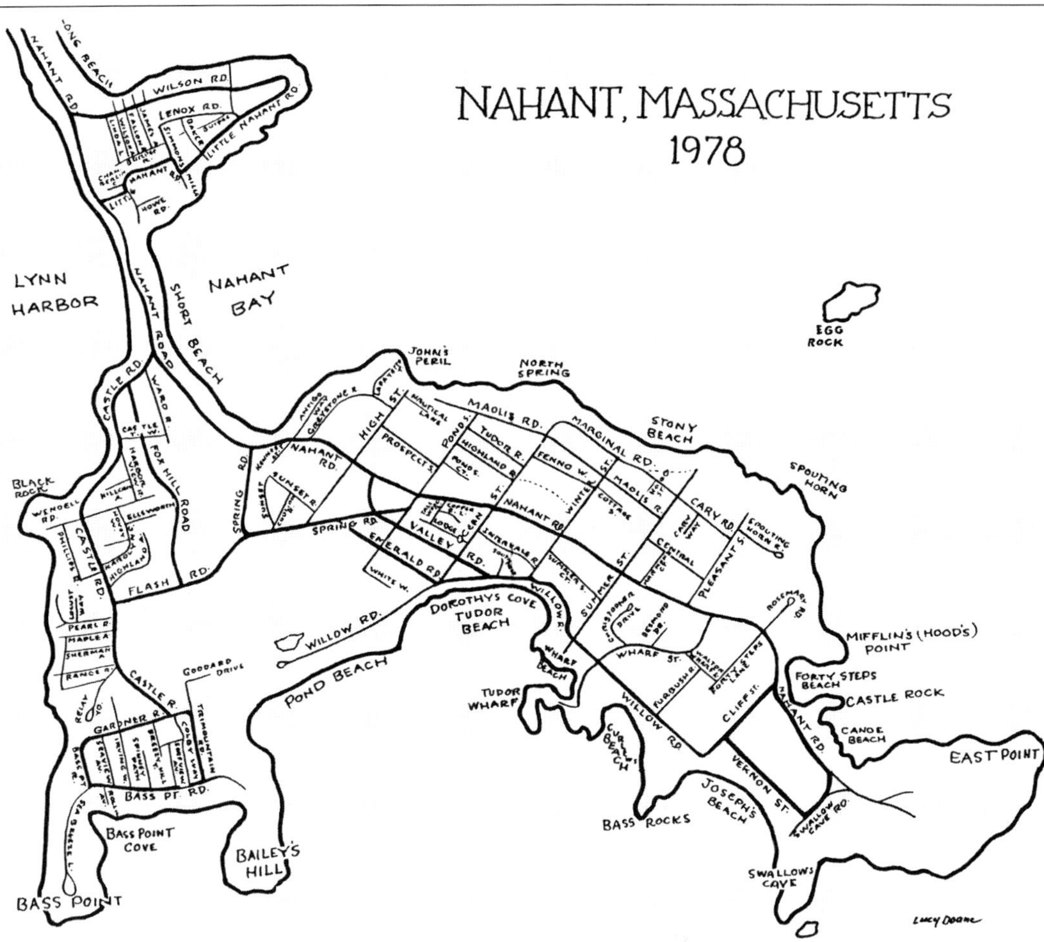

This very simple drawing of Nahant was done by artist Lucy Doane, who grew up in Nahant. After graduating from Teachers College, Columbia University, she taught art in New Hampshire and Vermont, and she returned home to Nahant in retirement. Doane was known for illustrating children's books, and later her paintings were widely shown in New England and New York. (Courtesy Nahant Historical Society.)

On the Cover: On July 4, 1897, a Nahant Dory Club regatta was held in Nahant. Seen here tied up to the float at Tudor Wharf are the sailing dories of the Swampscott and Nahant fleets with their crews. Some of the identified Nahanters are Samuel Covell, Winthrop T. Hodges, Lothrop Motley, and Arthur Johnson. In the left background is the Tudor Hotel on Willow Road. (Courtesy Nahant Historical Society.)

IMAGES
of America

NAHANT REVISITED

Christopher R. Mathias
and Robert A. Wilson

ARCADIA
PUBLISHING

ISBN 978-1-4671-0791-4

Published by Arcadia Publishing
Charleston, South Carolina

Printed in the United States of America

Library of Congress Control Number: 2021946496

For all general information, please contact Arcadia Publishing:
Telephone 843-853-2070
Fax 843-853-0044
E-mail sales@arcadiapublishing.com
For customer service and orders:
Toll-Free 1-888-313-2665

Visit us on the Internet at www.arcadiapublishing.com

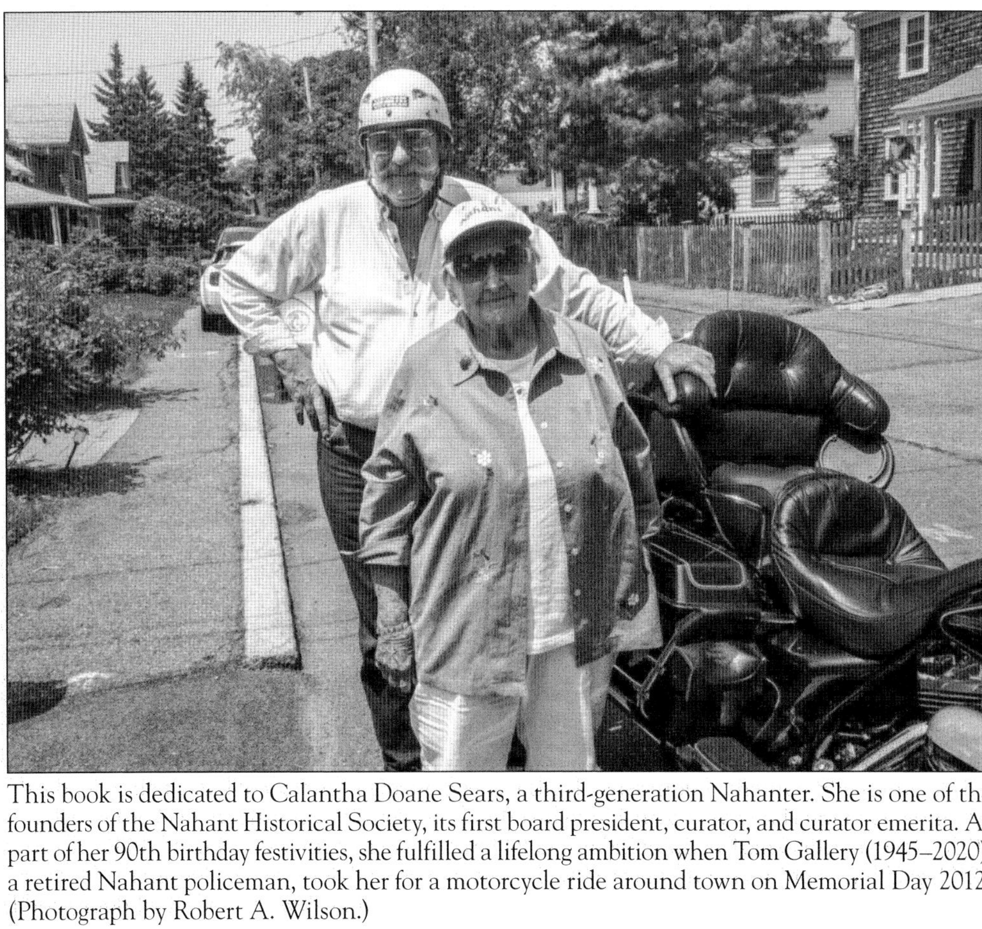

This book is dedicated to Calantha Doane Sears, a third-generation Nahanter. She is one of the founders of the Nahant Historical Society, its first board president, curator, and curator emerita. As part of her 90th birthday festivities, she fulfilled a lifelong ambition when Tom Gallery (1945–2020), a retired Nahant policeman, took her for a motorcycle ride around town on Memorial Day 2012. (Photograph by Robert A. Wilson.)

Contents

ACKNOWLEDGMENTS

The authors are deeply indebted to the Nahant Historical Society and its board of directors for permission to mine the collection for images and information relating to the history of Nahant. Julie Tarmy, executive director of the society, has been invaluable in finding relevant materials, giving access to the collections, and being our frontline editor. Calantha Sears, curator emerita, was absolutely essential to correcting mistakes and suggesting connections between images and people. Her deep personal history with Nahant and interest in sharing it is a great gift to this smallest town in Massachusetts. Suzanne Hamill is a wonderful editor of our sometimes rough manuscript who gave it the final polish. Great thanks to James Shea, former director of the Longfellow House, who gave important advise and editing for the "Longfellow in Nahant" chapter. Ken Turino gave great support, encouragement, advice, and the initial push to get this project started.

The basis for this book is the annual pictorial calendars that the society has produced over many years. Thanks are due to all those who helped assemble these. The realization that not everyone uses wall calendars now sparked the idea to share these images with a new audience in a familiar book format.

Thanks are also due to Lorna Condon, senior curator of the Historic New England Library and Archives, for use of several images. Sam Hammond Duncan generously donated the Hammond family albums to the society and provided further information about images. Abe Garfield generously gave permission to use images from the Fay/Garfield family collection.

Unless otherwise noted, all images appear courtesy of the Nahant Historical Society (NHS). All images from the National Park Service, Longfellow House–Washington Headquarters National Historic Site, are abbreviated NPS.

Introduction

The first Arcadia book on Nahant, Images of America: *Nahant*, was published in 1999 and covered briefly the whole history of the town. This second Arcadia title, Images of America: *Nahant Revisited*, is a thematic approach to this history and covers in more detail selected topics. It has been greatly enhanced because the Nahant Historical Society has had many donations and additions to the collections in the intervening 22 years. Other local institutions and individuals have allowed the use of materials related to Nahant. Many of the images used here have appeared in the society's annual pictorial calendar but have been brought together to tell a fuller story.

This book is divided into eight chapters. The first is entitled "East Point." It begins with the opening of the Nahant Hotel in 1823 by Thomas Handasyd Perkins on the model of European resort hotels. It drew vacationing Boston and East Coast elite families. Soon, the Bostonians built "cottages," and a summer colony was born. After a devastating fire destroyed the hotel in 1861, East Point was sold to the Lodge family. Sen. Henry Cabot Lodge built his summer home, East Point, and his sister Elizabeth Lodge James built her home, Lowland. The US military used the property during the Spanish-American War, World War I, and World War II for the defense of Boston Harbor. After the military occupation, Northeastern University and the town of Nahant have shared the site.

Henry Wadsworth Longfellow and his family lived seasonally in Nahant from the 1830s until 1896. He bought the former Wetmore house in 1860 with his brother-in-law Thomas Gold Appleton, an art collector, world traveler, and bon vivant. Through the use of extracts from his journals, letters, and poetry, Longfellow speaks directly about his life in Nahant and the inspiration he drew from living surrounded by the sea. Many of his friends and associates were literary stars and artists of the time. John Frederick Kensett painted in Nahant and visited with Longfellow. Frederic Auguste Bartholdi, the French sculptor, discussed the monumental sculpture he was designing to be placed in New York Harbor. James T. Fields, Longfellow's publisher, summered nearby.

The Samuel Hammond family of Boston is documented as an example of members of the summer colony and their seasonal activities. These images are taken from three family photograph albums dating from the 1850s to the 1940s and were donated to the Nahant Historical Society. His son Mason and daughter Susan saw duty in World War II and were decorated for heroic service. Susan drove ambulances in France and Belgium, evacuating nurses, women, and children from war zones, and was awarded the Croix de Guerre with Star from France. Mason was a Monuments Man saving European art and patrimony from certain destruction. He was awarded the Bronze Star and decorated by the governments of France, Holland, and Italy.

The "People and Places" chapter shows other extraordinary people, both locals and summer residents, who contributed greatly to the rich history of Nahant. Harriet Beecher Stowe visited regularly during the 1870s and 1880s. Oliver Wendell Holmes Sr. summered here in the 1870s and enhanced the pictorial record by his invention of the first successful handheld stereoscopic viewer. Gen. John C. Frémont, called the "Pathfinder of the West" and an 1856 candidate for president, summered here with his family. Thomas Roland came to Nahant in 1883 and established a commercial plant nursery with 20 greenhouses in Nahant and was an important contributor to the Massachusetts Horticultural Society.

"Seaside" is documented using stereoscopic views, postcards, and photographs of the period. People are seen using this maritime environment for recreation and inspiration. The rugged cliffs, rock outcroppings, and stony and sandy beaches show the forbidding and enticing landscapes that draw people to visit or live here. Accomplished photographer Dudley Bowditch Fay gives us views of delightful gardens bordering the sea and enduring images of the ocean in his early-20th-century photographs.

The "At Work" chapter covers what people did for employment. Henry Cabot Lodge, although spending most of his political life in Washington, DC, was also Nahant's town moderator for many years. He employed local individuals to maintain his estate and one local young man as a chauffeur both in Washington and while home in Nahant. A horse-drawn delivery van for William Hallbauer's ice cream shop in Bass Point is seen doing its rounds. Hallbauer went into partnership with Howard Johnson, and his recipe for ice cream made Howard Johnson a household name. Images show people employed in stores, such as Gove's fish market on Tudor Beach, selling fish and lobster right from the sea. Town facilities and infrastructure always needed upkeep. The much-loved Little Nahant boardwalk required constant repair. Howard Nichols and Fred Manter are busy renovating a portion of the walkway in a 1953 photograph.

"Civic Life" covers people involved in town government and institutions such as the Massachusetts Humane Society and its successor services to save lives and vessels at sea. Abbie May Roland, a significant force in the women's suffrage movement, is shown as well as the Nahant Woman's Club of the North Shore celebrating the 100th anniversary of the passage of the 19th Amendment. This club was formerly known as the Nahant Woman's Club. People's thoughts of the Covid 19 pandemic are juxtaposed against a period postcard message of concern during the 1918 influenza outbreak.

"At Play" concentrates on sports, parades, and entertainment. Three Nahant summer residents won first prizes in the first modern Olympic games, which took place in Athens in 1896, and the Nahant Lermond brothers competed in running events at the 1924 and 1928 Olympics. School sports teams and Little League games are pictured, some with amusing stories. Plays and musicals were presented regularly as a means of self-expression, entertainment, and support for local causes.

The collections of the Nahant Historical Society are greatly benefitted by donations of objects and archival material from individuals who have a personal history in Nahant and others who come upon treasures related to Nahant by happenstance. Authors' proceeds from the sale of this book benefit this very active society.

One

East Point

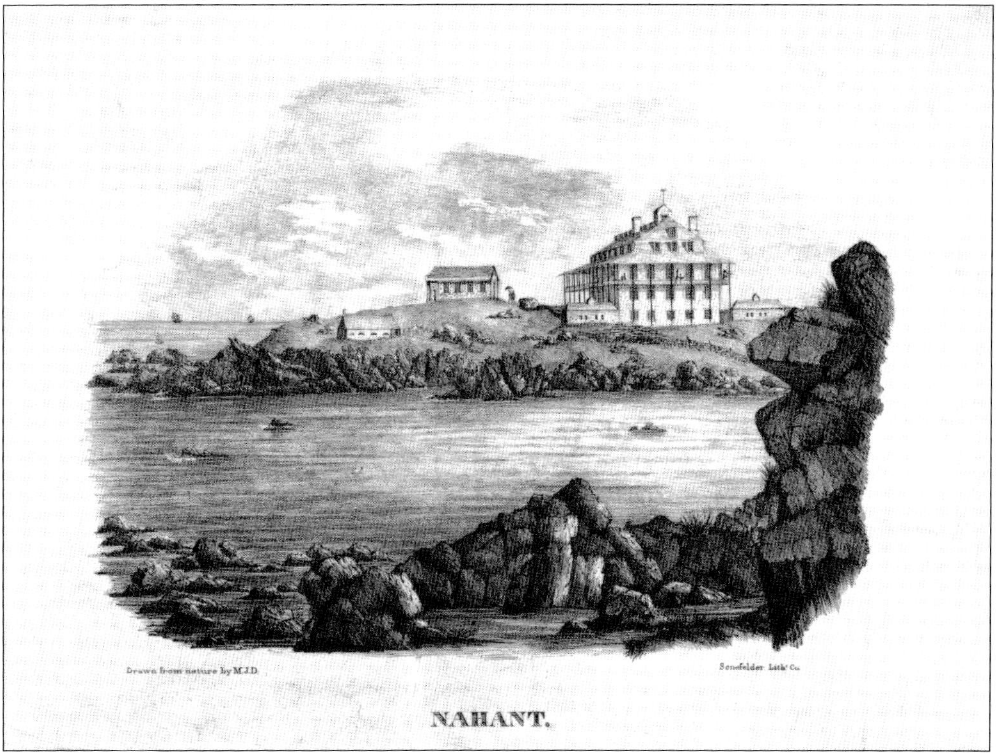

Thomas Handasyd Perkins (1764–1854) purchased 37 acres on East Point from the Breed family in 1821 and opened the Nahant Hotel on June 4, 1823. Consisting of four stories, it stood 86 feet high by 54 feet wide, with deep porches surrounding the two lower floors. The outbuildings included a billiard hall. This mid-1830s image is by Mary Jane Derby of Salem.

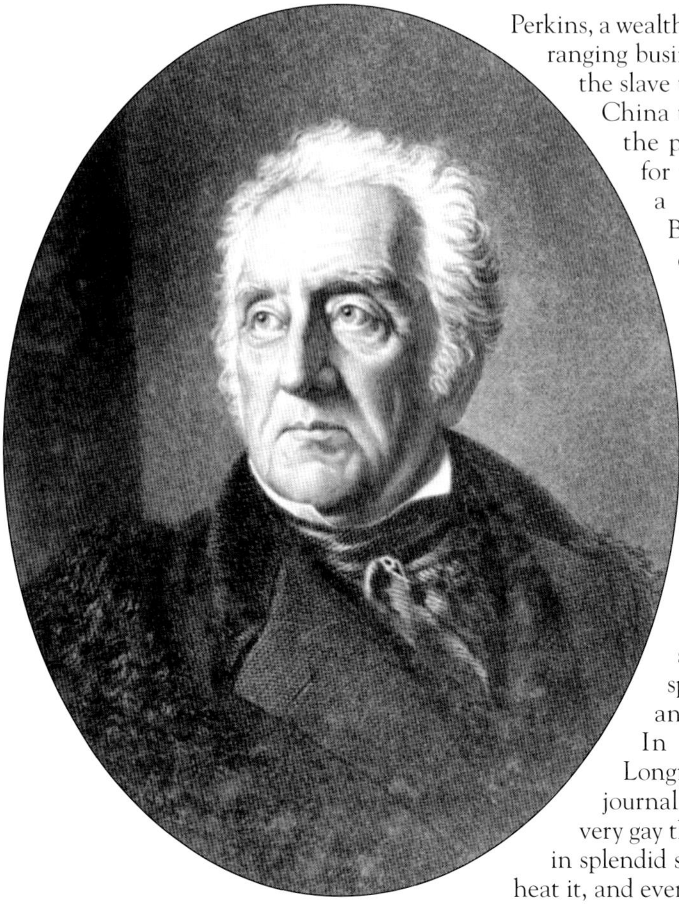

Perkins, a wealthy Boston merchant with wide-ranging business interests, was involved in the slave trade in Haiti by 1786 and the China trade by 1789, which included the purchase of opium in Turkey for resale in China. He was also a generous supporter of the Boston Athenaeum, a founder of the Massachusetts General Hospital, and a great patron of the Perkins School for the Blind.

Over time, the hotel expanded and could accommodate 1,000 guests. It had gardens and a school for children, and it sponsored musical performances and lectures by noted speakers. In 1854, Henry Wadsworth Longfellow's wife, Fanny, wrote in a journal entry, "Nahant promises to be very gay this summer, the hotel is rebuilt in splendid style with gas, and furnaces to heat it, and every luxury."

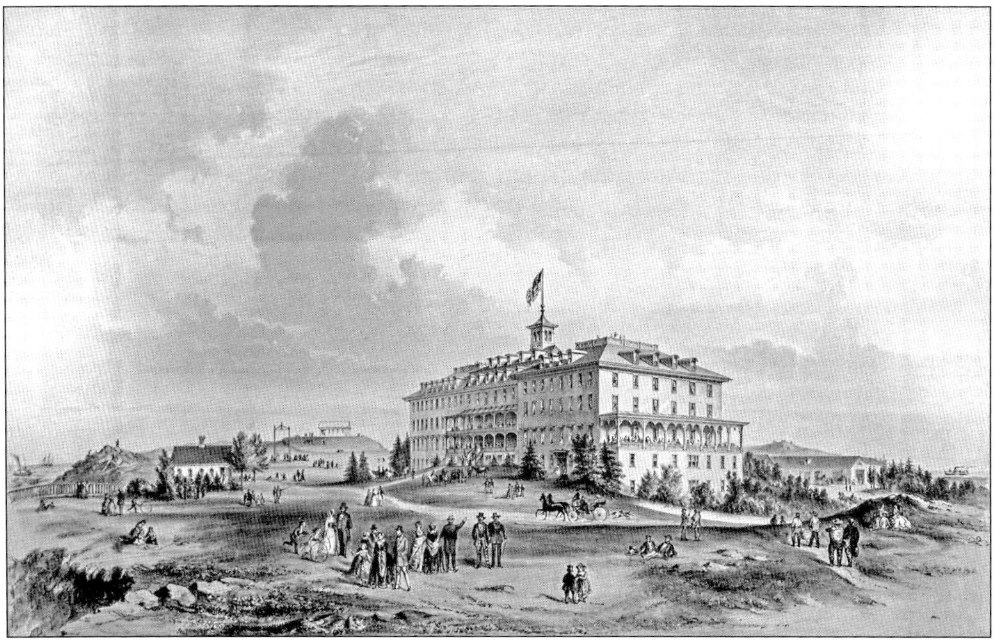

Phineas Drew (1808–1877) bought the Nahant Hotel from Perkins in 1842. He was successful until Lynn (which Nahant was a part of) adopted a state temperance act in 1852. The Temperance Watchmen raided the hotel in August 1852, seizing the supply of liquor. Drew and his Boston patrons petitioned the legislature for Nahant's separation from Lynn. With approval, Nahant became a town in 1853, and profits returned to the hotel.

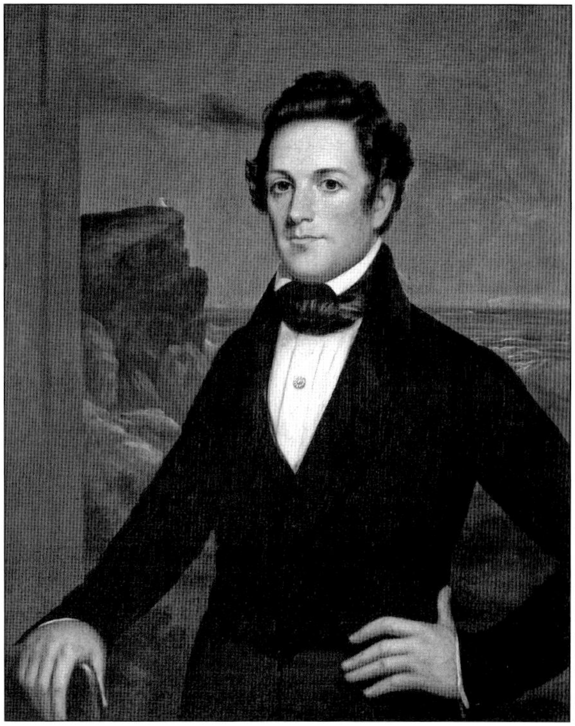

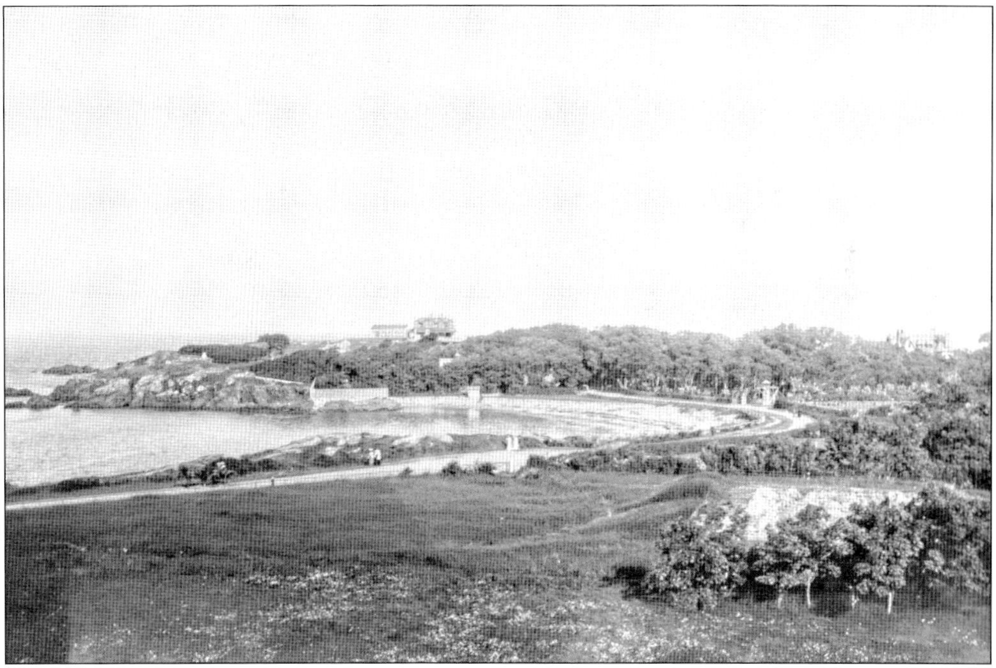

This 1904 view of East Point from the Samuel Hammond house demonstrates the overall topography after the 1861 Nahant Hotel fire. Looking across Nahant Road and the water are, on the left at the crest of the hill, the Lodge library and Lodge's house East Point, and on the extreme right, the James house Lowland. This landscape remained largely intact until the later military occupation of the site.

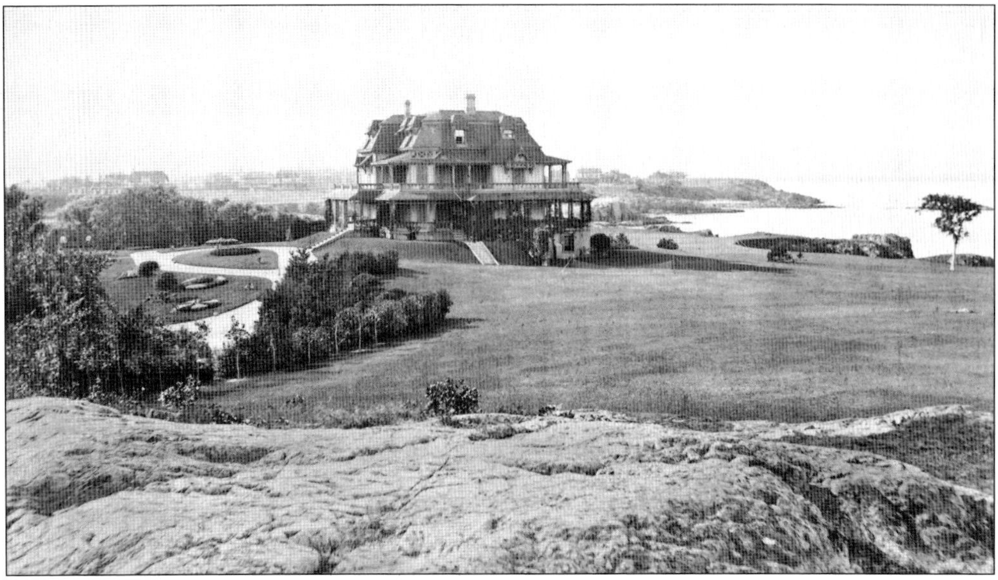

John Ellerton Lodge (1807–1862) purchased East Point in 1861 following the hotel fire. The property was passed to his son Sen. Henry Cabot Lodge (1850–1924) and daughter Elizabeth Lodge James (1843–1908). The Lodge house construction began in 1868, with a design by architect Charles Brigham, on the site of the hotel. Lodge and his wife, Anna Davis Lodge (1851–1915), moved into East Point in 1871.

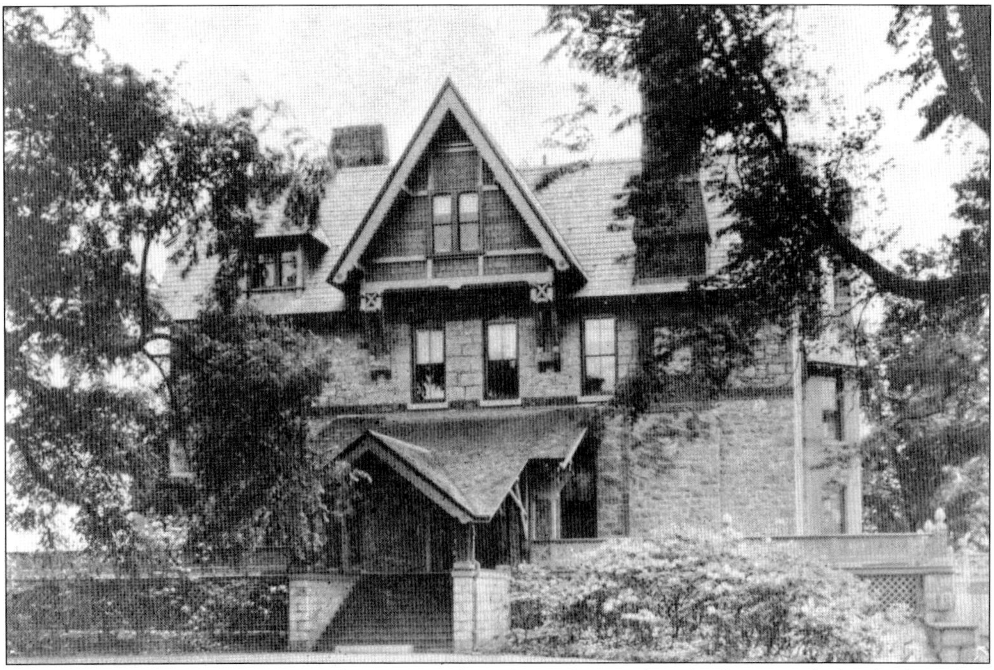

George Abbot James (1835–1919), a Harvard graduate from Ohio, had married Elizabeth Cabot Lodge and was now a trusted part of the family. He acted as Lodge's agent for the construction of East Point and when finished turned his attention to his own house. It was built of massive blocks of Quincy granite and located at a lower elevation than the Lodge home, hence the name Lowland.

This imposing gate of the Lodge and James estates still exists, with some alterations, at the entrance of Lodge Park and Northeastern University's Marine Science Center. On the higher pillar was a lantern, and on the lower pillar sat a Japanese stone Buddha. When the military acquired the property in 1941, then-owner Harmon Elliott moved the Buddha to his new home, Cas-el-ot, on Swallow Cave Road.

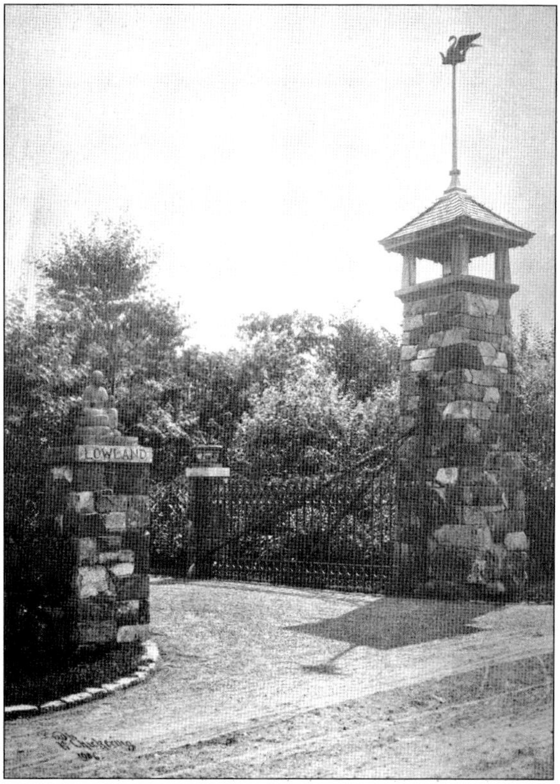

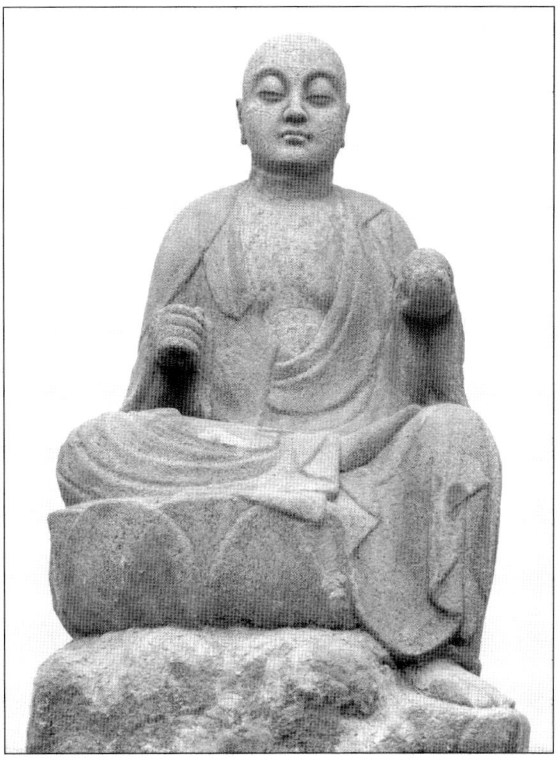

The Buddha, a representation of Jizo Bosatsu, suffered neglect and eventual decapitation in the 1980s. The most recent owner arranged for the conservation of the statue and the sculpting of a new head. Today, the Buddha is exhibited in the rotunda of the Nahant Community Center on a specially designed plinth. The Nahant Historical Society is grateful to the donor and all involved in this project.

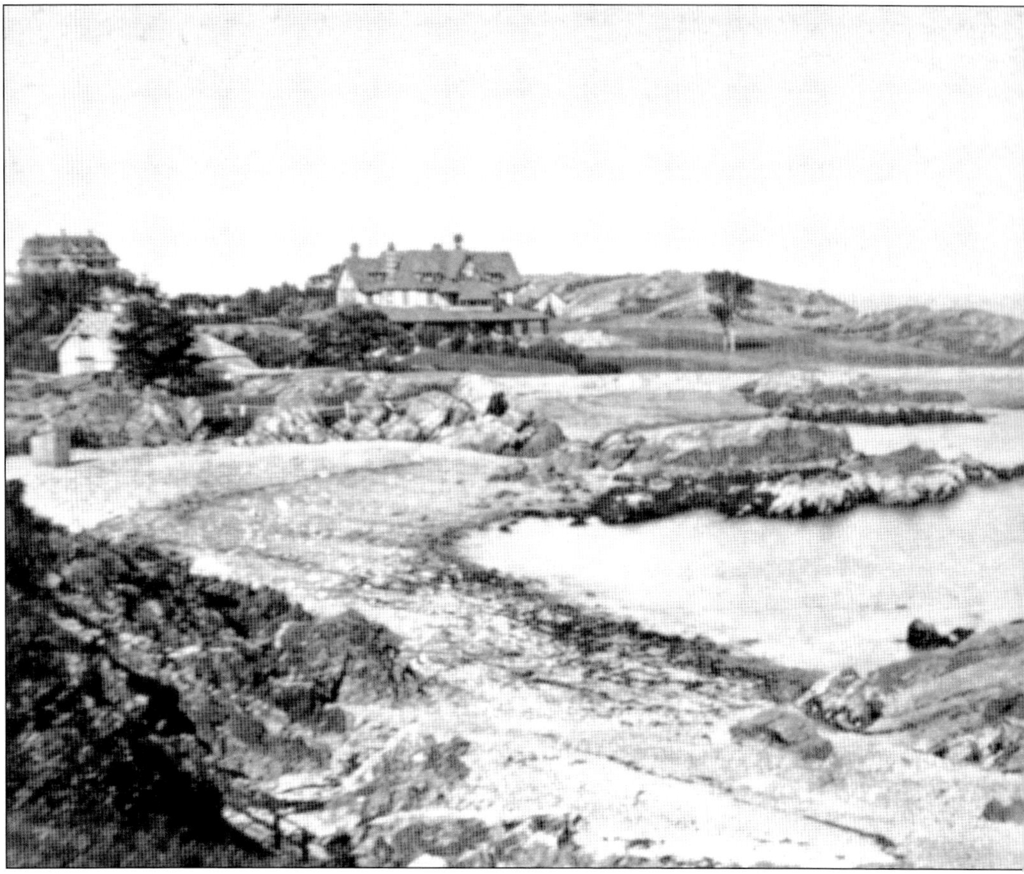

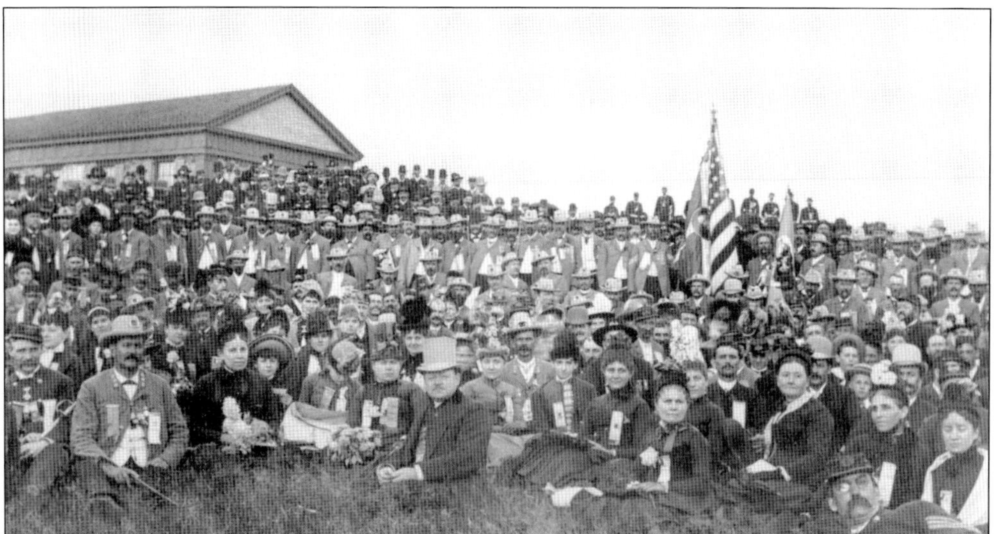

There were 18 known Nahant Civil War veterans who belonged to the General Lander Post 5 (Lynn) of the Grand Army of the Republic. On June 18, 1887, this group hosted a group of veterans from Richmond, Virginia, at the Lodge estate under the auspices of the National Order of Blue and Gray. A reciprocal visit was made to the Robert E. Lee Camp 1 (Richmond) on July 5, 1887.

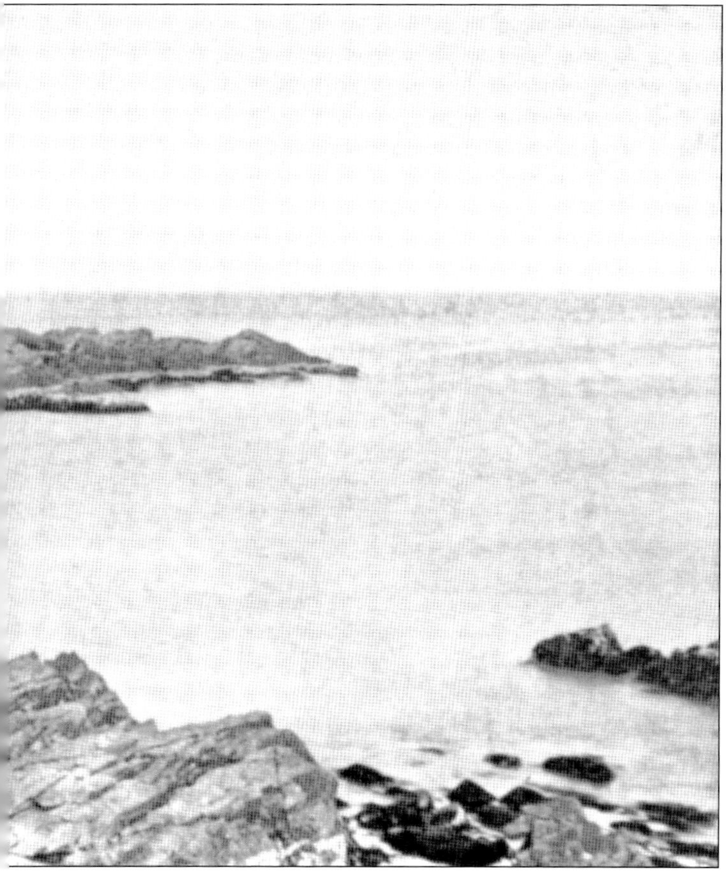

This 1879 image is titled *View from Prescott Cottage*, which was located at the end of Swallow Cave Road. Above the barn on the left is Lodge's East Point, and James's Lowland is to the right. Looking over the beach in the foreground, the seawall and the rocky beach of Lowland are clearly visible. The rock formation on the beach just to the right of the tree is the location of a seawater swimming pool that Harmon Elliott (a later owner) built into the rocks. In the distance to the right are the headlands without any alterations by the military that came later.

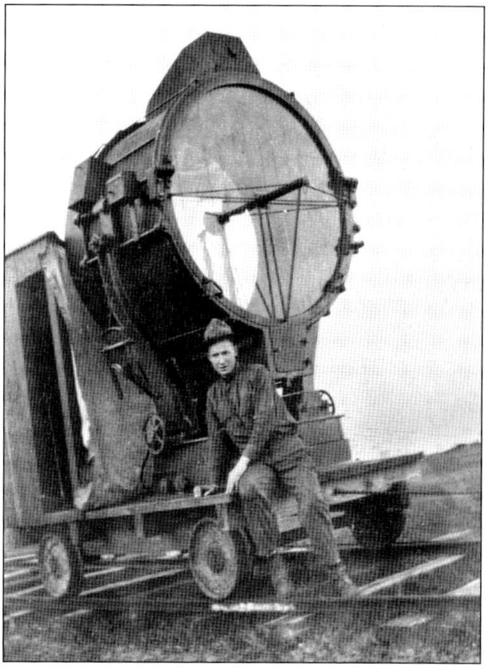

Working with Henry Cabot Lodge, the Army Corps of Engineers established a site for a 60-inch seacoast searchlight on East Point. This location was a key position for the surveillance and defense of Boston Harbor during World War I. Construction for this project included a shelter for the light, a powerhouse, and a gun emplacement.

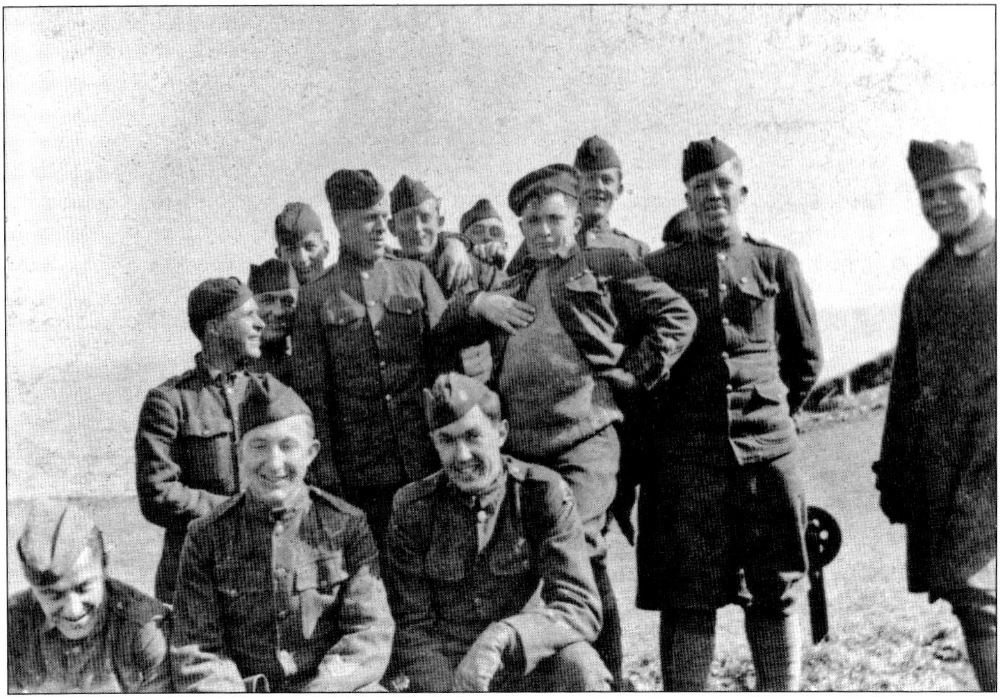

This group of soldiers served at East Point manning the searchlight and gun emplacement. As Senator Lodge requested, after the war, his property was returned to its prewar conditions. All equipment was removed, and the landscape was restored. Some of these soldiers may well have assisted in returning the estate to civilian use.

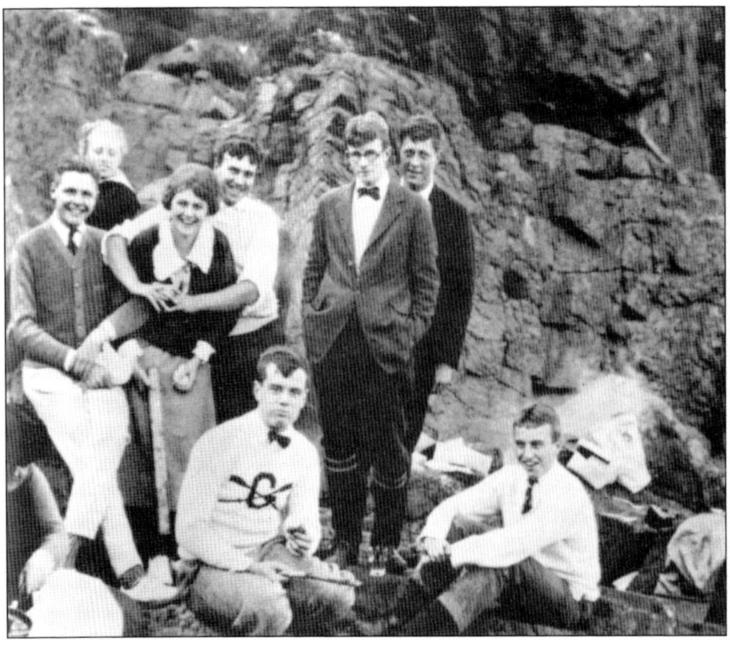

Seen here on the rocks at East Point are Henry Cabot Lodge Jr. (1902–1985) on the left and his sister Helena Lodge de Streel (1904–1998), being embraced by a friend. These grandchildren of the senator are joined by friends for an autumn picnic in 1921. After graduating from Harvard in 1924, Lodge Jr. had a long political career, including serving as ambassador to South Vietnam and the Vatican.

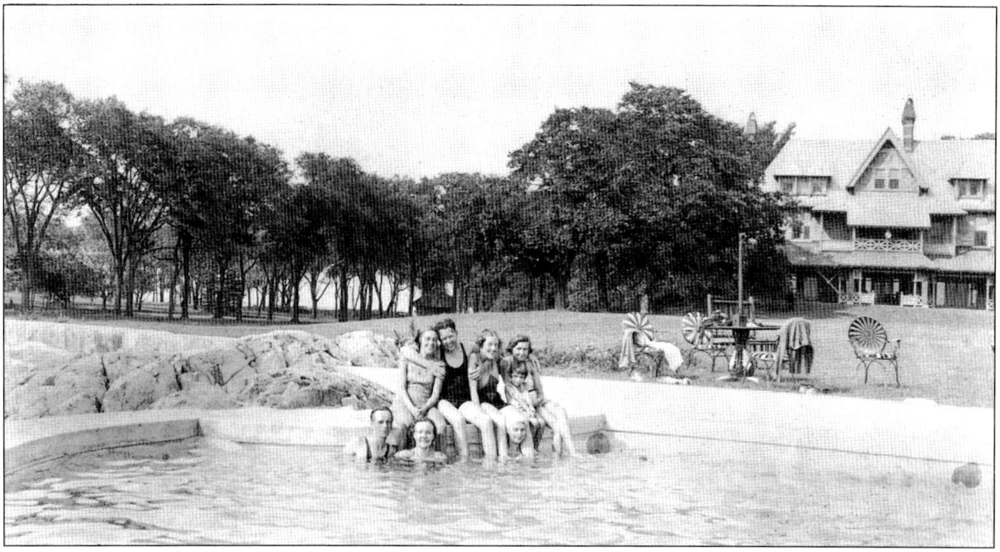

Harmon P. Elliott (1887–1969), a friend of longtime summer resident Charles Hammond Gibson, bought Lowland in 1928. His alterations to the estate included this seawater swimming pool in 1930. From left to right are (in the pool) George Downs, Kitty Levitt, and unidentified; (sitting on the ledge) Roberta Greenhalgh, Richard Kirkman, Jean Greenhalgh Kirkman, and two unidentified.

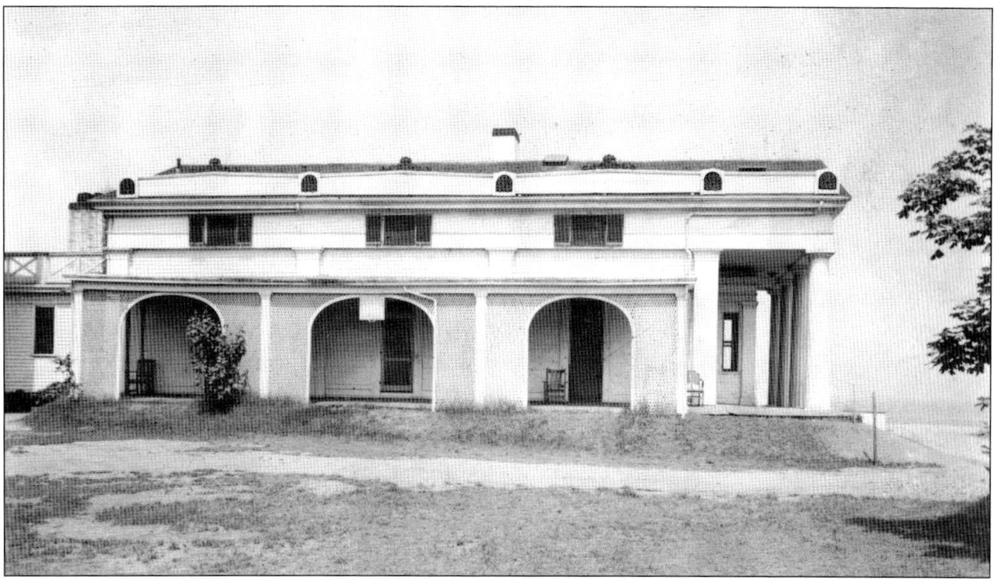

The Lodge house came down in 1941, shortly after the military took all of East Point and some adjacent areas by eminent domain. One such property was the Mifflin house on Nahant Road above Forty Steps Beach, which became the commander's residence. An observation tower was built adjoining the house where military specialists could search for enemy ships in Boston Harbor. This and three other towers remain in Nahant.

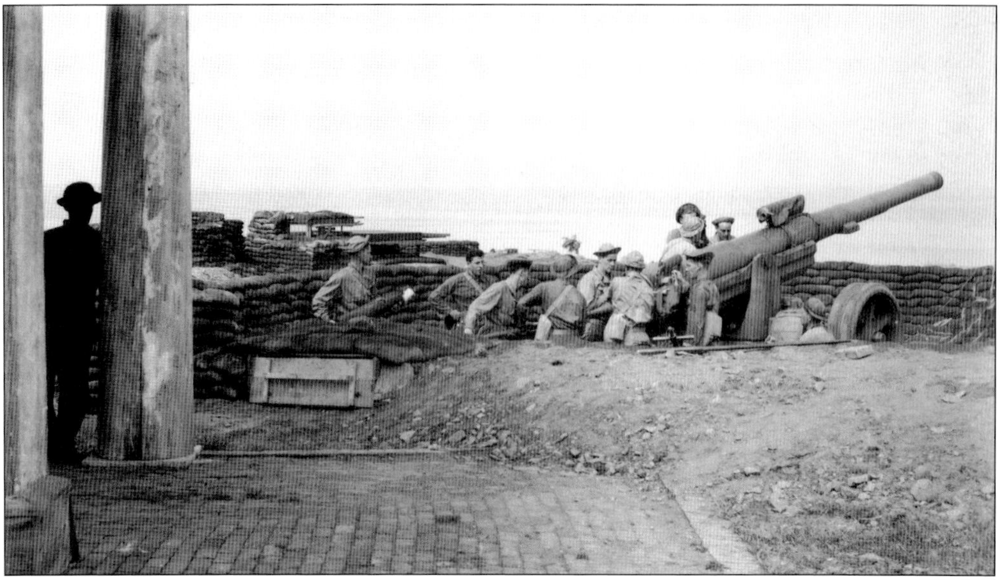

This 155-millimeter gun was deployed as a heavy field weapon during World War II and was additionally classed as a secondary armament for seacoast defense with a range of 14 miles. The gun was located on East Point next to Lodge's stone library. This building, in the then-popular Greek Revival style, was formerly the Nahant Hotel billiard hall. Note the portico columns on the left.

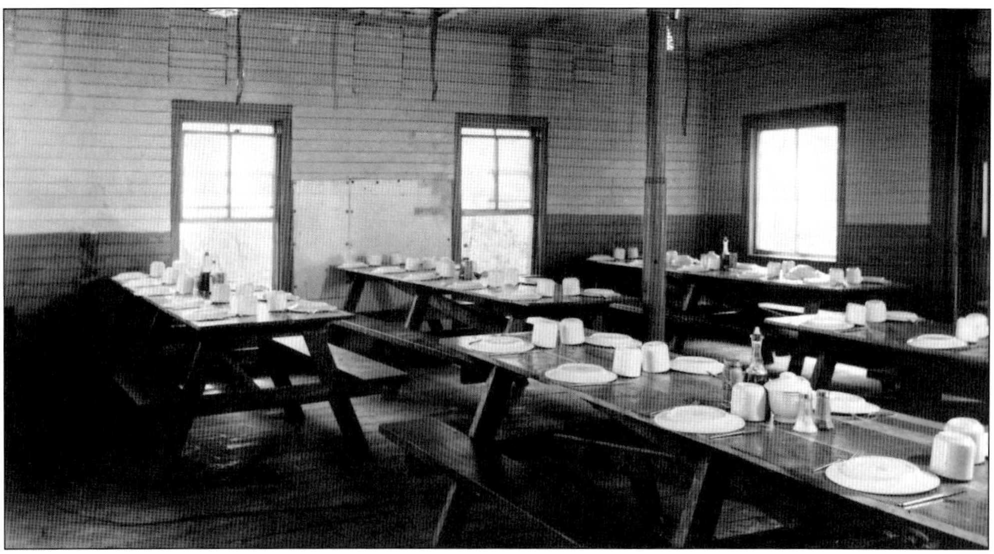

The Lowland house was designated as the headquarters building for the East Point Military Reservation. Here is one of the outbuildings, possibly the barn, that was converted into the mess hall. At this point, the military began radically altering the landscape by constructing bunkers at East Point as well as Bailey's Hill.

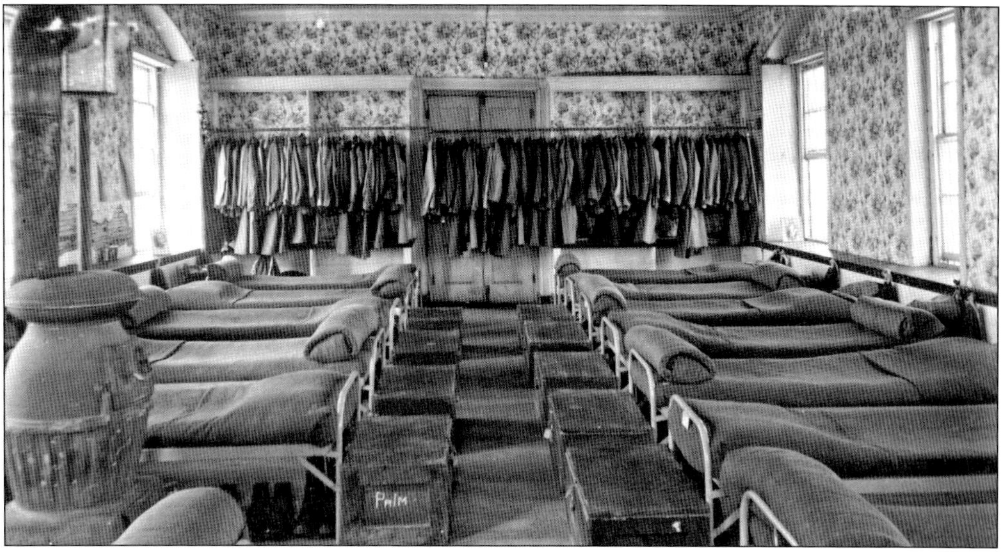

Another use of an outbuilding was for a bunkhouse. Note some of the soldiers' personal effects such as photographs of loved ones on the windowsills and clothing at the end of the room. When the military left after the war, the granite mansion was abandoned, and it finally burned on May 9, 1965. One of the enlisted men, Daniel Zeitz, married a local woman, Betty Mitchell, and settled in Nahant.

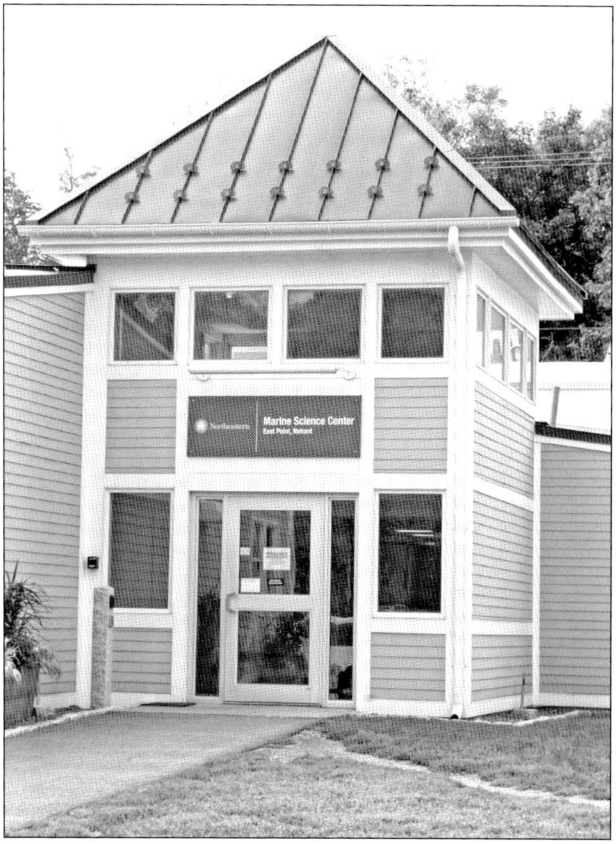

Following World War II, the military mothballed East Point. In 1966, Northeastern University acquired part of the property (cost-free) for use as its Marine Science Center. Seen here is the entrance to the Edwards building, dedicated in 1969. It is a former military building that has been expanded over time. Smaller structures, water storage tanks, and a greenhouse have been added. (Courtesy Robert A. Wilson.)

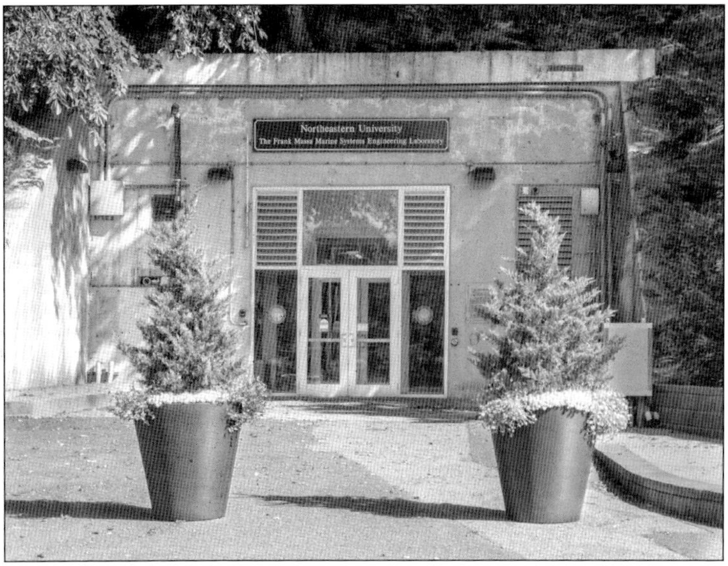

The Murphy bunker, a vast concrete construction, is now used by Northeastern as lab space. When built, it was covered over with soil and plantings to disguise it from potential enemy ships. This landscape, after more than 70 years, has now become a habitat for diverse flora and fauna with a successful ecosystem that includes hills, meadows, and wetlands. (Courtesy Robert A. Wilson.)

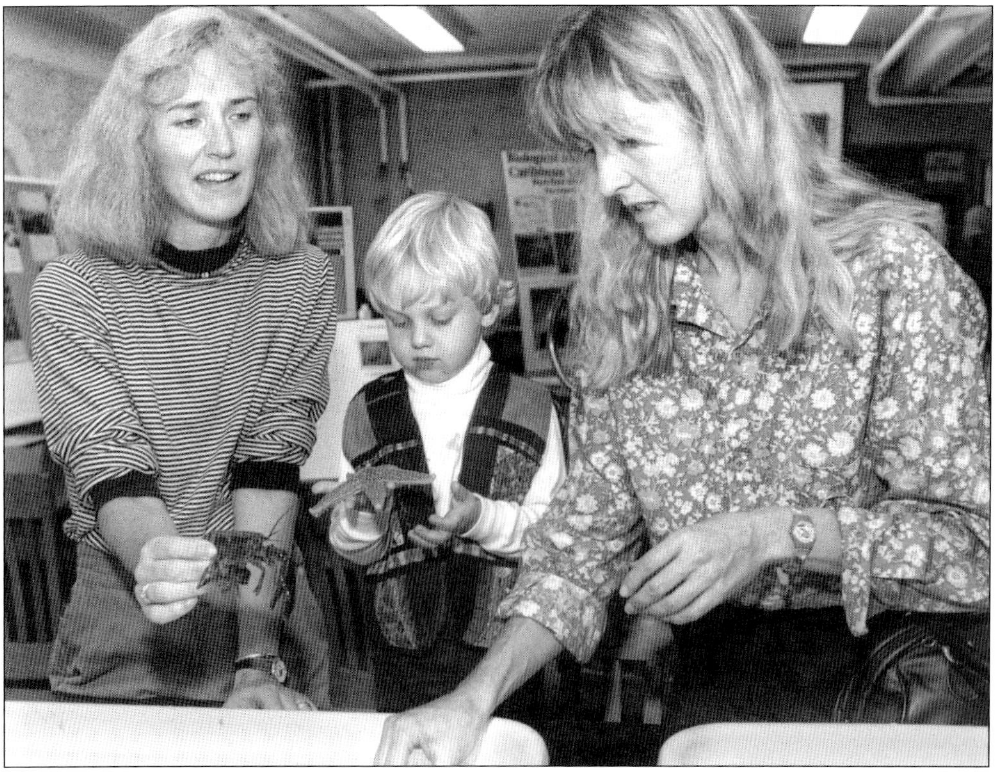

The Marine Science Center has had students visit to observe experiments being conducted, tour the research labs, and examine the rocky shore environments unique to East Point. In this Walter Hoey image of 1990, from left to right, Morgan Hardwick Whitman (a Northeastern staff member) shows a small lobster to Nahanter Ryan Hambleton and his mother, Sheila Hambleton.

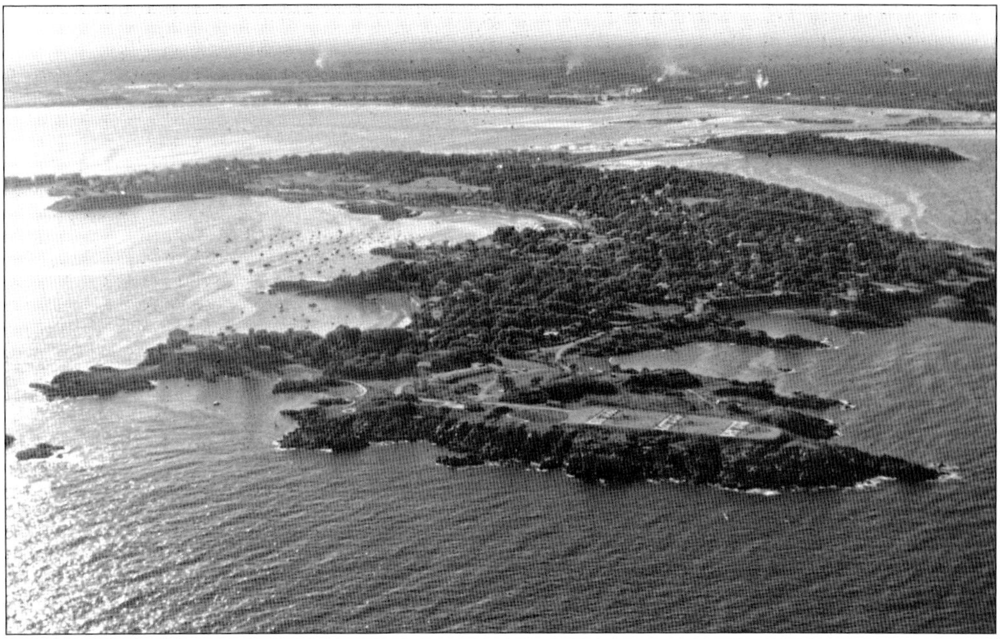

In 1954, the US government announced that a Nike missile station was planned for East Point. This aerial photograph shows the three completed missile storage magazines. These were constructed of reinforced concrete deep into the bedrock and were each 63 feet long by 49 feet wide. They were decommissioned along with the rest of East Point. In 1976, Nahant purchased this portion, which is now the site of Lodge Park.

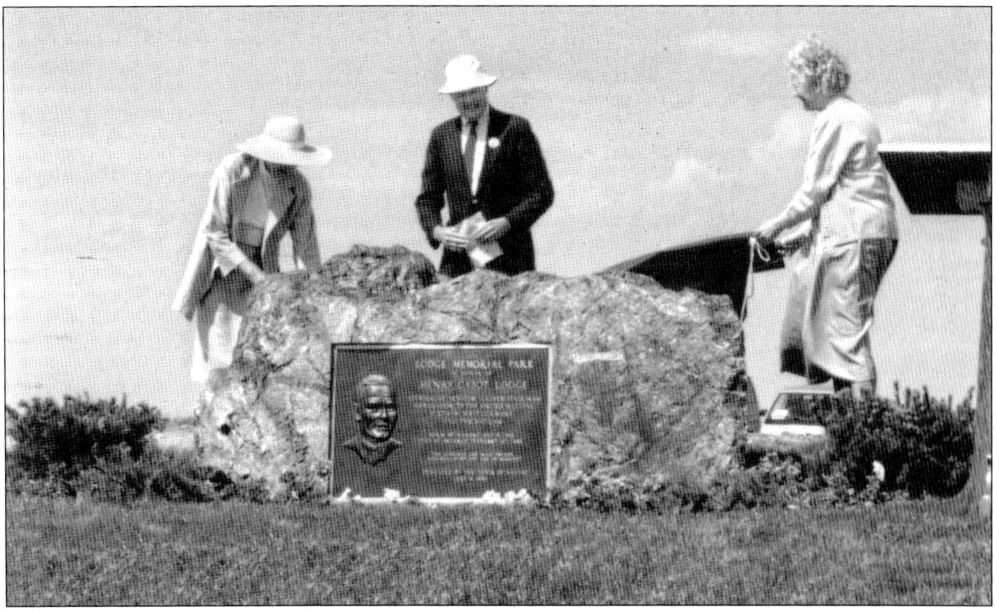

The dedication ceremony of Lodge Park took place on July 4, 1988. The memorial plaque of Henry Cabot Lodge Jr. was unveiled by, from left to right, Baroness Helena de Streel (Lodge's sister), John Lowell (speaker), and Emily Lodge Clark (Lodge's widow). In part, it reads, "Journalist, Senator, Ambassador . . . Born at Nahant, July 5, 1902, . . . *The Earliest and Most Prized Memories of My Life Are of Nahant.*"

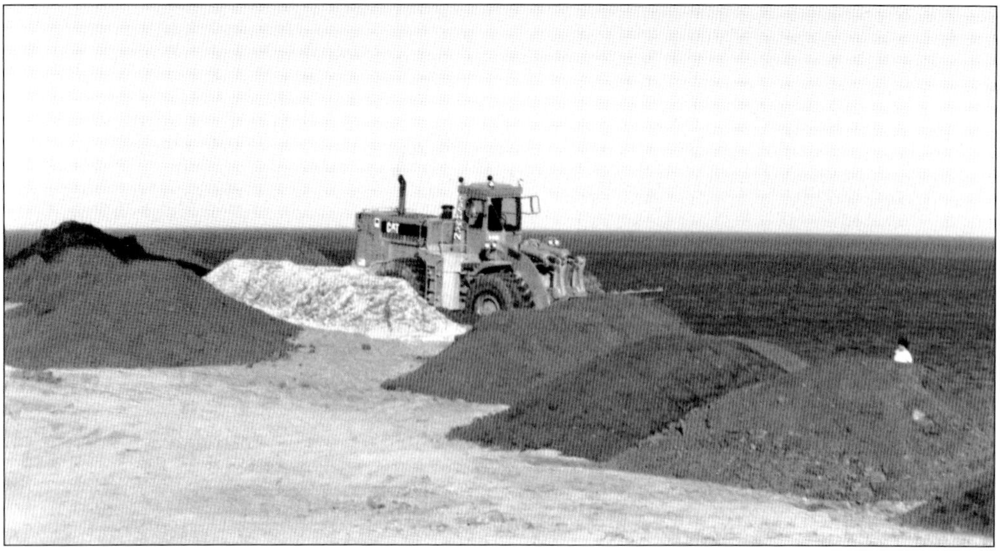

In 1990, the Nahant town meeting approved $30,000 for further implementation of the master plan for Lodge Park and amended the zoning bylaw map to declare the entire East Point zone to be a natural resource district. The missile silos were filled in with clean excavation material from the Big Dig project in Boston. Tons of topsoil were brought in and graded off in preparation for seeding.

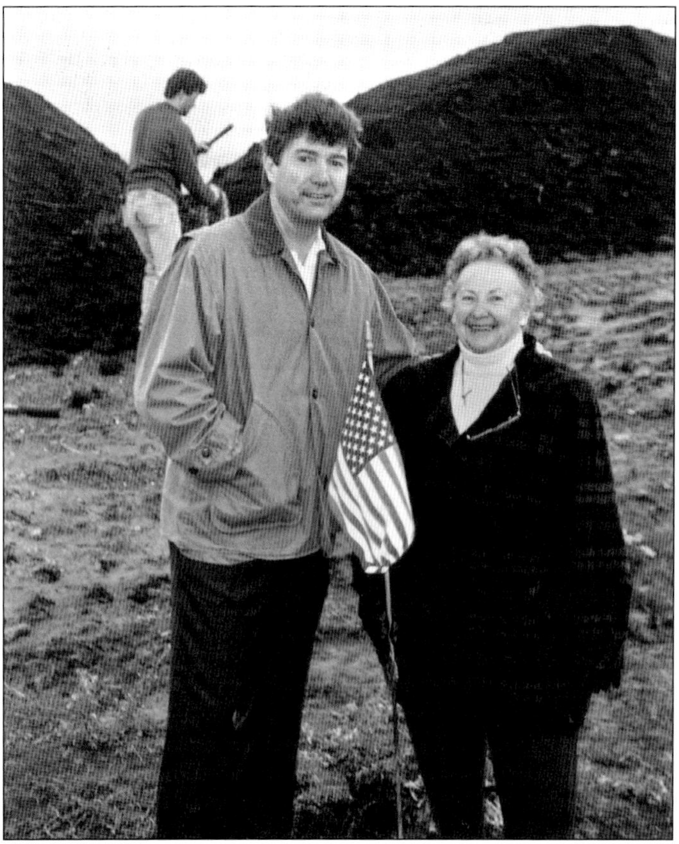

A particular concern was to reestablish the native plants appropriate to this exposed scenic environment, enabling the wild populations of animals to return. Inspections were made regularly. Gene Canty, the chair of the Conservation Commission, and Calantha Sears from the historical society appear pleased with the progress. These efforts have encouraged the passive recreation of East Point by town residents and visitors.

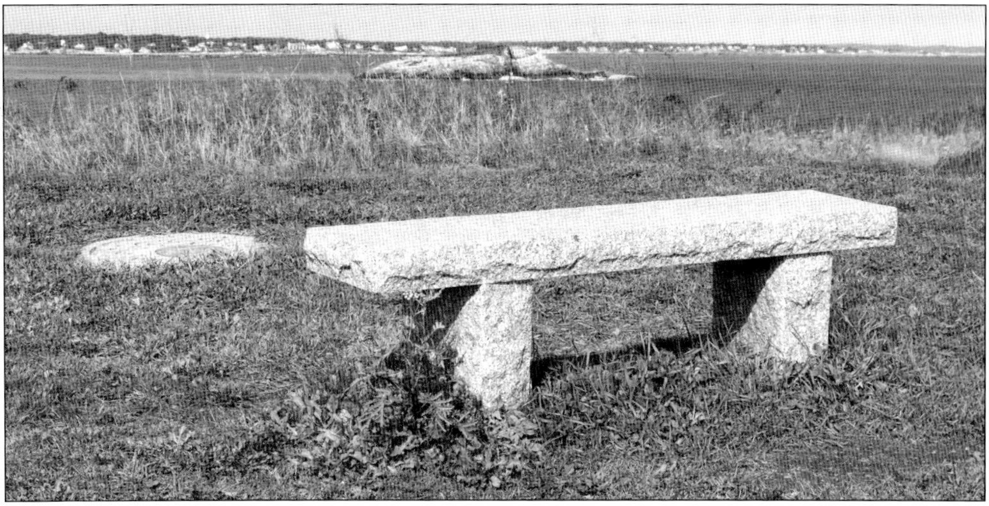

John Volpe (1908–1994) was a two-term governor of Massachusetts, ambassador to Italy, and Nahant citizen. His memorial in Lodge Park consists of a granite bench and a circular granite and bronze compass set into the grass. It reads, "A Gift in Memory of . . . Hon. John Anthony Volpe . . . Hon. Henry Cabot Lodge . . . May 1997 . . . *Friends and Colleagues.*" (Photograph by Robert A. Wilson.)

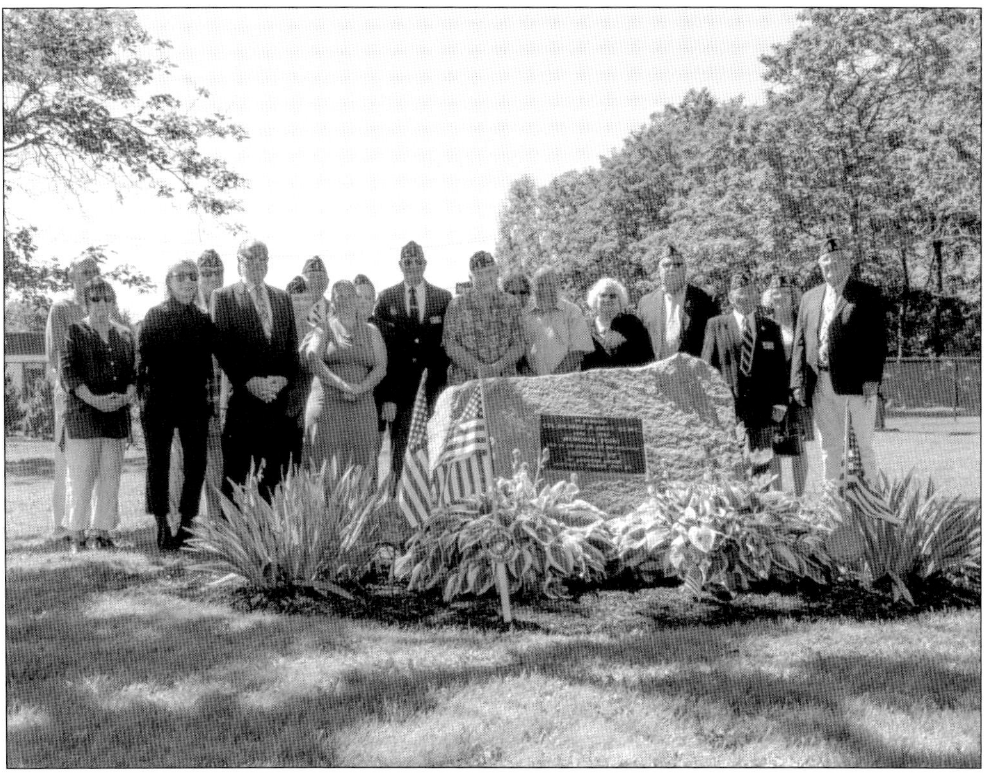

Memorial Point is a grassy area at the entrance to East Point. A bronze plaque set in stone remembers Cpl. Richard R. Davis, USMC (1947–1967), who gave his life during the Vietnam War. The memorial was dedicated by the American Legion Mortimer G. Robbins Post 215. Family, friends, veterans, and town officials gather on the 50th anniversary of his passing on July 9, 2017.

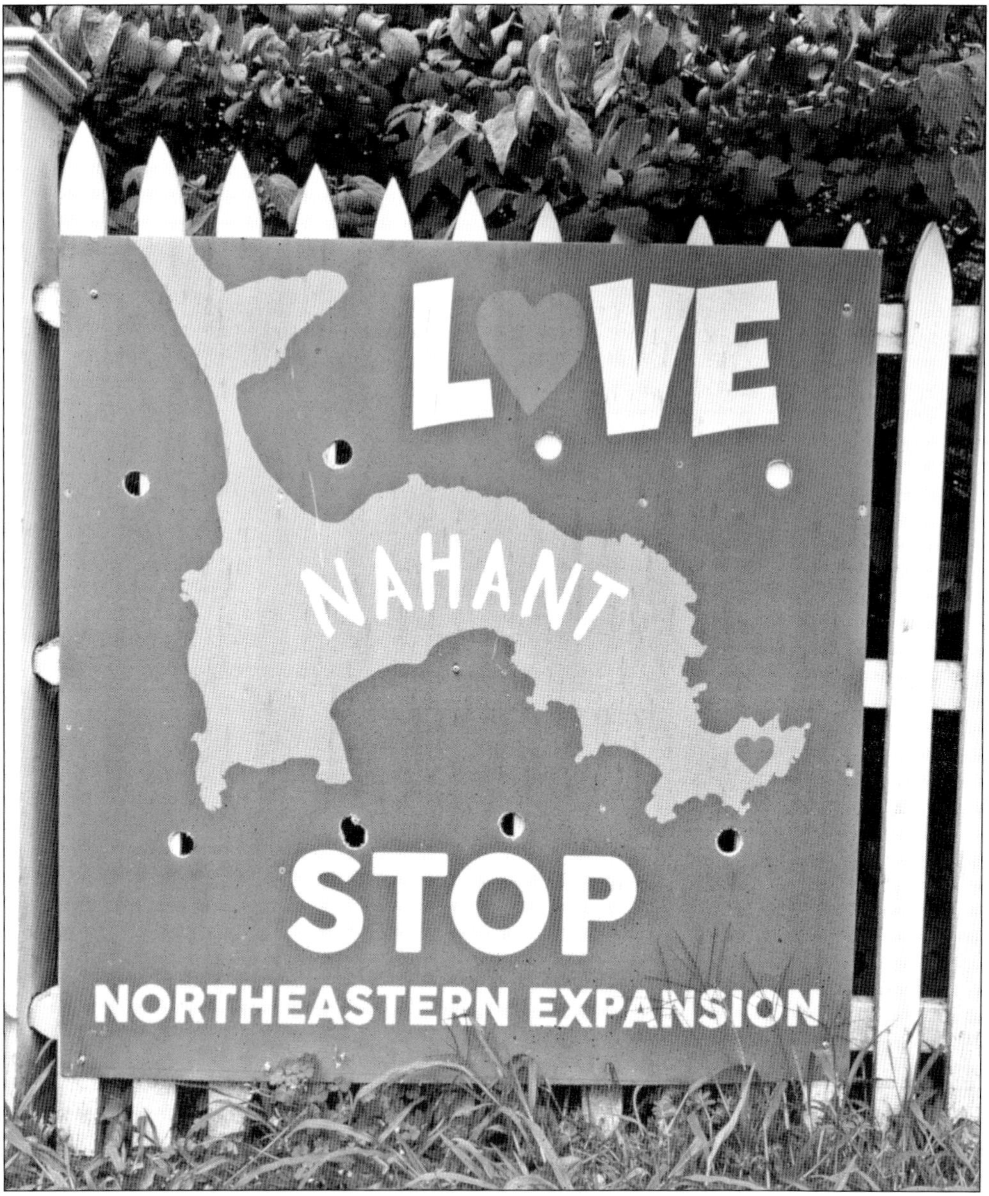

This sign, which can be seen throughout town in 2021, concisely states the sentiment of many people in Nahant. Northeastern University has proposed the construction of a 55,000-square-foot glass-enclosed building on top of the Murphy bunker at East Point. It would completely dominate this end of Nahant, overshadow Lodge Park, and endanger this important natural resource area. The project would require parking for 250 cars and a new access road, resulting in damage to wetlands areas. This site is on an important Atlantic coast migration path for many species of birds that would be at risk of collision with the glass facades of the building. Increased seawater pumping capacity for more experimentation tanks and the resulting outflow of warmed seawater increases the risk of beach erosion and threatens nearby lobster breeding environments. Other vital flora and fauna habitat may be harmed by this urbanization of East Point. Space for this project has been offered by nearby communities, but the upper levels of the Northeastern administration, so far, are unwilling to consider these options.

Two

Longfellow in Nahant

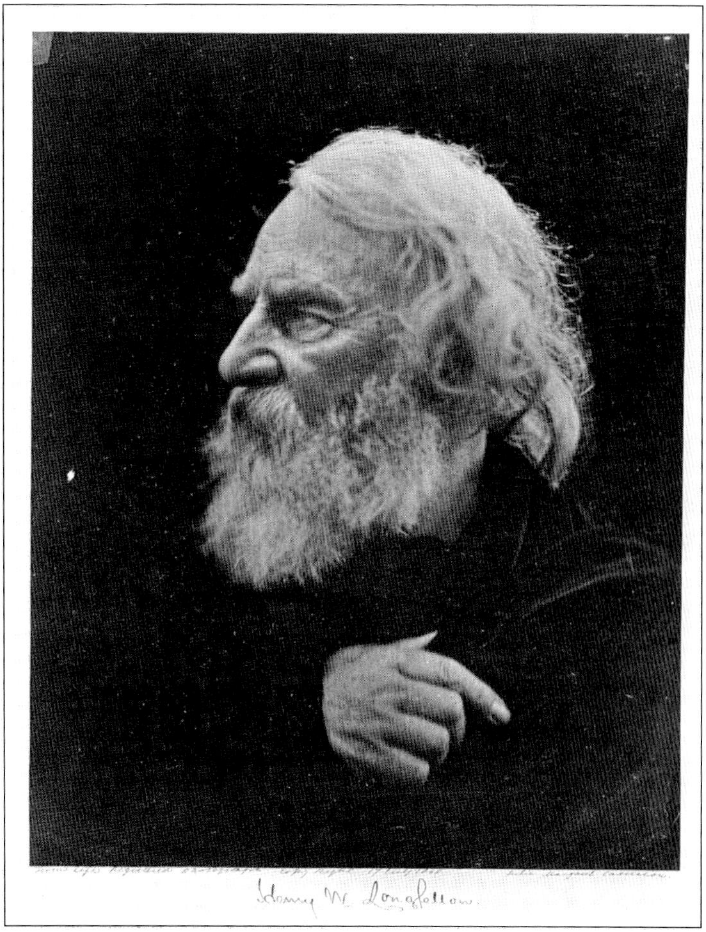

Henry Wadsworth Longfellow (1807–1882) was the most well-known and beloved American poet of the 19th century. He was born in Portland, Maine, and graduated from Bowdoin College in 1825. Following years of European travel and teaching, he was made professor of modern languages at Bowdoin and later at Harvard in 1836. This portrait, from 1868, is by Julia Margaret Cameron. (Courtesy NPS.)

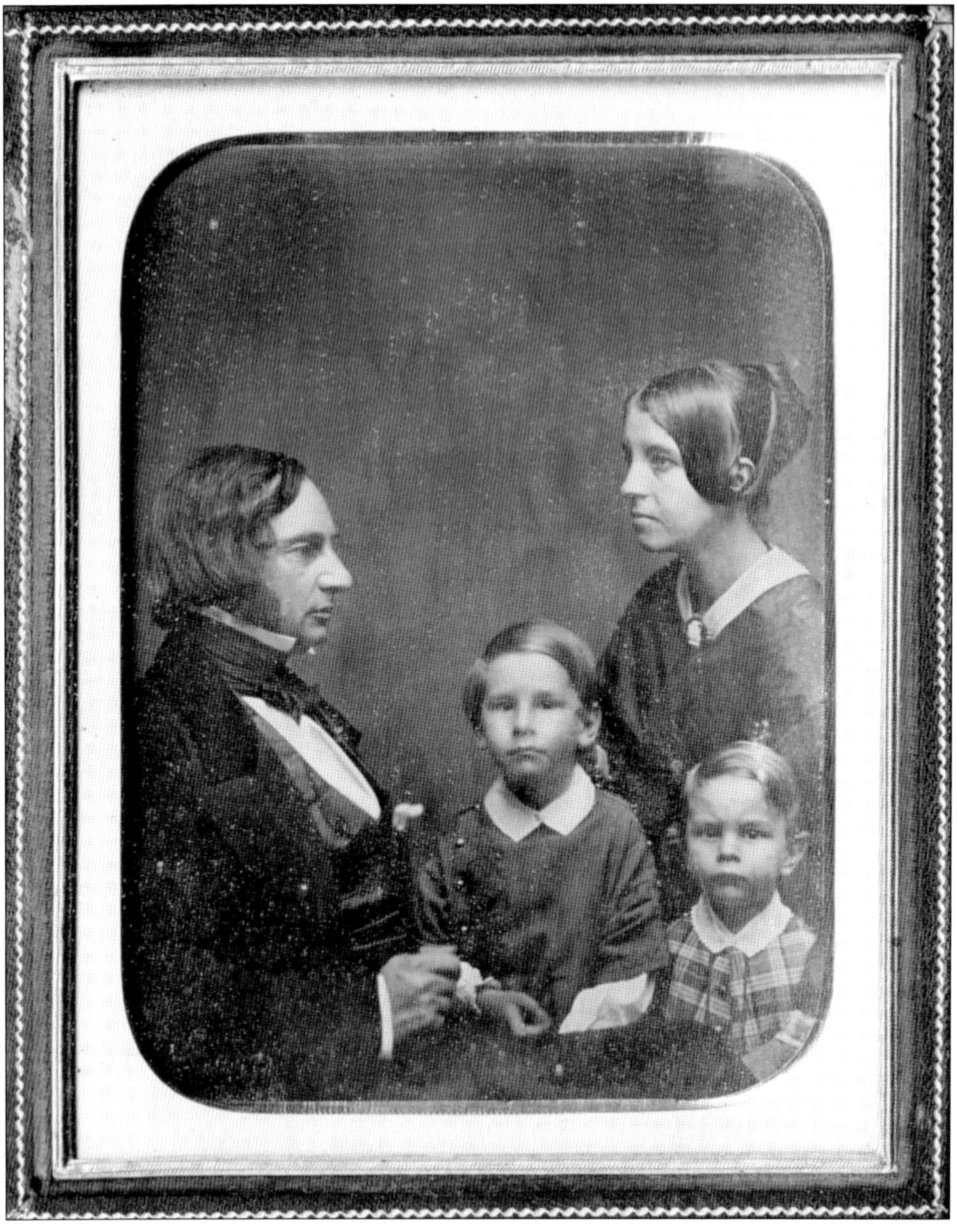

Longfellow met his wife, Fanny Appleton (1817–1861), in 1838 while traveling in Europe. She was accompanied by her father, Nathan Appleton (one of the wealthiest men in Boston), her sister Mary, and her brother Thomas Gold Appleton. With Tom's encouragement, Longfellow pursued a courtship with Fanny, and after a few years of missteps, they married in 1843. Nathan Appleton made a wedding gift of the already historic Craigie mansion on Brattle Street in Cambridge to the new couple. This house was built in 1759 for John Vassall and served as Gen. George Washington's headquarters during the Siege of Boston (1775–1776) during the American Revolution. Andrew Craigie, Washington's apothecary general, bought it in 1791, and when he died in 1819, his widow took in boarders. Longfellow was a boarder for several years before his marriage. It would remain Longfellow's in-town residence for the rest of his life. This 1849 image shows the devoted couple and their first children, Charles (left) and Ernest. (Courtesy NPS.)

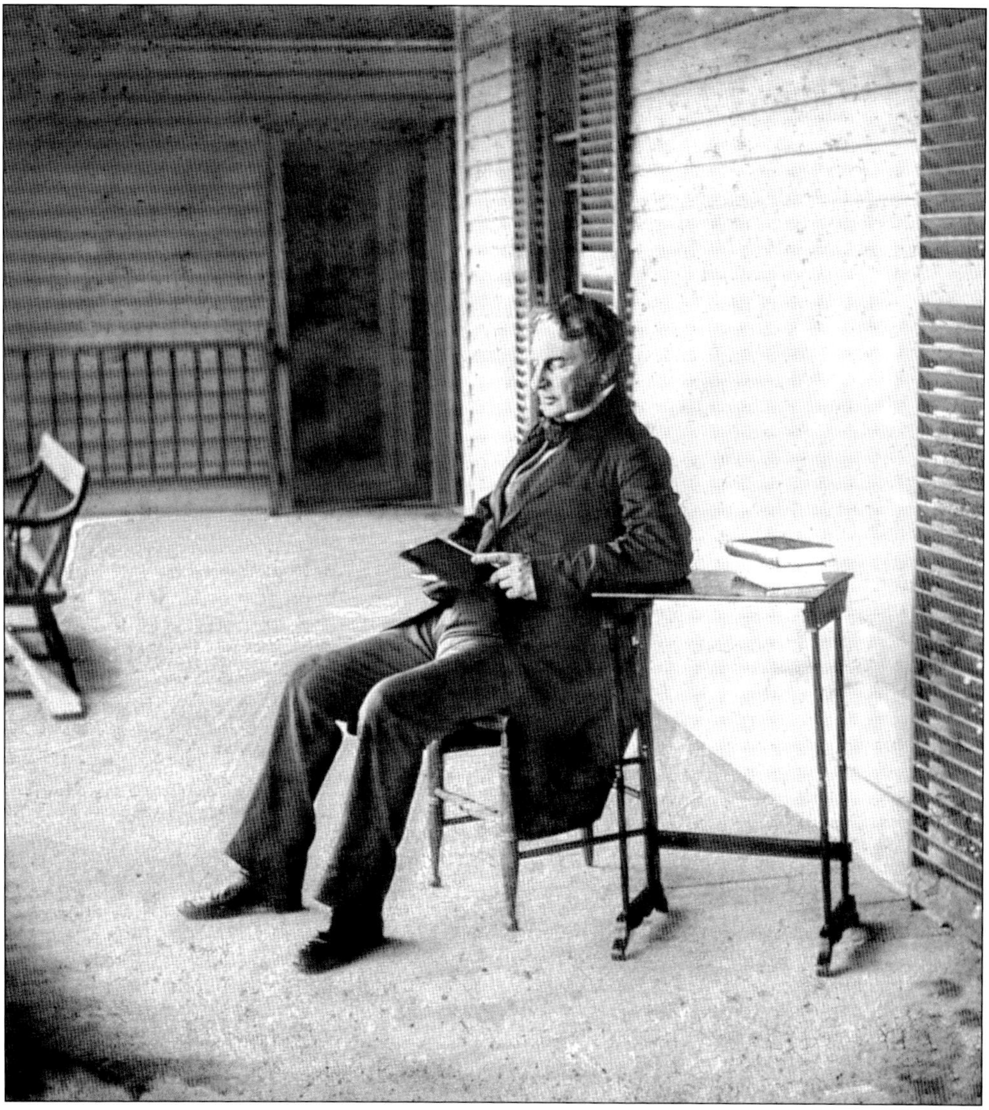

Although Longfellow had been coming to the Nahant Hotel since the 1830s, it was not until later that he stayed for longer periods. In 1850, 1851, 1853, and 1854, he and his growing family boarded at the Jonathan Johnson house on Nahant Road in the village. In 1856, he rented the Mountford cottage on Swallow Cave Road. The year 1857 found him in the Hood house at 368 Nahant Road. During the 1858 and 1859 seasons, he rented the William Wetmore house near 201 Willow Road. This serene c. 1850–1858 image of Longfellow shows him on a porch in Nahant. One might imagine him here on his piazza overlooking the sea contemplating the sights and sounds that he later formed into his poem of 1880 called "Four by the Clock." In part, it reads, "Four by the clock! And not yet day; But the great world rolls and wheels away, With its cities on land, and its ships at sea, Into the dawn that is to be!" (Courtesy NPS.)

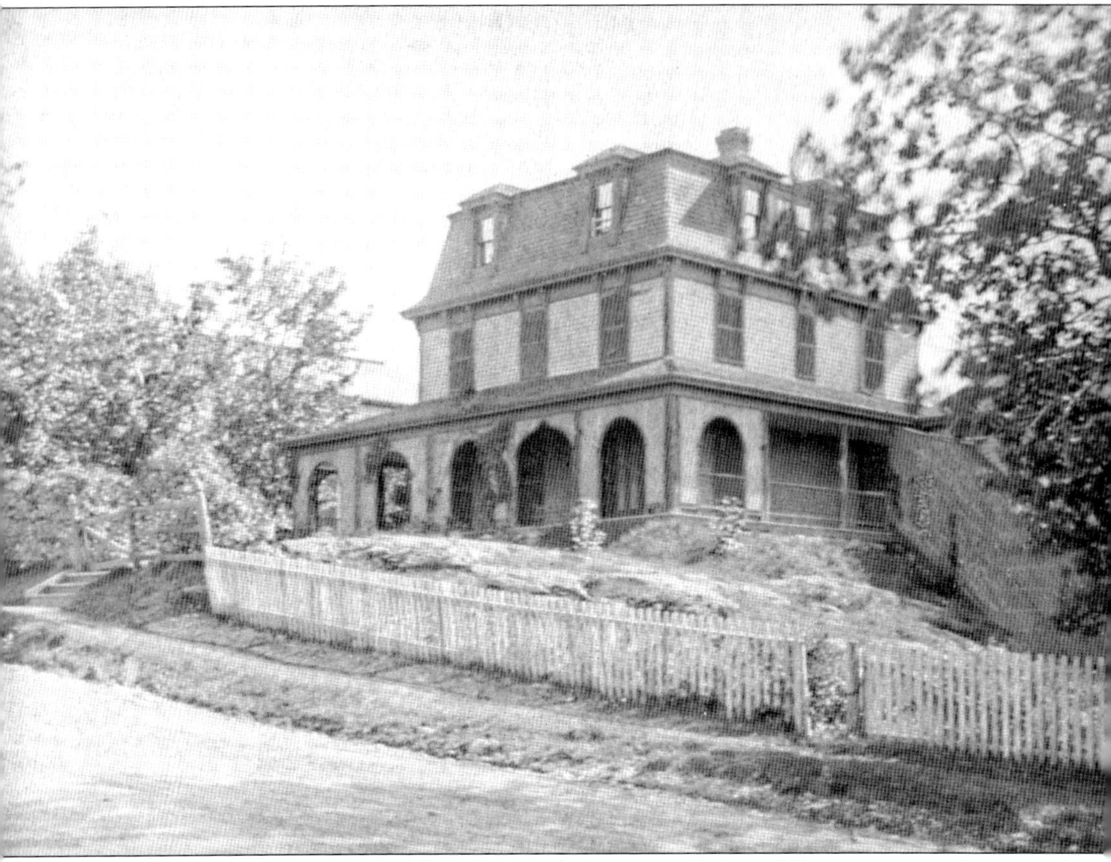

Reflecting on his purchase of the Wetmore house in 1860, Longfellow writes in a January 12, 1861, letter to his brother-in-law Thomas Gold Appleton, "I bought the Nahant cottage with you, at 5,000 dollars. . . . I had not time to consult you . . . the heirs being rather in a hurry." Both were pleased and spent many years enjoying the seaside from here. This image reflects additions Longfellow made to the house. In a June 3, 1866, letter to Ernest (his son) he notes that "at Nahant, where we have been enlarging the house, by an attic with a French roof and an addition to Uncle Tom's quarters of two rooms, making six more bedrooms in all." On July 22, 1866, in a further letter to Ernest, Longfellow comments, "The new roof leaks, and the pump will not draw. You will like the upstairs rooms." In a letter dated August 9, 1866, to his nephew William Longfellow, he complains that "nor has the painter finished his work." Such seems to be the universal experience of homeowners.

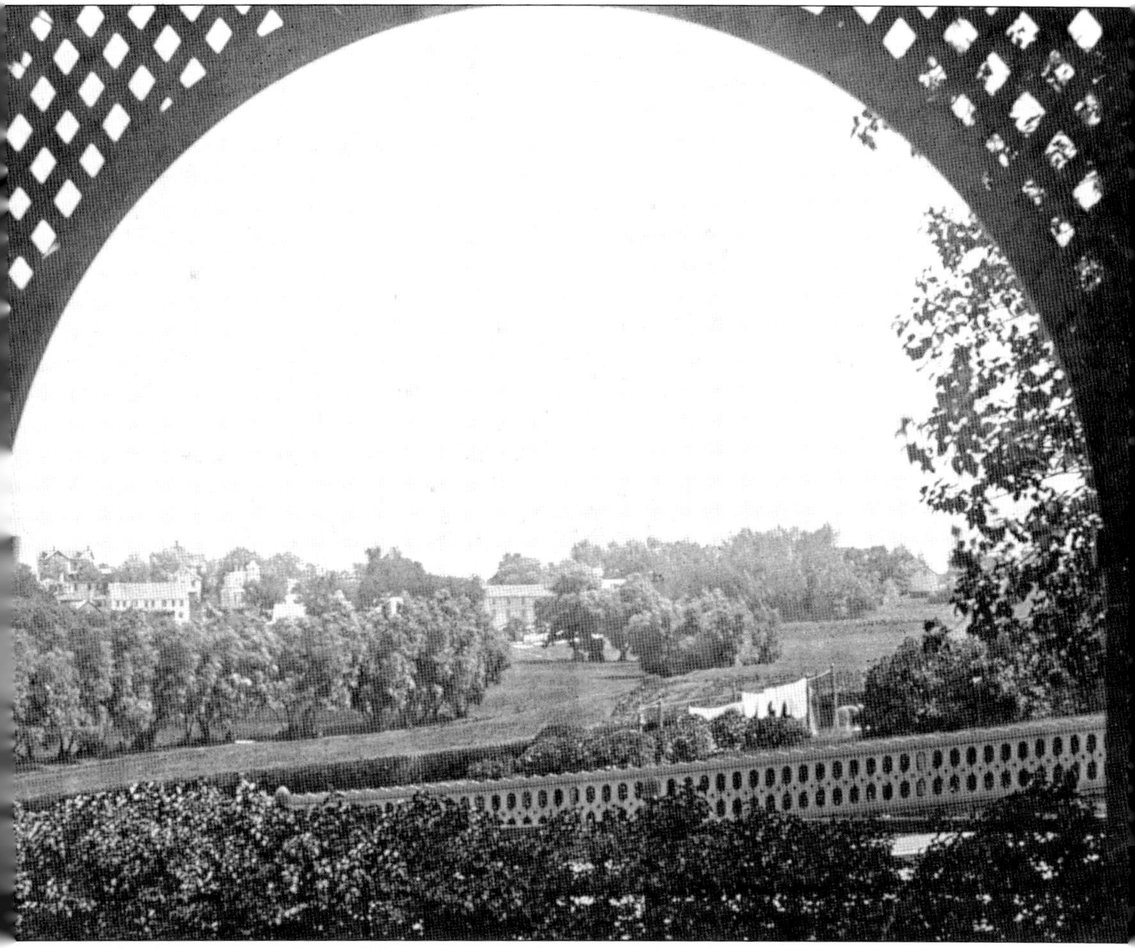

From the front piazza of Longfellow's cottage, the view included some of the village houses; the Whitney Hotel with its outbuildings and agricultural fields; and meadows. Note the decorative fencing of the Blanchard house across the street. Although Nahant had been denuded of its trees in the 18th century, by the mid-1800s, Frederic Tudor's efforts to replant trees in Nahant had been successful. The resulting romantic landscape could be enjoyed by family and guests when they were tired of the seascapes on the other side of the house. In a journal entry of August 18, 1850, Longfellow writes, "The pathway through the fields under the willows is very rural and pretty." Another of July 14, 1851, notes, "Met Mr. Tudor climbing over a stone fence. . . . He showed us his wheat field by the sea." On August 13, 1851, he writes, "We were to meet the Storys at the Whitney's bowling alley in the field under the willows but they came not." (Courtesy NPS.)

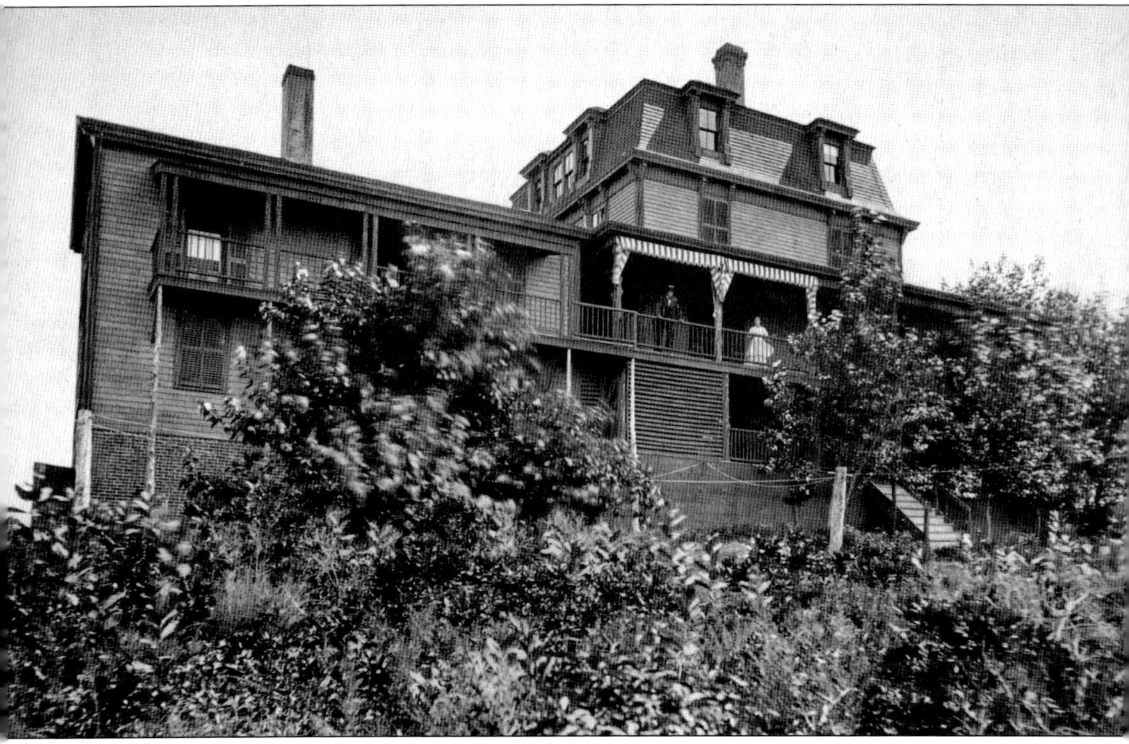

This view of the water-side facade of Longfellow's house demonstrates how steep the site is as it descends to the rocks and waves below. It had a view of the open Atlantic, anchored ships, Bailey's Hill, and Boston in the distance. In his 1922 book *Random Memories*, Ernest Longfellow remembers, "On the back piazza overlooking the bay, my father passed a great deal of his time." From this vantage point on a clear evening could be heard sounds coming from the mainland. Longfellow captured this still atmosphere in a poem written on July 28, 1859, entitled "The Bells of Lynn." In part, it reads, "O curfew of the setting sun! O Bells of Lynn! O requiem of the dying day! O Bells of Lynn! Borne on the evening wind across the crimson twilight, O'er land and sea they rise and fall, O Bells of Lynn! Till from the shuddering sea, with your wild incantations, Ye summon up the spectral moon, O Bells of Lynn!"

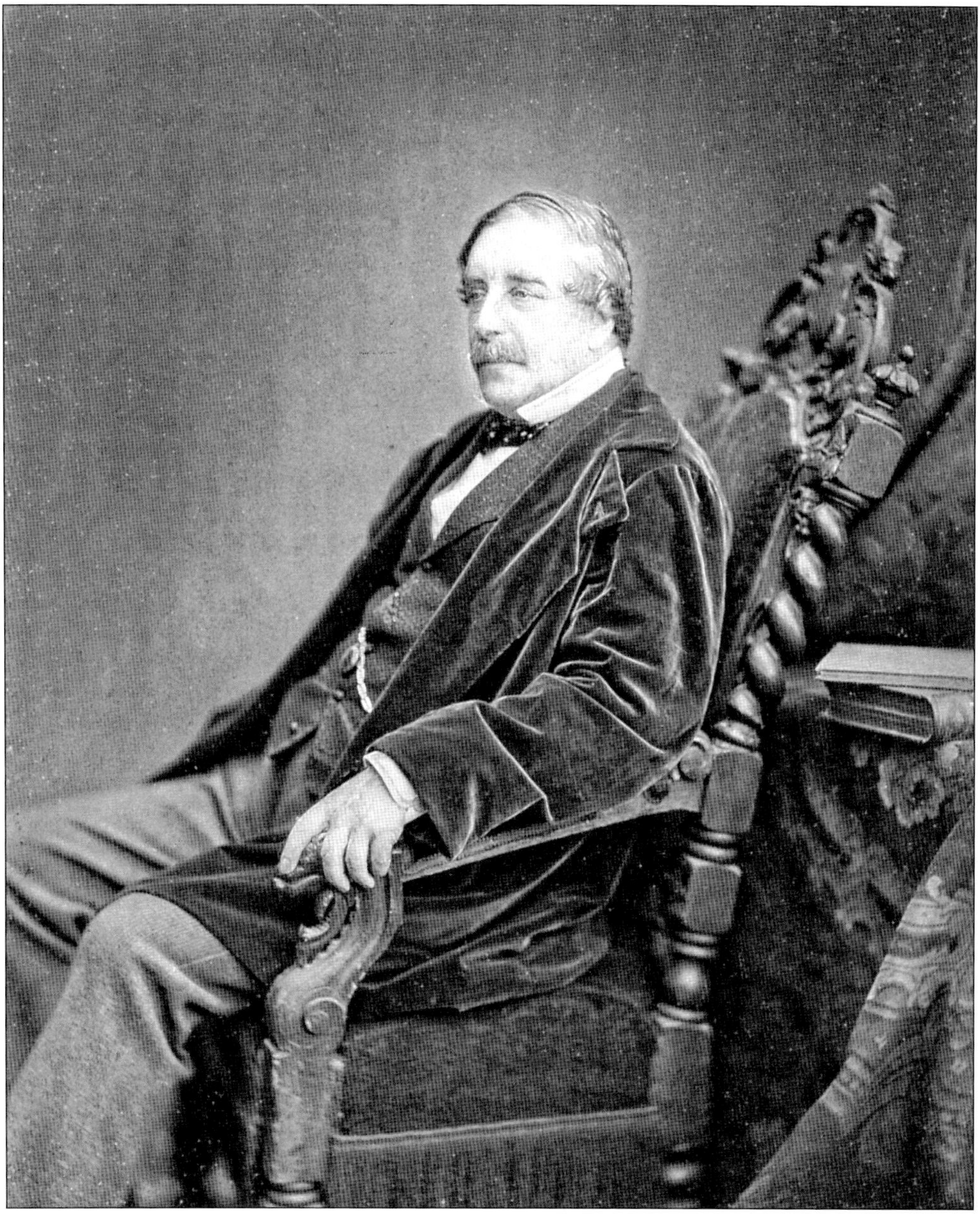

Thomas Gold Appleton (1812–1884) graduated from Harvard in 1831 and spent his life traveling and acquiring art. He endowed the Boston Public Library and was a founding member of the Boston Museum of Fine Arts. Many pieces from his collections of European and Asian art formed the initial holdings of the museum. A lifelong bachelor, he greatly enjoyed his many nephews and nieces, including the Longfellow children. Ernest Longfellow recalls, "My uncle, Mr. Appleton, formed a part of our household, much to our delight. He lived in a semi-detached ell, where he had his own suite of rooms." Susan Hale, in her biography, *Life and Letters of Thomas Gold Appleton*, quotes his sister Mary Macintosh: "Uncle Tom was . . . always turning up with his hands full and then disappearing without warning." In a letter dated July 12, 1870, to Edith and Anne Allegra (his daughters), Longfellow writes, "Uncle Tom, Ernest, and Mr. Peterson [artist Johann Erik Christian Peterson] have just got back from Marblehead in the *Alice*." (Courtesy NPS.)

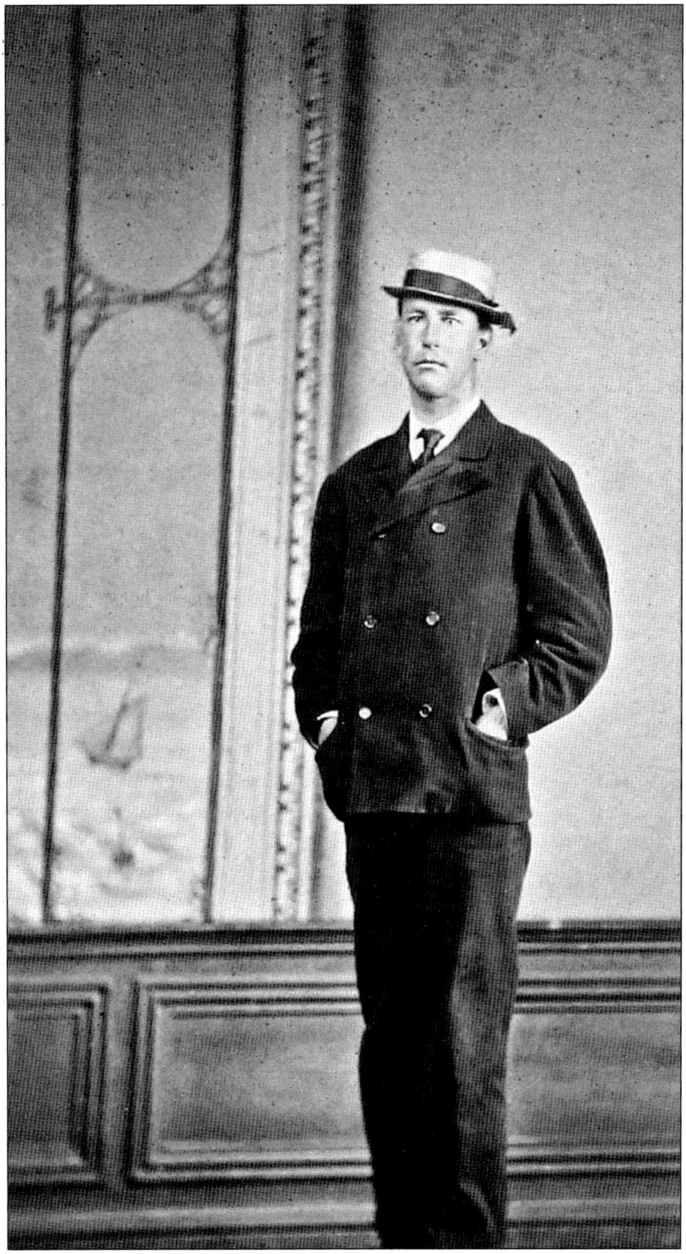

Charles Appleton Longfellow (1844–1893) was the oldest child of Henry and Fanny Longfellow. Charley was a rather headstrong youth but lived a charmed life summering in Nahant. On July 28, 1853, Longfellow noted, "The boys were up early today to receive their boat. After breakfast, Charley rowed me about in it." And on August 15, 1853, he wrote, "Charley has a bad hand from too much rowing." Much to Longfellow's objection, Charley enlisted in the Union army in March 1863. In June, he was ill with camp fever and spent time recovering in Nahant but returned to the fighting. He was honorably discharged on February 15, 1864. Following his uncle Tom Appleton's example, Charley occupied the rest of his life with worldwide travel. He particularly enjoyed Japan, where he lived for almost two years beginning in 1871. He also collected extensively and returned to Cambridge with many treasured items and his body covered in Japanese tattoos. (Courtesy NPS.)

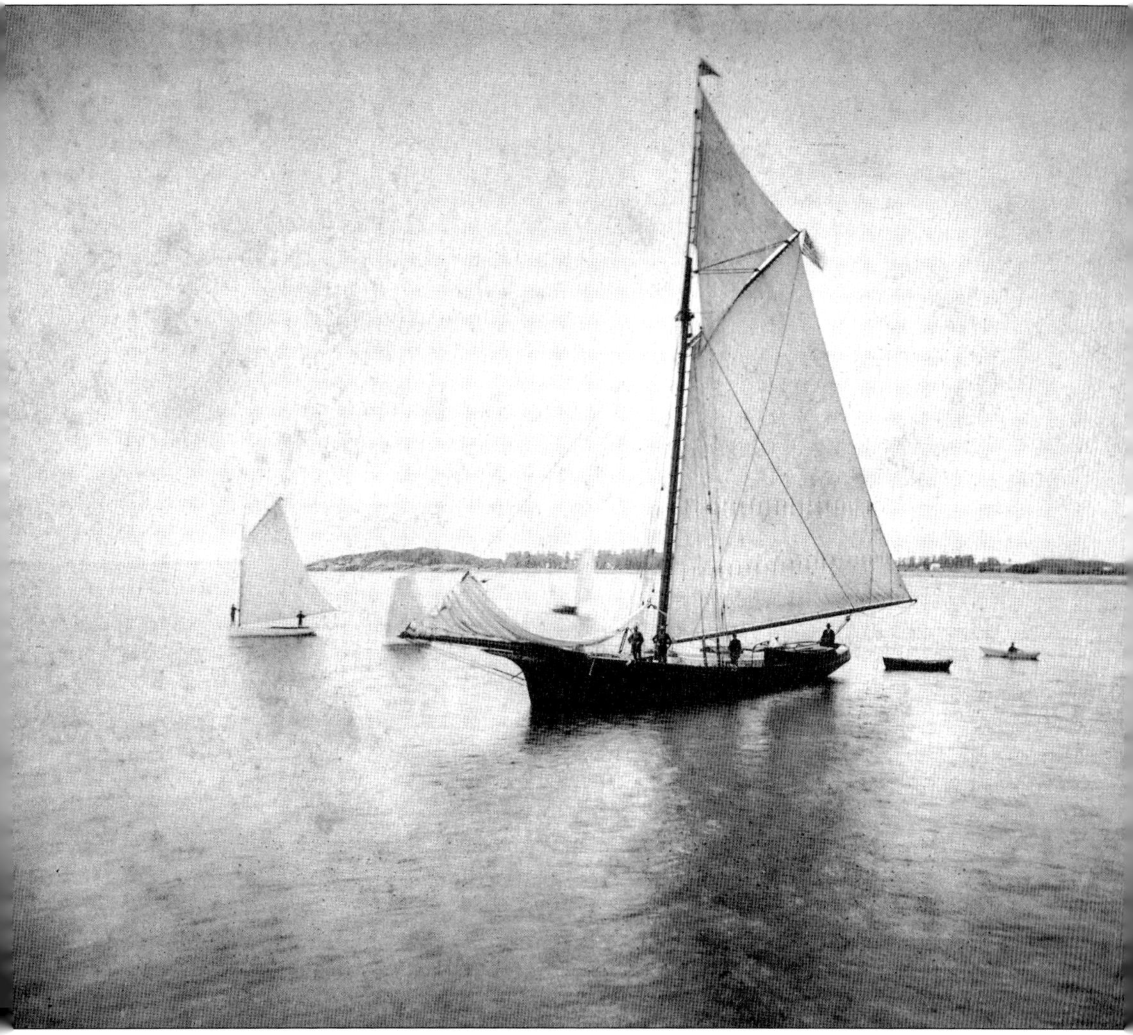

The yacht *Alice*, owned by Tom Appleton, was a seaworthy 27-ton sloop of 50 feet built by Townsend at Portsmouth, New Hampshire, in 1866. It was named after Alice Longfellow, the poet's first daughter, and modeled on the Boston pilot boat. Seen here at anchor off the house in Nahant with Bailey's Hill in the background, it made history in 1866. Longfellow writes to Ernest on June 3, 1866, "Arthur and Charley are all eagerness and excitement." The *Alice* was one of the first small yachts to cross the Atlantic. Leaving from Nahant, it arrived in the English racing center of Cowes on the Isle of Wight in just over 19 days and won the fastest crossing record. The captain was Arthur H. Clark, son of summer resident Benjamin C. Clark, and on the crew were Charley Longfellow and Harry Stanfield, all friends. (Courtesy NPS.)

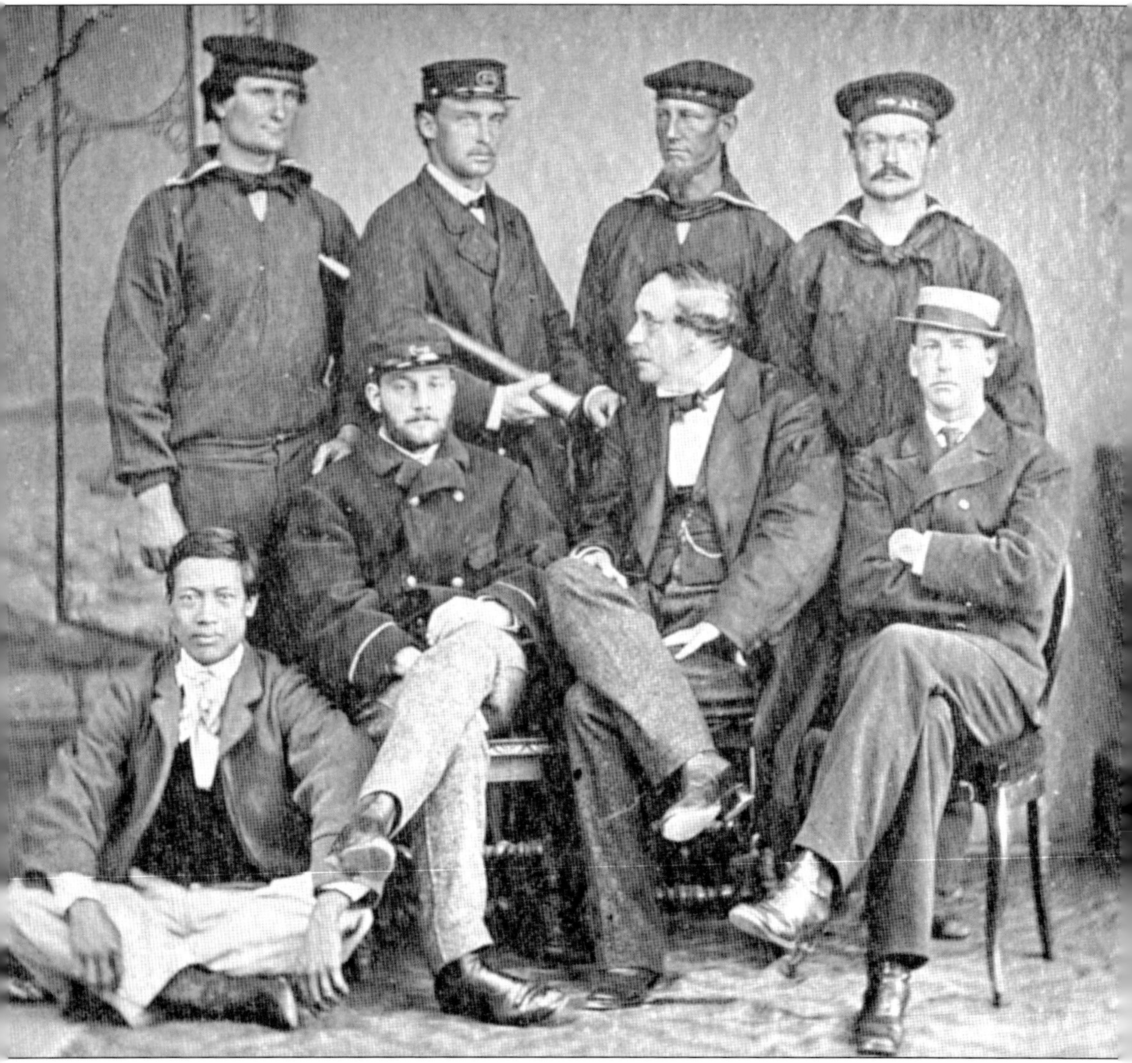

On June 3, 1866, Henry Longfellow noted in a letter to his son Ernest, "Uncle Tom's yacht, the *Alice*, is launched. When ready she is to sail for England . . . but I do not believe [Tom] will go in his yacht." In fact, Tom Appleton did not suffer the deprivations of a small boat but sailed on the Cunard line's *China,* an iron-hulled, screw-propelled steamer that carried only saloon passengers. He enjoyed a stateroom and all the latest amenities during the passage, while the crew of the *Alice* enjoyed the thrill of the competition. This formal portrait of the people associated with the *Alice*'s voyage was most likely taken in England after the successful arrival in Cowes on July 31, 1866. From left to right are (first row) sitting on the floor, the ship steward (presumed), sitting in chairs Harry Stanfield, Tom Appleton, and Charles Longfellow; (second row) unidentified, Capt. Arthur Clark, and two unidentified men. (Courtesy NPS.)

In the image at right, four men relax on the deck of the *Alice* after the voyage, with the shoreline of Cowes in the distance. Charley is assumed to be the central figure standing with his hand in his pocket. The exceedingly rare image below is a glimpse inside the cabin. The accommodations, although compact, look very comfortable and certainly to the taste of Tom Appleton, who enjoyed sailing in regional waters. From left to right are Harry Stanfield, lying in the berth; unidentified, looking at a chart; and Charley. (Both, courtesy NPS.)

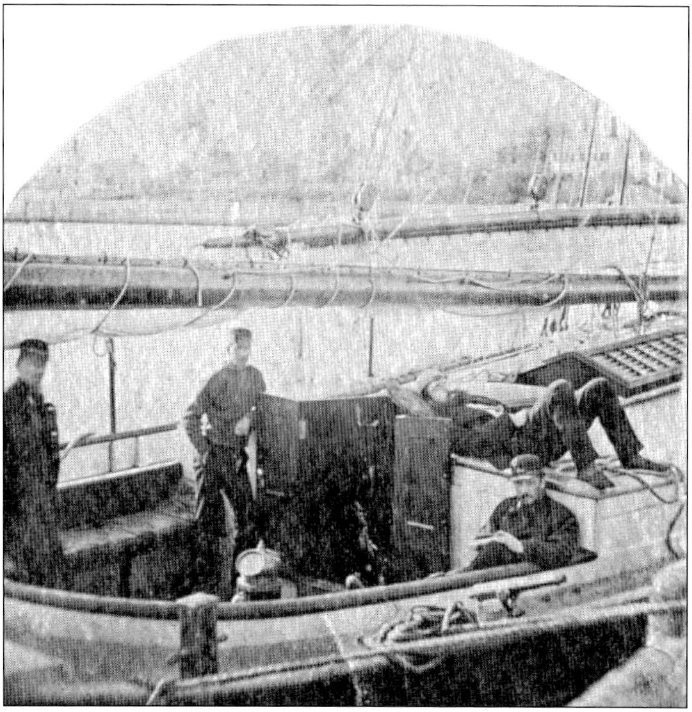

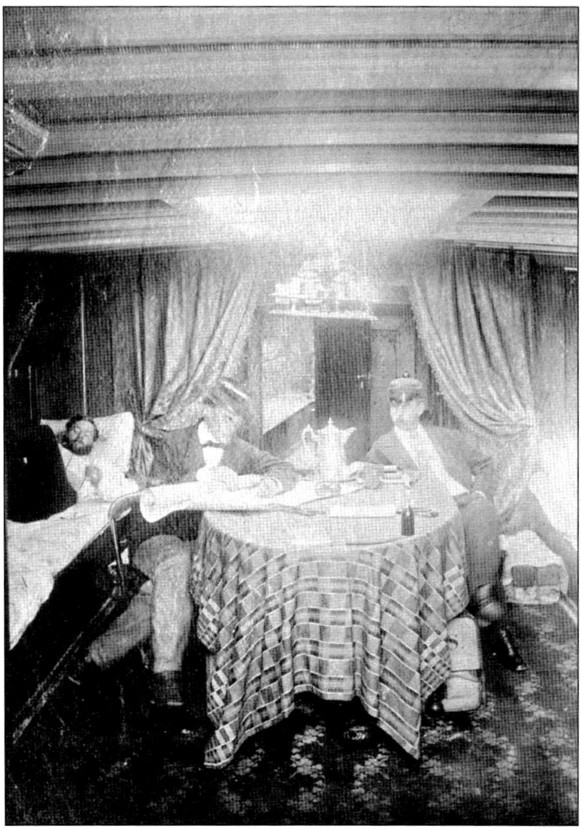

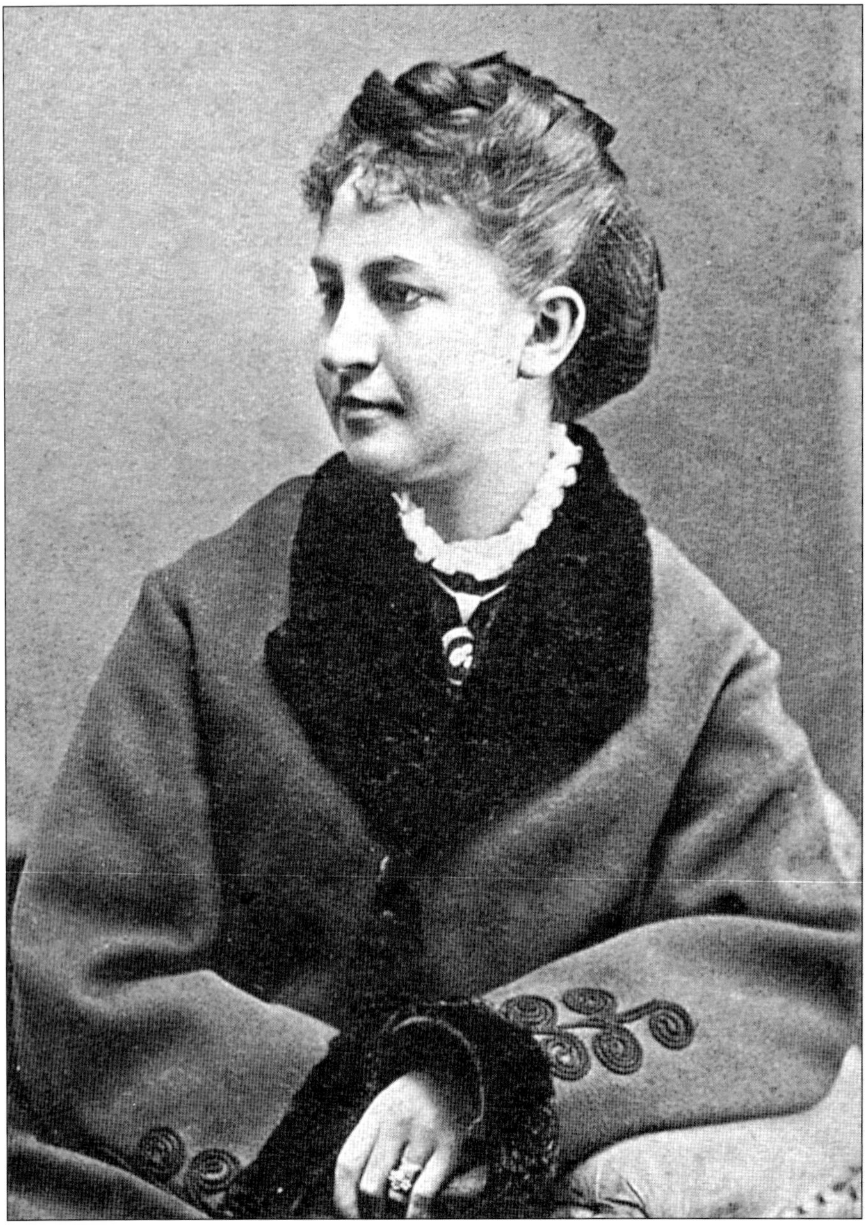

Alice Mary Longfellow (1850–1928) was the eldest daughter of the Longfellows. In a letter dated August 18, 1859, Longfellow writes, "My three little girls [Alice, Edith and Anne Allegra] . . . bathe in the sea, dig in the sand, and patter about the piazza . . . and sometimes go to see the Indians encamped on the shore and buy baskets." Given great support in childhood, Alice grew into an adulthood of confidence and service. She and Elizabeth Cary Agassiz helped found Radcliffe College, first as a women's annex to Harvard and finally as a fully integrated part of the university. Considered an early preservationist, Alice was instrumental in making Craigie House into a museum not only of her father's life and work but also of Gen. George Washington's headquarters during the Siege of Boston (July 1775–April 1776). She served on the Cambridge school committee and gave generously to many deserving institutions. Alice was the last owner of the Longfellow house in Nahant when it burned in 1896. (Courtesy NPS.)

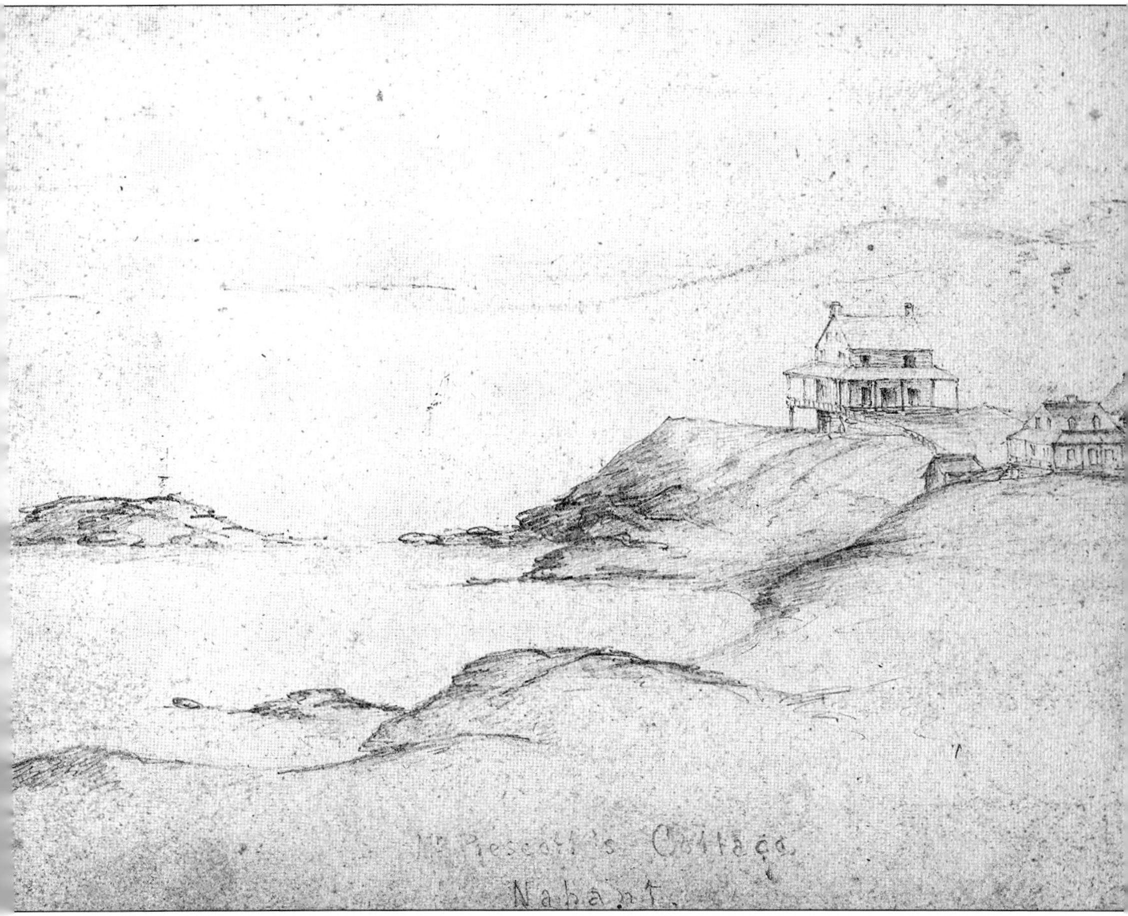

Judge William Prescott, from Salem and later Boston, built his summer residence Fitful Head at the present site of 3 Swallow Cave Road in 1828. His family, including his son William Hickling Prescott, his daughter-in-law Susan Amory Prescott, and their four children, enjoyed the property until 1853. On August 22, 1847, Longfellow records that he "called on Prescott. His cottage is one of the pleasantest here." This drawing by Longfellow shows, from left to right, Pea Island, the Prescott cottage, the Crowninshield (later Mountford) cottage, and the Dr. Edward H. Robbins/Rice cottage. While staying at the Nahant Hotel, he writes in his journal entry of July 10, 1839, "I will now go up to the belvedere [cupola] and sketch the scene. There, three sketches; Egg Rock, Pulpit Rock [in reality Castle Rock], and Prescott's cottage. Now for a bath." (Courtesy NPS.)

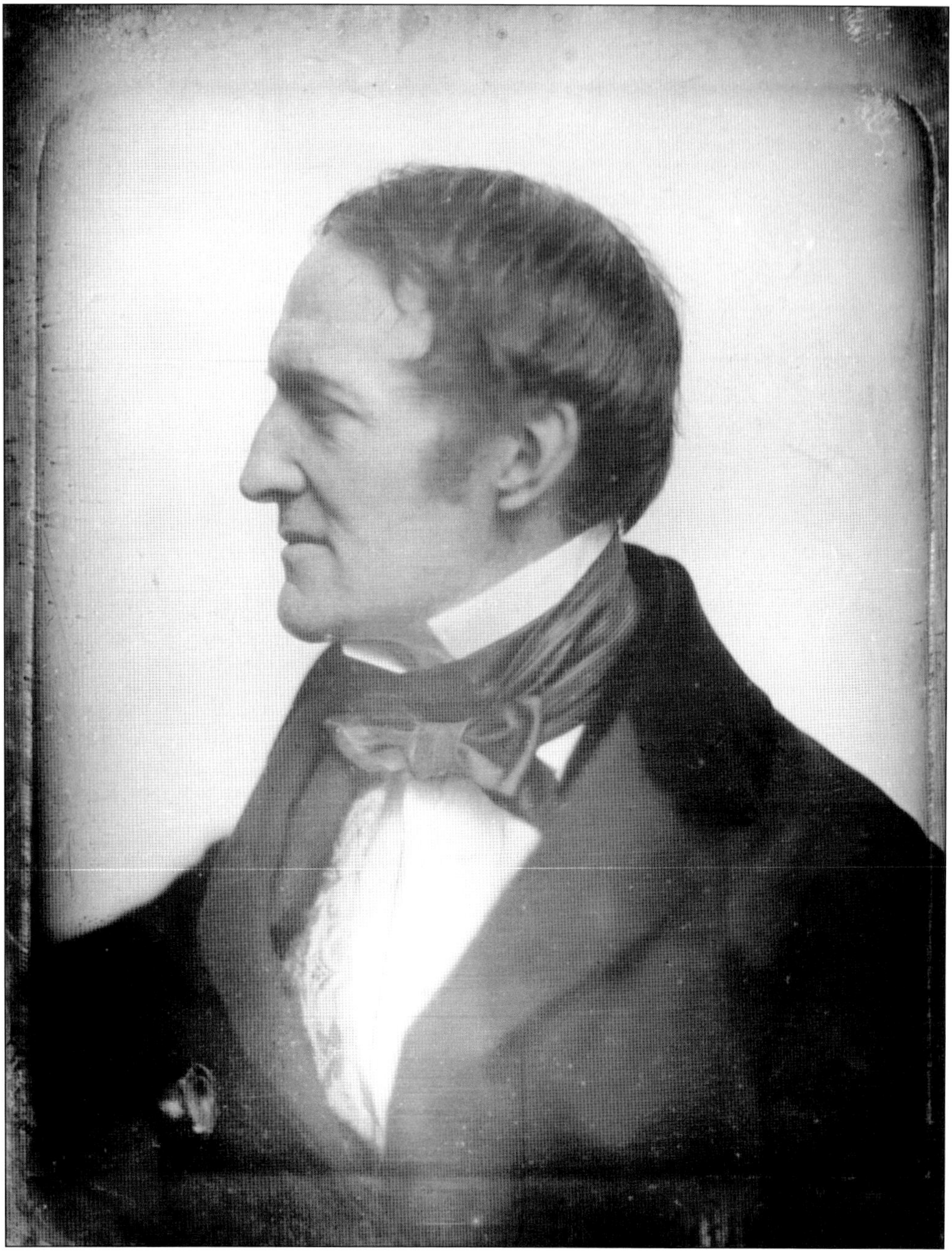

William Hickling Prescott (1796–1859) was one of the first great American writers of history. While attending Harvard, he was hit in the left eye by a crust of bread in a dining room food fight. He lost sight in that eye and had only partial vision in the other. He was assisted in his writing by a secretary and a noctograph, which had been invented for use by the blind. Despite this, he was noted for his rigorous research methods. His books on the history of Spanish America are considered models in the art of writing history. This Southworth and Hawes studio portrait was taken in 1859. Longfellow notes on July 26, 1851, "Dined with [Charles] Sumner at Prescott's . . . after dinner, sat chatting on the piazza. The sea beautiful, changing its hue with the changing hour."

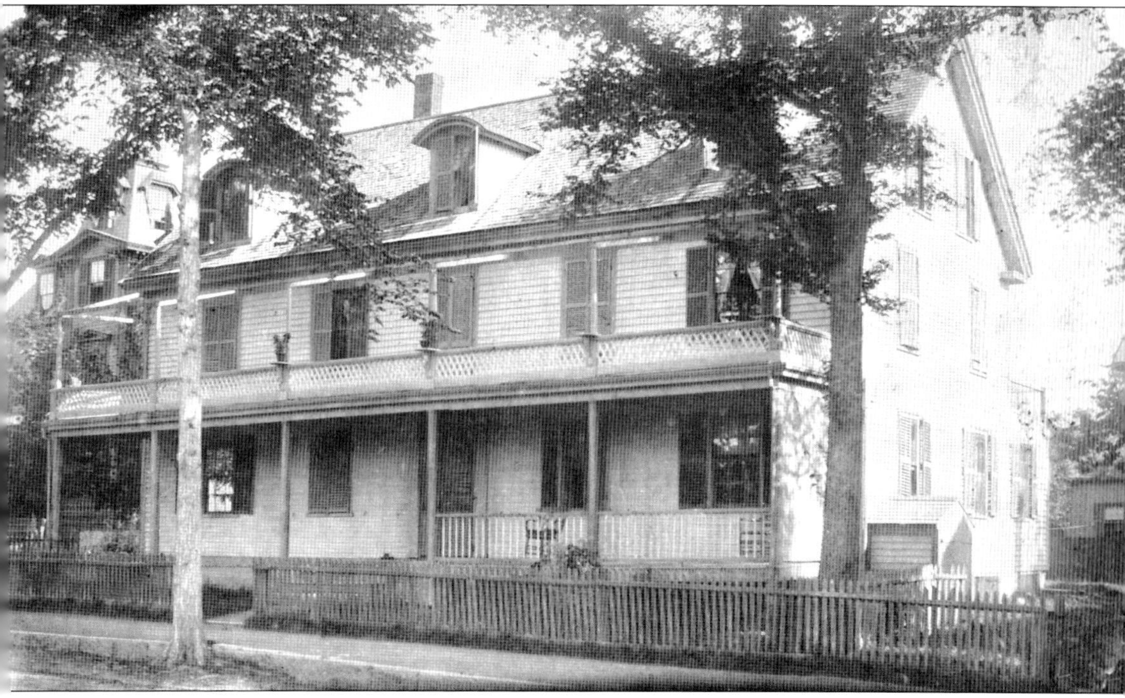

The Jonathan Johnson house was located at 332 Nahant Road, where the post office and Richland store are. It was Johnson's home but also was run as a boardinghouse for summer residents. Longfellow describes it as "the long low house in the village." Excerpted from his journals, on April 27, 1850, he "closed the matter with Jonathan Johnson touching the Nahant cottage . . . we take it for nine weeks." Also, on July 16, 1850, he writes, "Nothing could be pleasanter than our cottage, sheltered but near the sea. . . . Mr. Johnson is a jovial fisherman, and his laugh is as deep and merry as the sea." The Longfellow family stayed here in the summers of 1850, 1851, 1853, and 1854. The house was later moved to the corner of Willow Road and Wharf Street to be the front portion of the Rockledge Hotel, which is now condominiums.

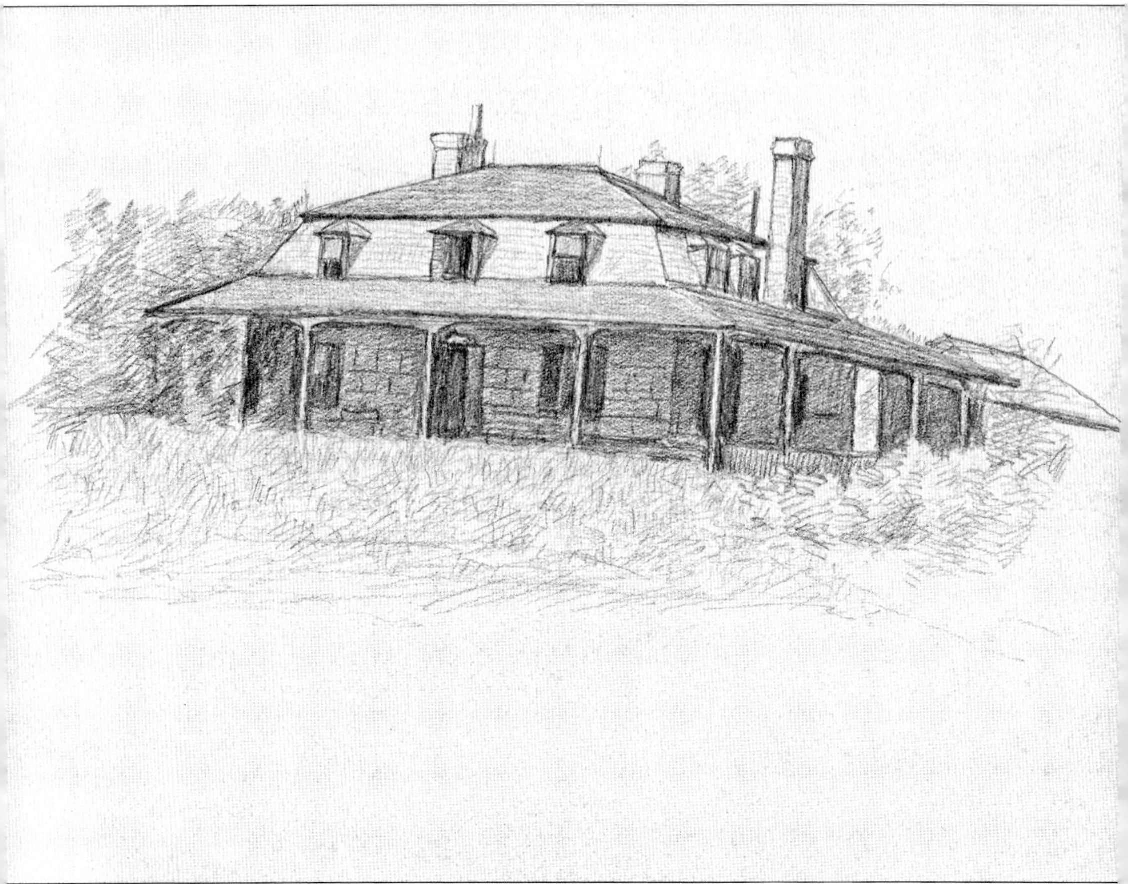

The Thomas Handasyd Perkins/Cary house, shown in this unattributed drawing, was built in 1817 of stone blocks brought by ship from Weymouth, Massachusetts. It was located on the shore near Spouting Horn. Perkins's son-in-law, Thomas G. Cary, had a daughter, Mary Louise, who in 1846 married Cornelius C. Felton, a professor of Greek and later president of Harvard. In 1850, another daughter, Elizabeth, married Louis Agassiz, a professor of zoology and geology at Harvard. Both were good friends of Longfellow. On July 18, 1857, Longfellow commented, "We stroll on the cliff and go down to the Spouting Horn to see the waves dash and roar in the moonlight." In a July 18, 1872, letter to Elizabeth Cary Agassiz, he writes, "Yesterday I was at your mother's. I found her in the hall at dinner surrounded by . . . many children and grandchildren. All seemed well and happy."

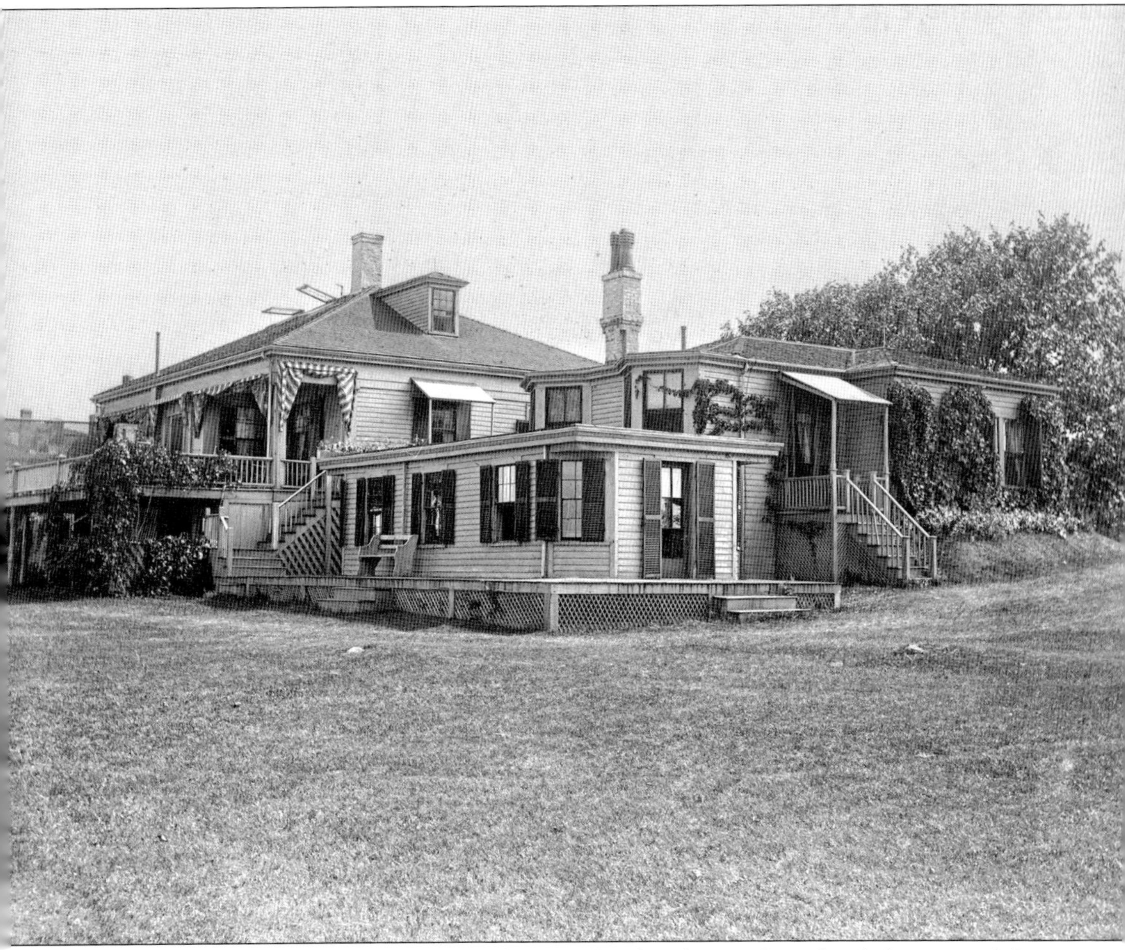

When Swiss-born Louis Agassiz came into the Cary family, Thomas Cary decided to expand the compound. He bought a small house known as the Butter Box, which had been built near Nahant Road and Summer Street by the Codman family. Cary moved it to the field next to his house near present-day Pleasant and Cary Streets. The Felton and Agassiz families were moved there. Wings were added over time, and it finally reached over 100 feet, plenty of room for frequent visitors and Agassiz's summer laboratories. This 1907 Baldwin Coolidge image shows it fully developed. Longfellow records on August 4, 1851, "Went to the steamboat landing. Agassiz and his wife arrive, Ah, Agassiz says, it is curious that to meet one's friends it is necessary to come to Nahant." Again, on July 18, 1857, Longfellow notes, "We go to Agassiz who shows us a beautiful Medusa he has just pulled from the sea, a new species not yet described in books." (Courtesy Historic New England.)

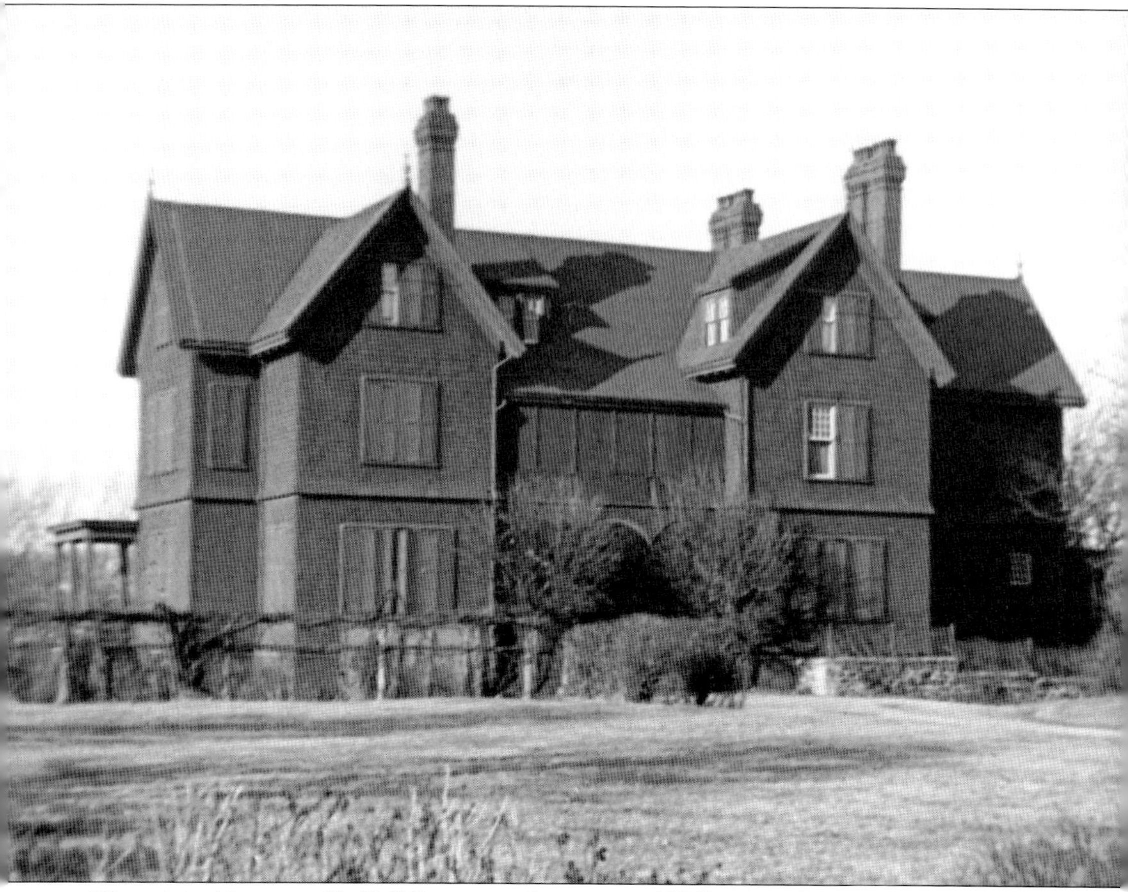

The original house at 51 Cliff Street, on the corner of Willow Road across the street from the Longfellow house, was built for John C. Gray in the 1850s. It was later owned by John Adams Blanchard and Laura Smith (Dove) Blanchard. In 1887, after her husband's death, Laura had the architect Alexander Wadsworth "Waddy" Longfellow, the poet's nephew, redesign the house with the landscape plan by Frederick Law Olmsted. The 1896 fire that destroyed Longfellow's house also took this house and three others nearby. Laura, now married to George Duncan, a London engineer, hired Longfellow again. He designed the present house in 1898, and it remains little changed today. Longfellow, by this time, had designed many buildings in and around Cambridge but was especially known for his work on the campuses of Radcliffe and Harvard Colleges.

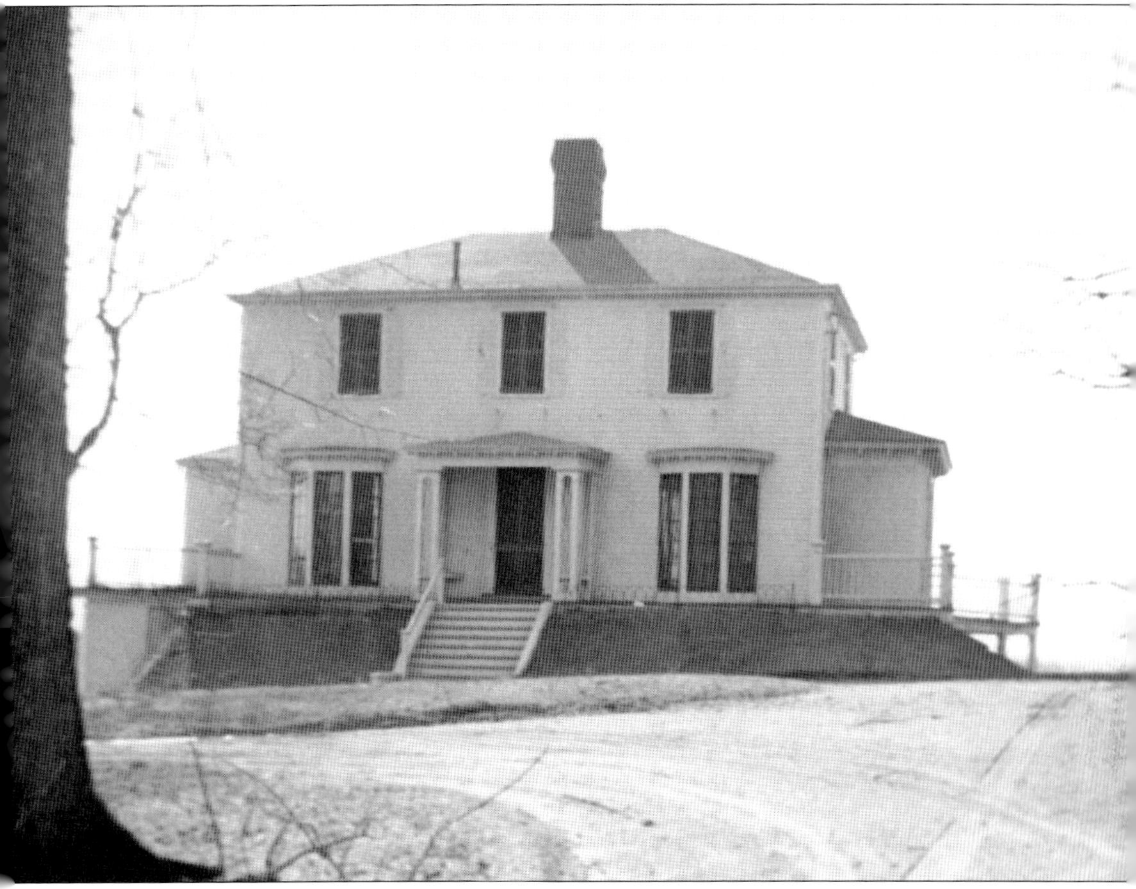

The initial portion of the house at 339 Nahant Road (the right side of the current house) was built in 1829. Later, this property was acquired by James W. Paige of Boston, a broker for textile manufacturers. He was also a partner in Nathan Appleton's textile mills in Lowell and the brother-in-law of Daniel Webster, the prominent orator and statesman. A wing on the left side was added in 1874 by J.T. Wilson; it was removed in 1939 and moved next door to create a separate house (345 Nahant Road). Longfellow noted in his journal on July 22, 1850, "Later the moon rose, and lightning flashed from the cloud fortress . . . like a cloaked assassin brandishing his blade. So, it seemed to me as I stood on Mrs. Paige's piazza." Also noted for July 19, 1851, "Daniel Webster is here dining with Mr. Paige."

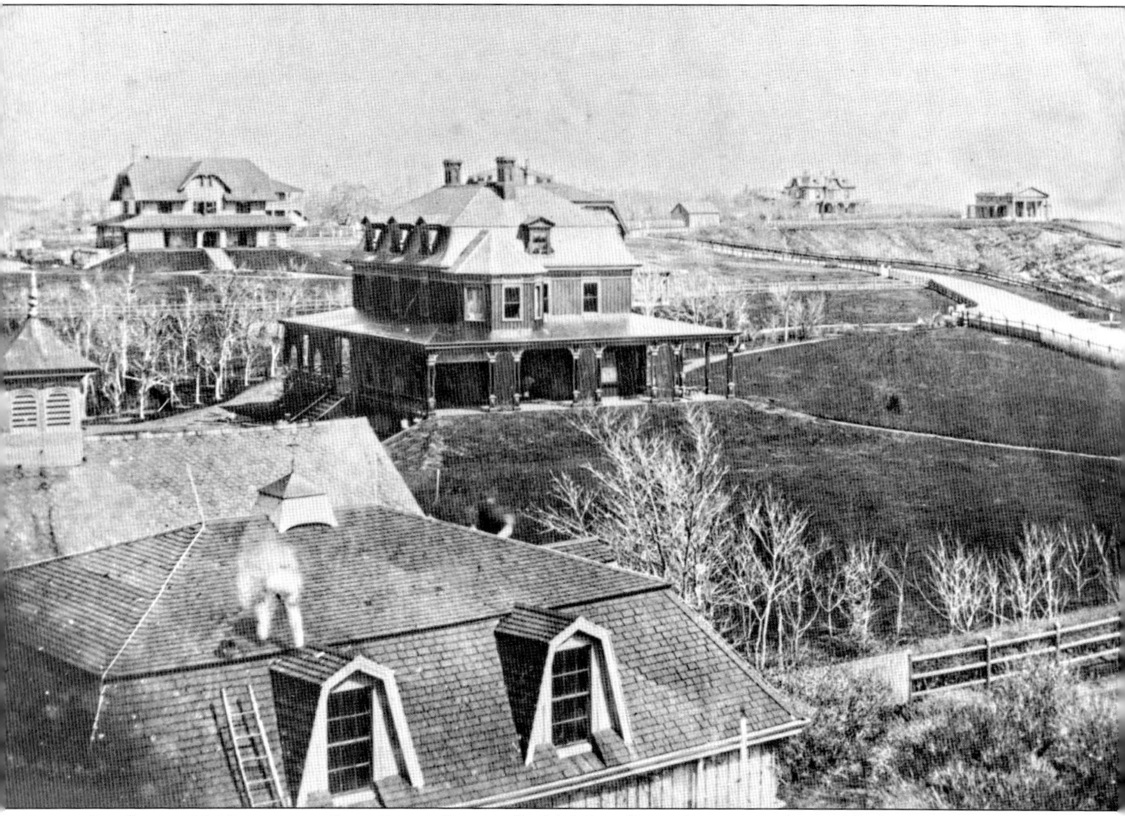

In this c. 1880 image taken from the roof of 36 Swallow Cave Road, visible beyond the barn in the foreground are (from left to right) the Hammond house, the Beal house, and the Upham and Mifflin houses. James Henry Beal (1823–1904), a Boston banker, was one of the men instrumental in financing the Civil War for the Union. James Holland Beal, a grandson, remembers a complaint by Mrs. Russell (a neighbor) of nude bathing by male Beal family members and friends on Cupid Rock below the cliff, which was part of the Beal estate. It was ignored, and later a sign forbidding swimming was placed on the rock in concrete by a Russell. No Beal admitted to it, but the sign was blown up, and a cavity was created, which James said was still visible. Longfellow, in a letter to James T. Fields, his publisher, on September 9, 1873, says, "Mr. and Mrs. Beal have just been here." Louisa Beal was the sister-in-law of James Fields.

Three

Hammond Family Albums

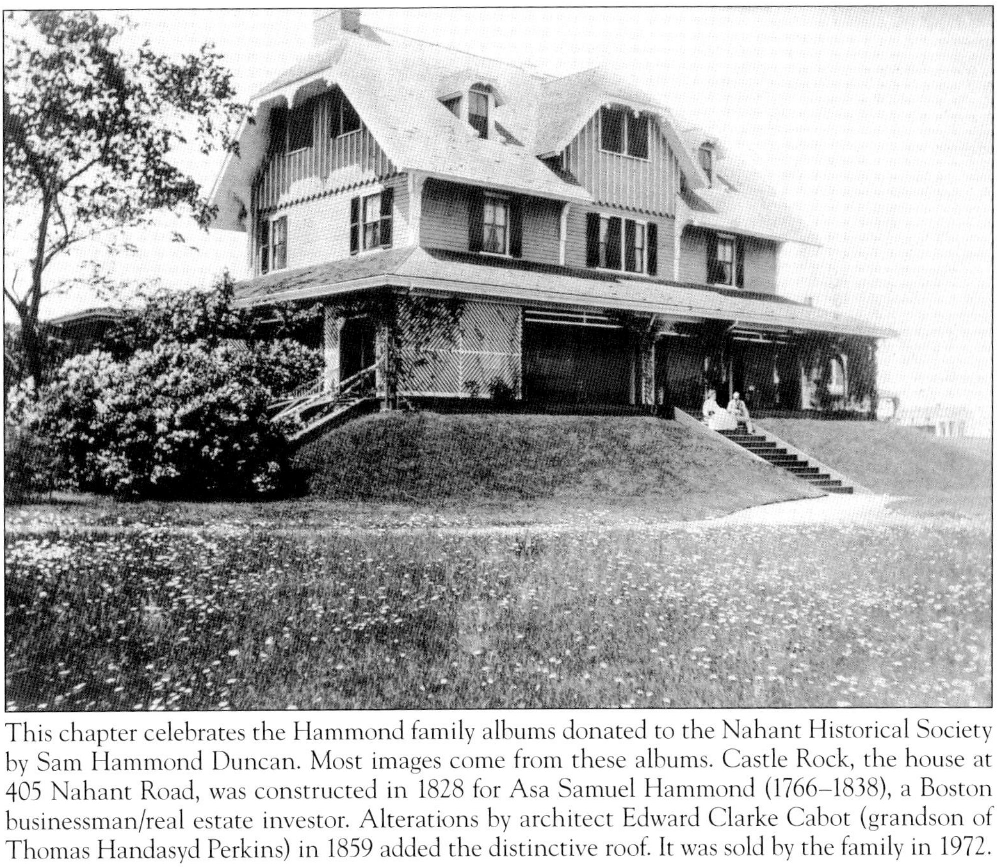

This chapter celebrates the Hammond family albums donated to the Nahant Historical Society by Sam Hammond Duncan. Most images come from these albums. Castle Rock, the house at 405 Nahant Road, was constructed in 1828 for Asa Samuel Hammond (1766–1838), a Boston businessman/real estate investor. Alterations by architect Edward Clarke Cabot (grandson of Thomas Handasyd Perkins) in 1859 added the distinctive roof. It was sold by the family in 1972.

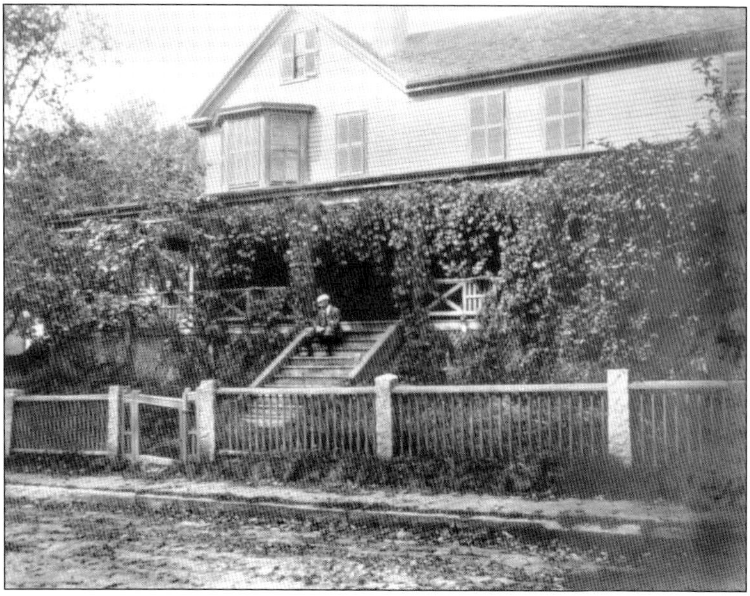

Because of the construction at Castle Rock during the 1859 season, the family had leased the cottage owned by Elizabeth Elliot Spooner. Seen here in 1904, with Samuel Hammond IV on the steps, it was located on Pleasant Street on the site of the current town hall. This image is entitled *Birthplace of Samuel Hammond IV.*

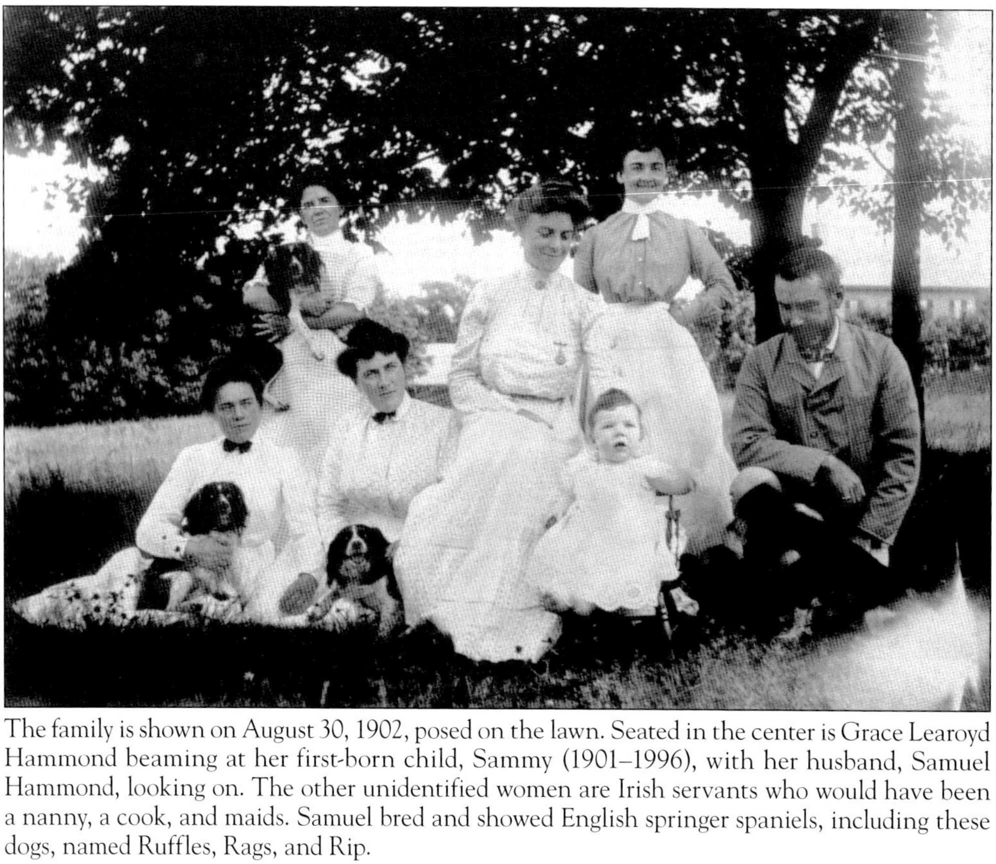

The family is shown on August 30, 1902, posed on the lawn. Seated in the center is Grace Learoyd Hammond beaming at her first-born child, Sammy (1901–1996), with her husband, Samuel Hammond, looking on. The other unidentified women are Irish servants who would have been a nanny, a cook, and maids. Samuel bred and showed English springer spaniels, including these dogs, named Ruffles, Rags, and Rip.

Samuel Hammond IV (1859–1934), of Boston and Nahant, graduated from Harvard in 1881 and was a deputy collector in Boston. He served as a Navy ensign during the 1898 Spanish-American War and married Grace Learoyd in 1900. Although not engaged in business after 1901, he was active in many Nahant civic affairs. He was a member and president of the New England Kennel Club for many years.

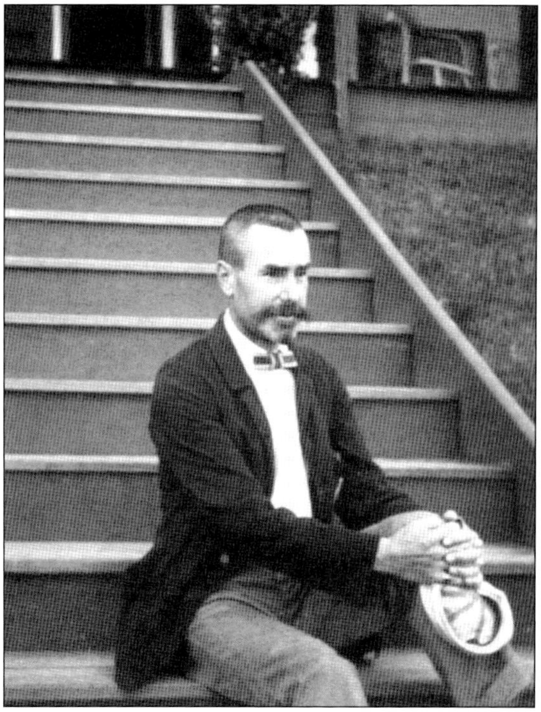

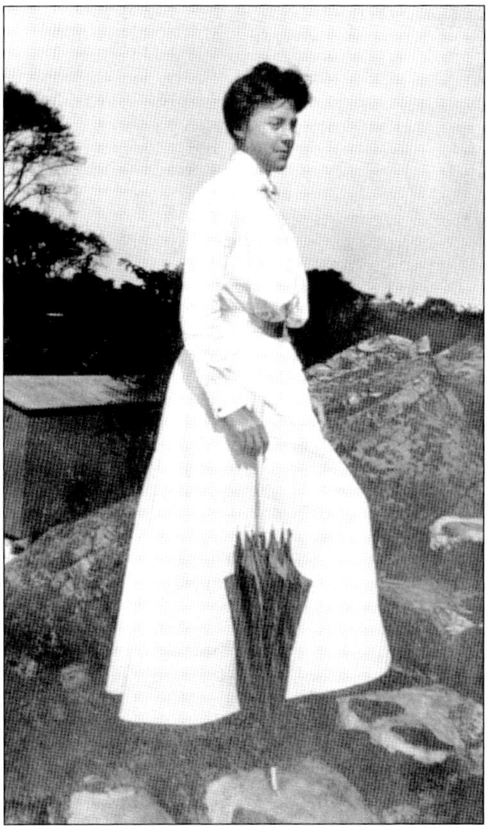

Grace Learoyd Hammond (1874–1972) is seen here in 1903 on the steps built into Cupid Rock, located on the headland adjacent to Castle Rock. She was the president of the board of managers of the Vincent Memorial Hospital in Boston, formed in 1891 to "give aid to women of any race or creed." Led and staffed by women, it was brought into the Massachusetts General Hospital system in 1941.

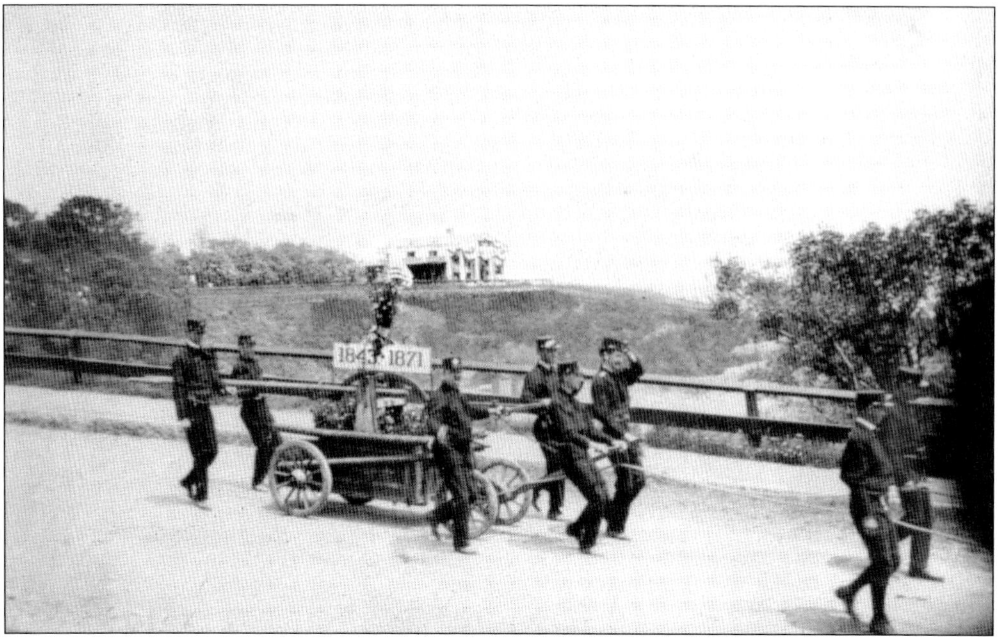

The semicentennial celebration of 1903 marked the 50th anniversary of Nahant's separation from Lynn in 1853. The parade route passed in front of Castle Rock, giving the Hammond family a perfect view. In the photograph above, firemen pull Nahant's first hand-pump fire engine, Eagle, used from 1843 until 1871. It can still be seen exhibited in the lobby of the town hall. Note the 1820s Mifflin house seen in the distance. The outdated Eagle was replaced with the Dexter No. 1 (below), which served until 1882. Its advantage was the ability to pump water into the tank as well as out to fight the fire.

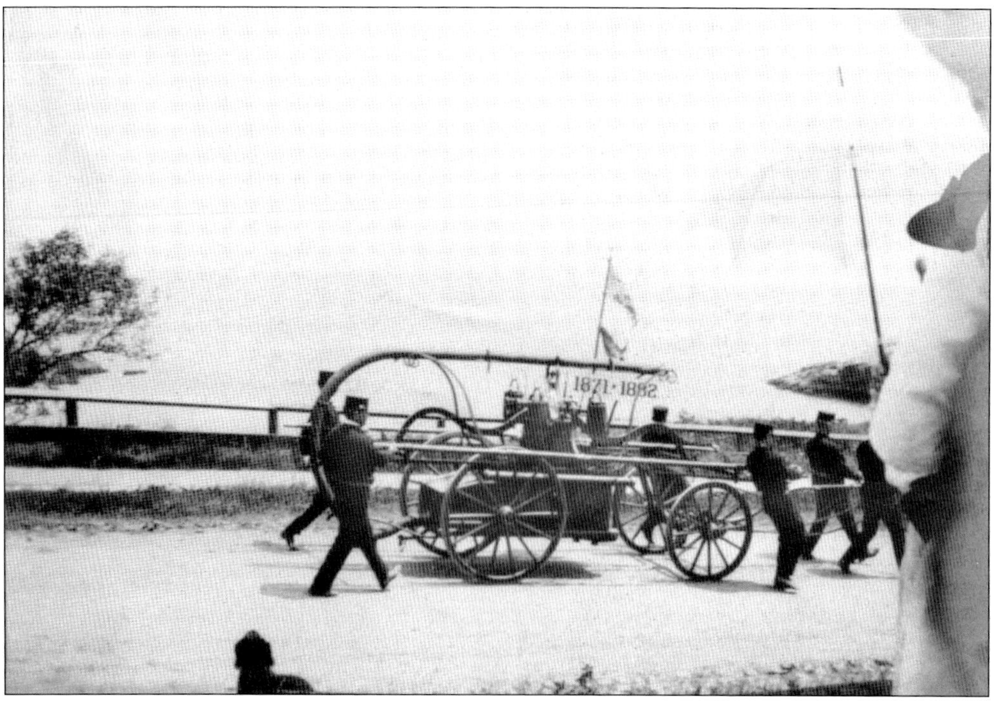

Samuel Hammond is posing on his white horse in his capacity as chief marshal of the parade. His family had been summering in Nahant for 75 years and were well integrated into town life. He served on committees, such as the one planning this celebration. In 1911, he was a significant force in the effort to build the new town hall, which was dedicated on November 9, 1912. (Courtesy NHS.)

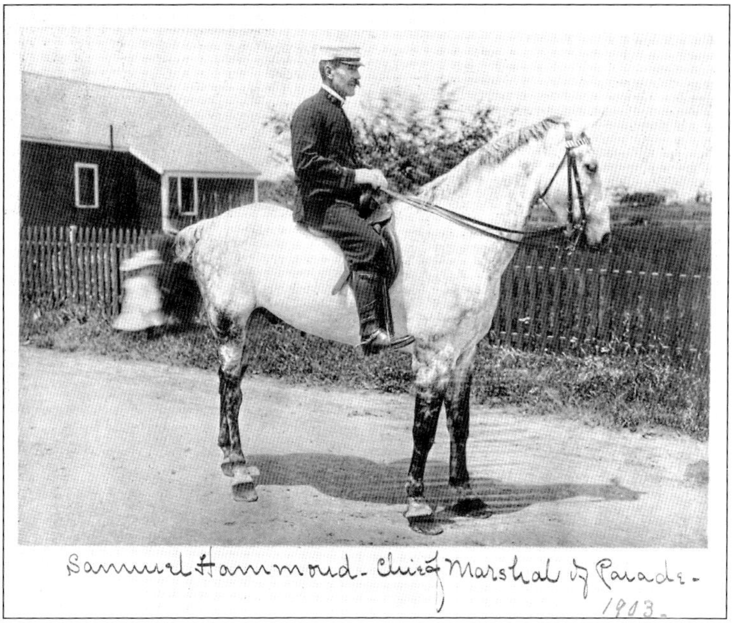

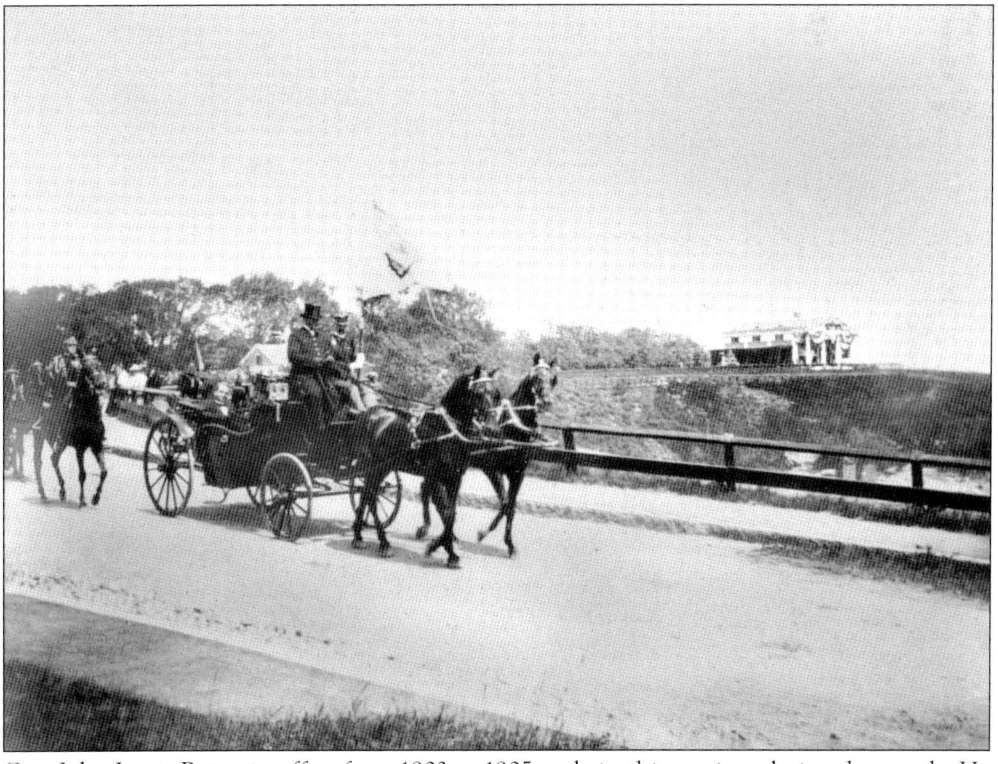

Gov. John Lewis Bates, in office from 1903 to 1905, rode in this carriage during the parade. He was a vocal supporter of women's suffrage. One of his accomplishments was the construction of the East Boston tunnel, which opened in 1904. This was the first underwater streetcar tunnel in the country and ran from downtown Boston to Maverick Square. It still serves as part of the MBTA subway system on the Blue Line.

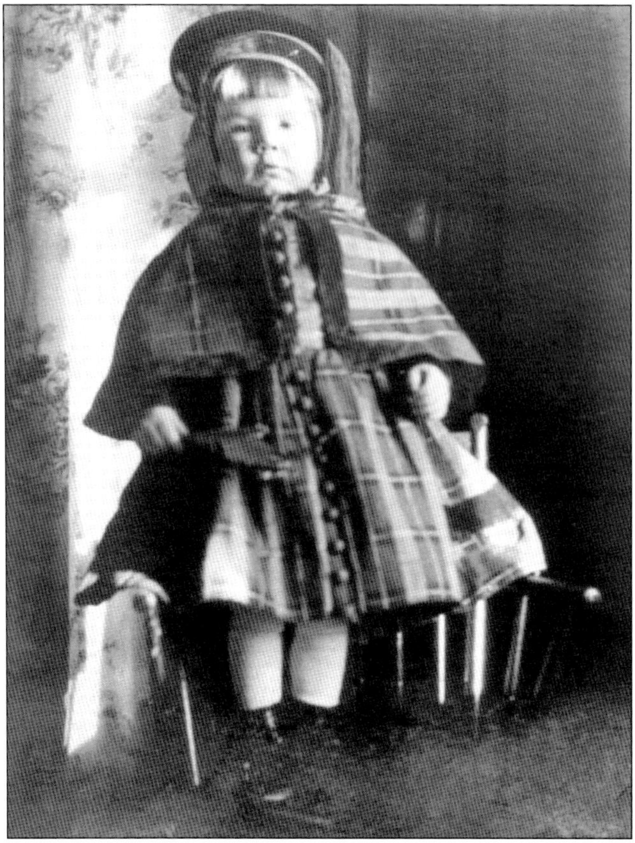

These two images from 1904 reflect the fashion of dressing children in exotic clothing for special occasions. The photograph at left, *Uncle Col's Dress*, shows John Collins Warren in the 1840s. Dr. Warren (1842–1927) was a surgeon whose expertise was the removal of cancerous breast tumors. Below, *Sammy as a Highlander* shows a suit of clothing worn by generations of Hammonds. It was donated to the Museum of Fine Arts (MFA), Boston, in 1996 by Samuel Hammond Duncan. It has been featured in two exhibitions at the MFA: Dressing Up: Children's Fashions, 1720–1920, in 1996, and Gender Bending Fashion in 2019. Most of the pieces in this set were made in France in the 1870s.

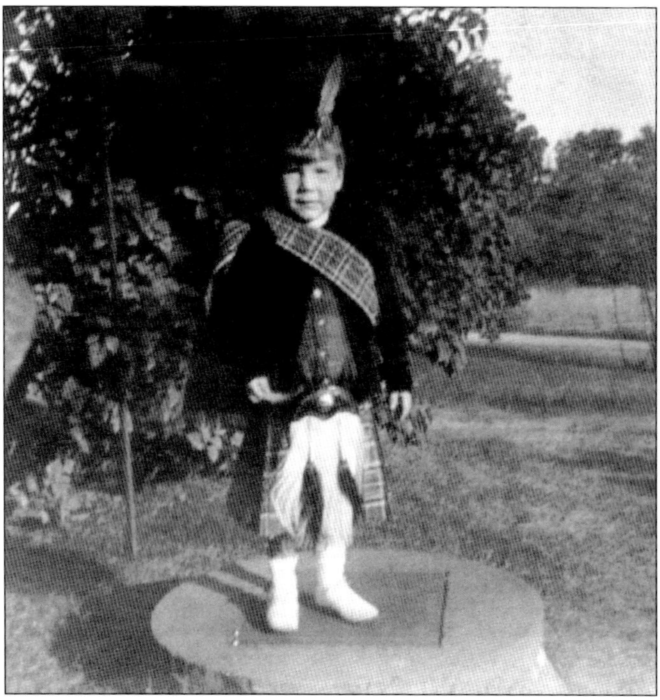

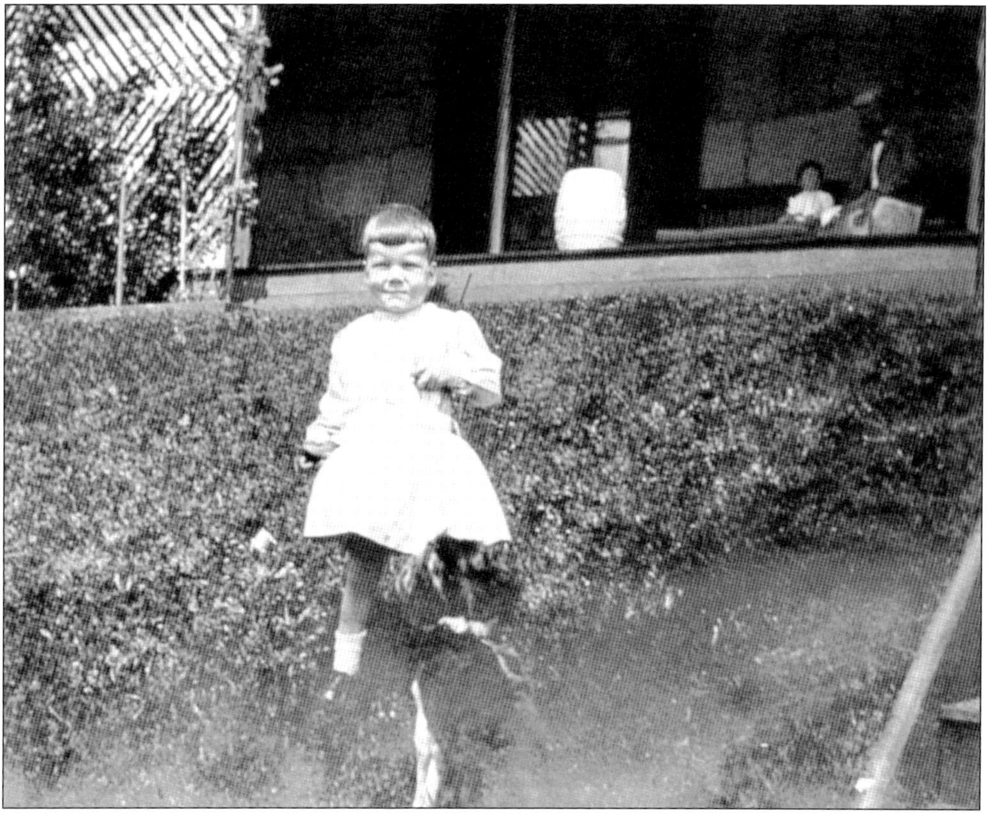

New parents have always had a great interest in documenting their first child. Since the advent of photography, these types of images have appeared in family albums. The above photograph shows Sammy, very pleased with himself, after his first haircut on June 28, 1904. The image to the right, from August 29, 1904, is titled *First Trousers*. These made the statement that he was no longer a baby and that he now entered the sphere of masculinity. In a world of specific gender differentiation, these were significant events for the individuals and their families.

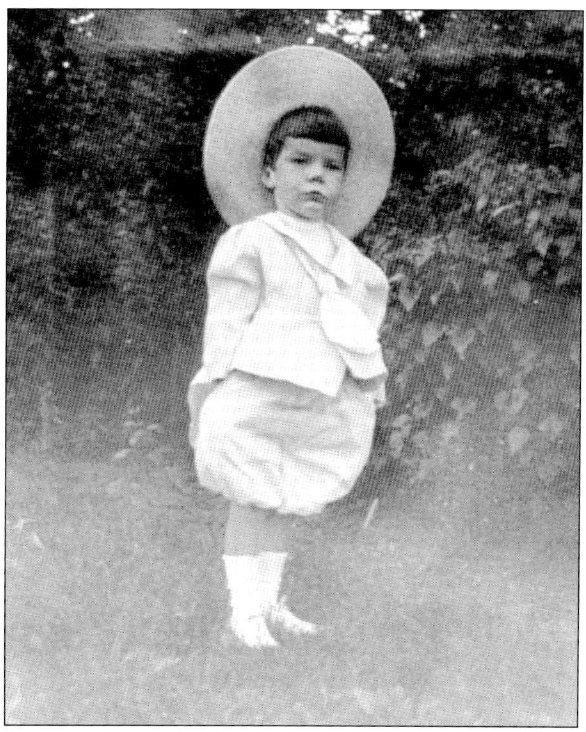

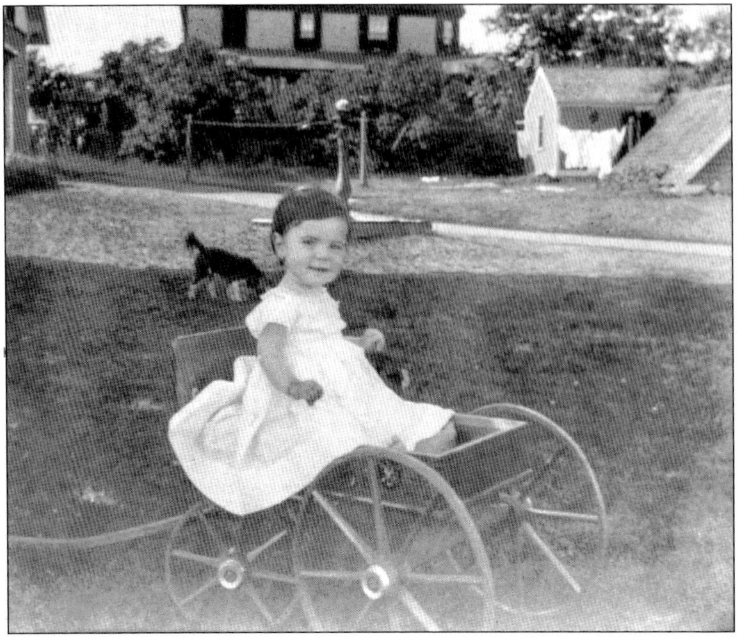

Mason Hammond (1903–2002) was just 18 months when he was photographed on the lawn of Castle Rock. A sweet smile can always melt the heart of a viewer. After a happy childhood. Mason graduated from Harvard in 1925 and earned a second degree at Oxford University as a Rhodes Scholar. In 1928, he returned to Harvard to begin his long career as a professor of classics and history.

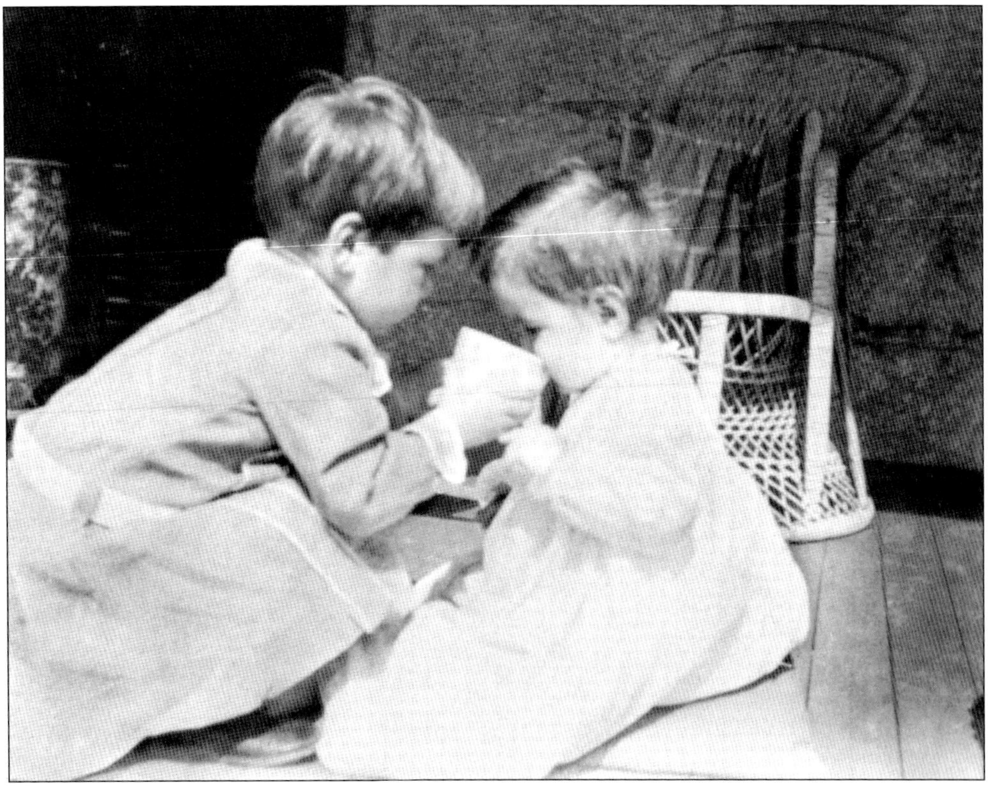

Sammy and Mason are shown on the generously sized wrap-around piazza of Castle Rock that was typical of early Nahant cottages. Titled *Brotherly Care, August 19, 1904*, this image was sure to delight parents, grandparents, aunts, and uncles. It looks like they really were fond of each other, which was proved true in later photographs and written remembrances.

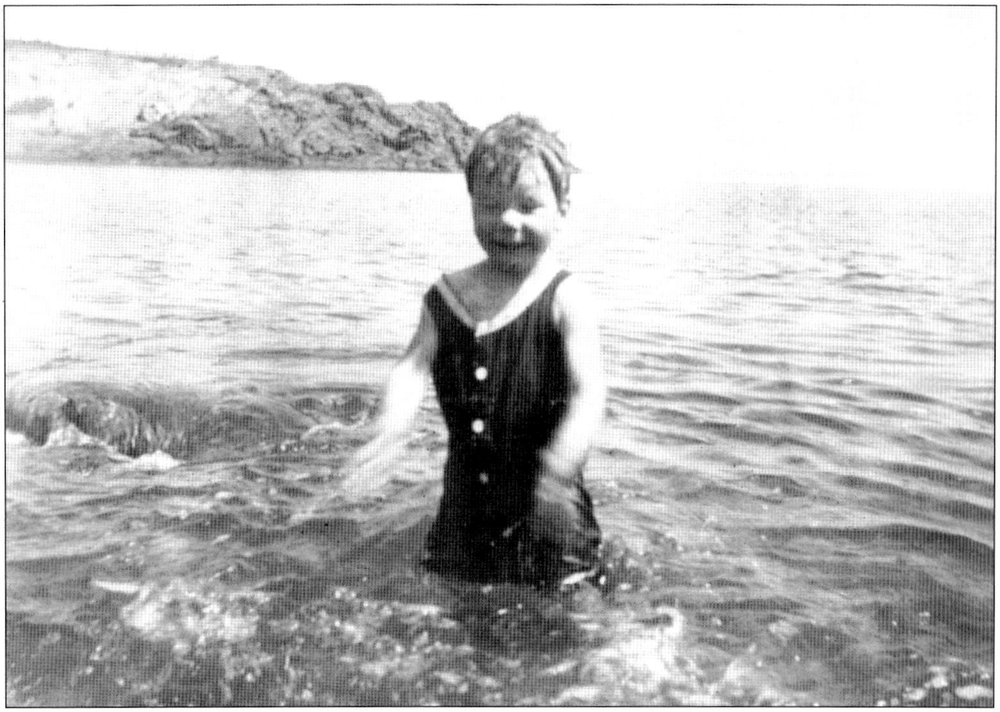

These candid shots of August 25, 1904, are titled *Sammy's First Bath*, which meant sea bathing or swimming. He seems excited but a little disconcerted to be standing alone in the water at Forty Steps Beach just below the family house. What child would not be thrilled to be riding on mother's back above the cold sea? This was the site of many summer water activities by the seasonal residents. The picture of Sammy alone was taken by his mother, and the other was captured by his father.

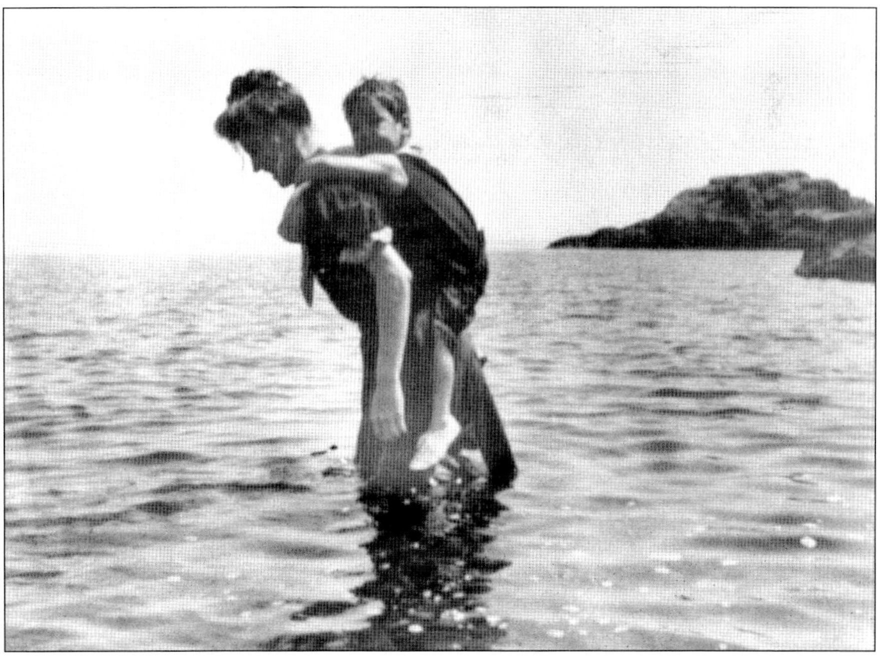

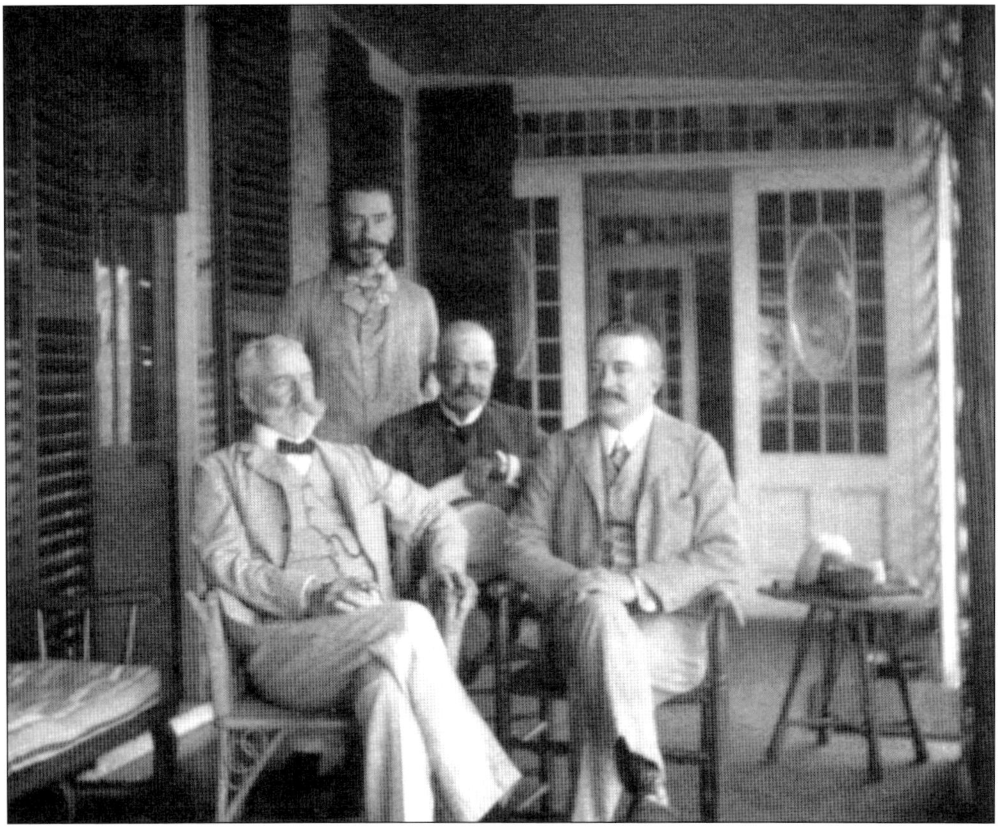

The "Four Fathers," as they were called, were neighbors in Boston and closer neighbors in Nahant. They are posed on the Hammond piazza on July 4, 1904. Sitting from left to right are Frank Merriam (1850–1924), Charles T. Lovering (1846–1915), and Dudley Bowditch Fay (1860–1921). Standing in the back is their host, Samuel Hammond. They and their families were great friends, and some were closely related.

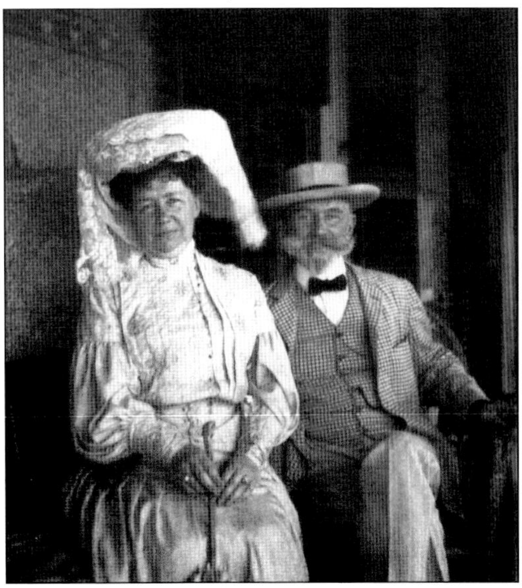

Another photograph taken on July 4, 1904, is of Rosamond Warren Gibson (1846–1934) and neighbor Frank Merriam. "Aunt Ros" summered next door at Forty Steps, a house she built on the westerly end of the Hammond property. She was a constant presence in the family, acting as grandmother to the Hammond children until her death in 1934. Her son, Charles Hammond Gibson Jr. (1874–1954), continued to summer there into the 1950s.

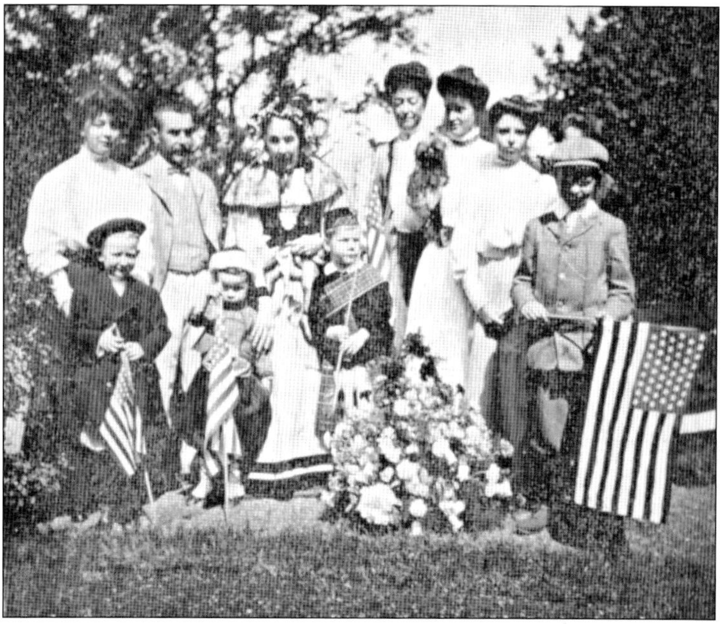

Mary Russell (1826–1918), standing in the center, started a relief fund in gratitude to the Nahant Fire Department for saving her Vernon Street home, Rose Cottage, from the 1896 fire that consumed five nearby houses. During the Memorial Day festivities, the firemen would pass by Rose Cottage to receive her annual donation. She is seen here after the 1906 event with her family and neighbors. (Courtesy Fay/Garfield family.)

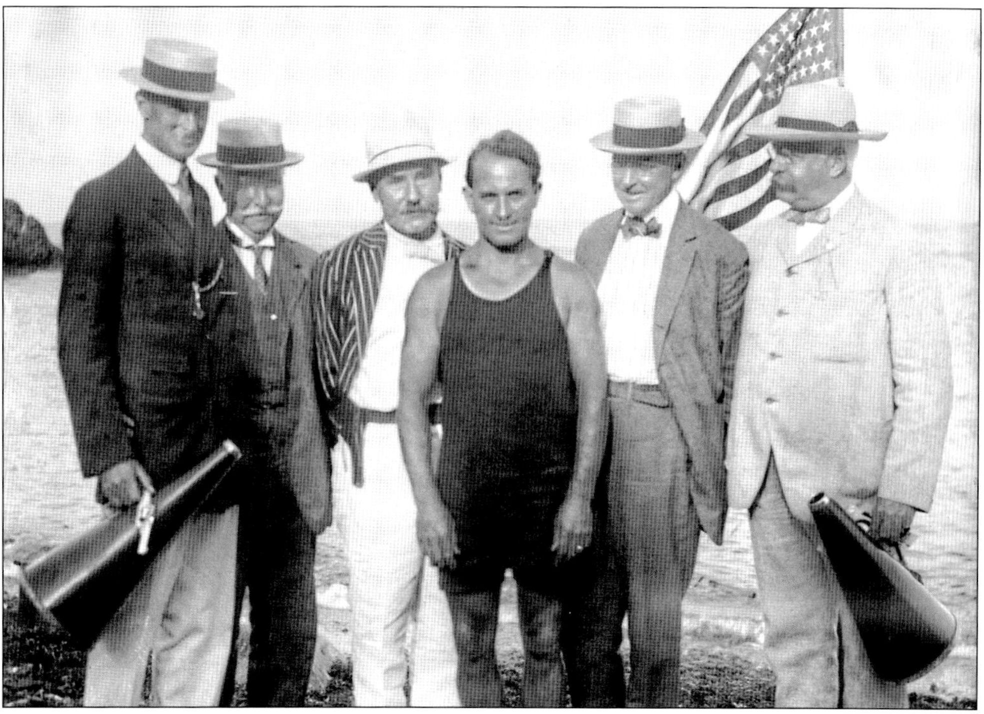

The annual water carnival, begun in 1909, took place at Forty Steps Beach. It was an event for the summer family children to show off their newly acquired water skills. Seen here, from left to right, are the 1913 officials, Arthur Johnson, John Denny, Samuel Hammond, George Emerson (instructor), James Newell, and George Inches. George Emerson was the athletics director at Boston University and continued summer instruction in Nahant for many years.

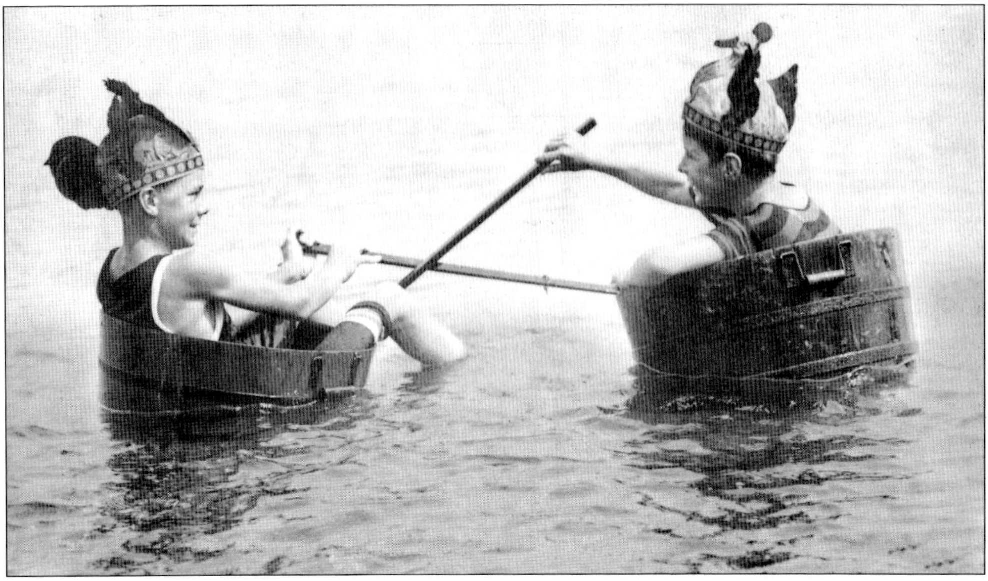

Not every event in the water carnival was serious. Featured here in 1914 are Sam Hammond on the left and Mason in the tub tilting contest. Sam remembers, "In the basement were . . . wooden wash tubs. . . . Mason and I discovered we could paddle around in the water. We'd get long poles and try to upset each other. It was quite a lot of fun." This year, Mason placed first. (Courtesy NHS.)

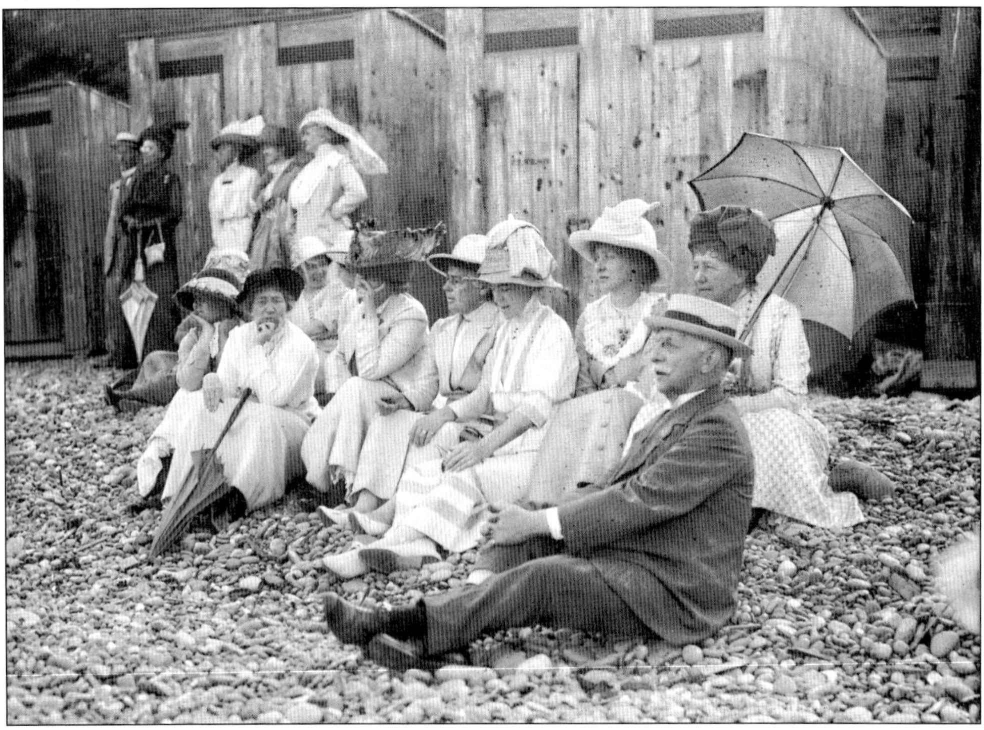

John Denny sits on the beach with unidentified seasonal residents and their guests in this 1910s image. Their focus is on one of the competitions in this year's water carnival. This event regularly drew hundreds of people lining the street above and crowding the beach. It was also reported in the Boston and Lynn papers.

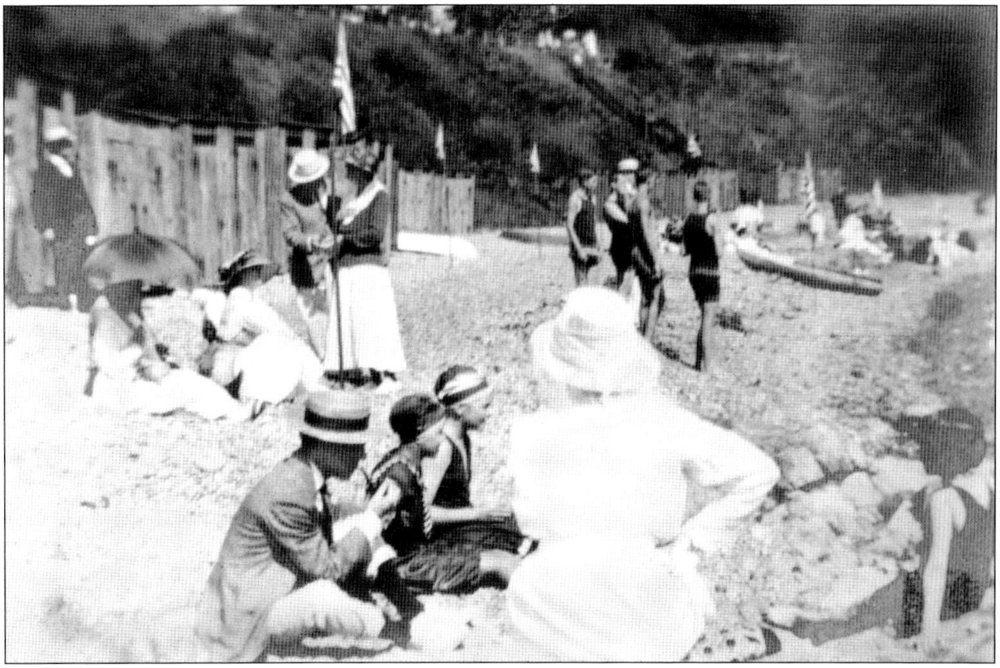

Observers and participants are gathered at Forty Steps Beach for the 1918 Water Carnival. In the foreground, sitting on the rocks between two adults, are Susan Hammond (1907–1967) on the left and her friend Helena Lodge (1904–1998). In the background are the wooden changing booths rented to each family by J.T. Wilson. Above the standing boys is the long and steep stairway to Nahant Road that gave the beach its name.

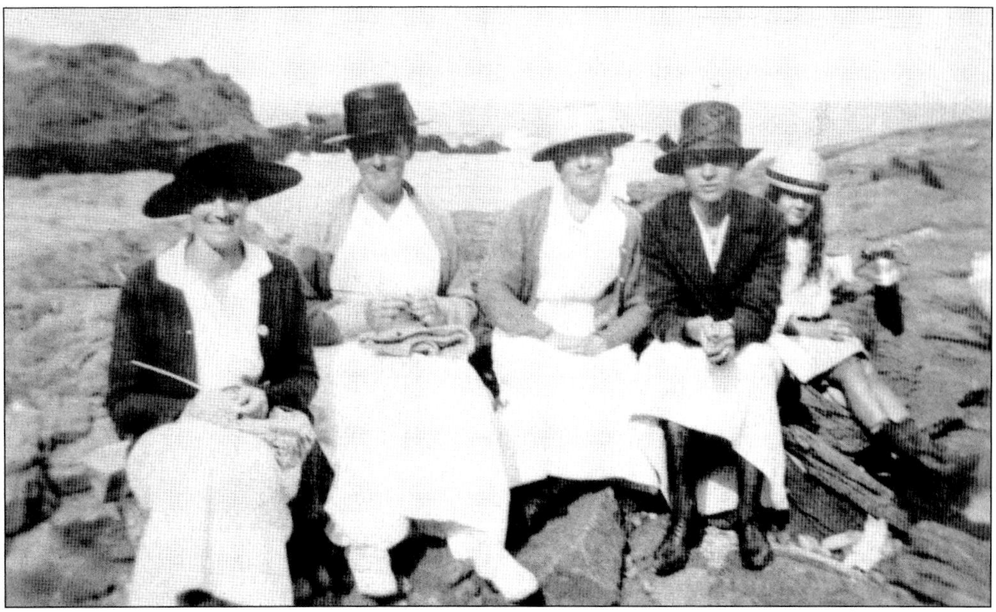

Four unidentified nurses are enjoying a pleasant September day on the rocks near Forty Steps Beach. They are likely relaxing from their duties during the 1918 flu epidemic ravaging the country or may be from the Vincent Hospital in Boston, where Grace Hammond devoted her time and energy. The nurses are joined by Ruth Lovering, daughter of Hammond neighbor Charles Lovering.

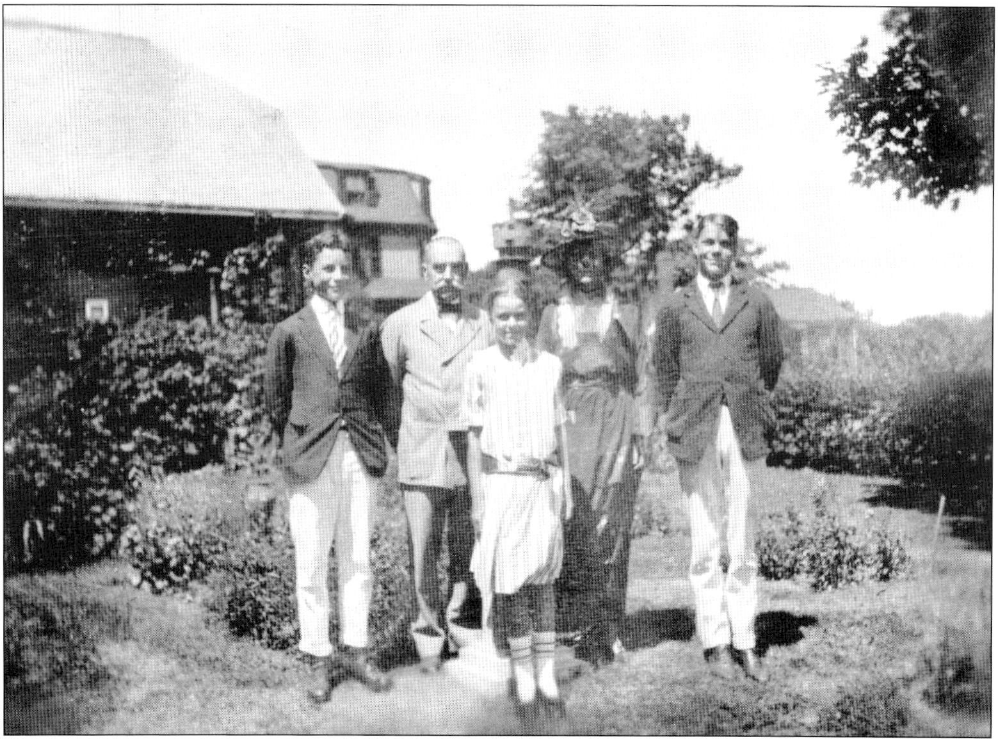

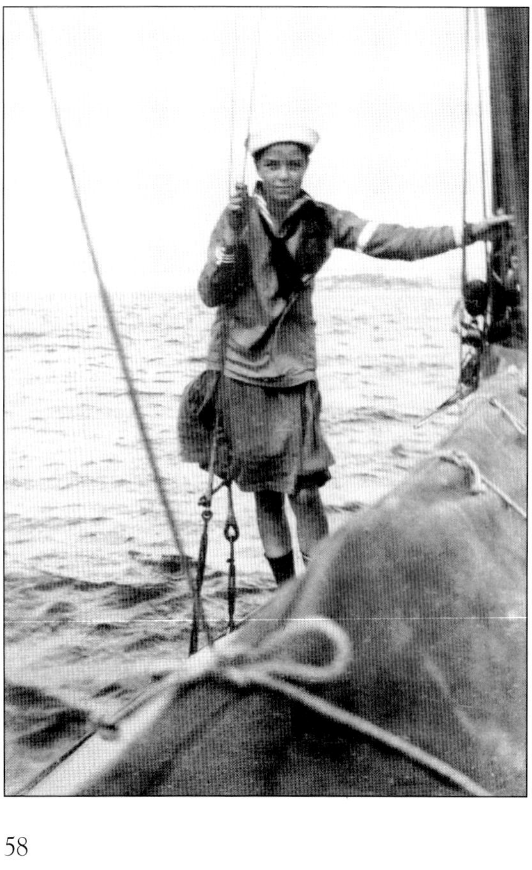

In 1918, the maturing family poses in the garden of Castle Rock near the stable with the Lewis and Laurence Curtis house in the background. From left to right are Mason (15 years old), Samuel (59), Susan (11), Grace (44), and Sam (17). Both parents shared the joy of gardening. Samuel liked doing the vegetables and flowers for cutting, and Grace enjoyed more decorative gardening.

Susan is posing on the *Nettie* in 1920 with Bailey's Hill in the background. By this time, she was becoming a good sailor. She had her debutante ball on Beacon Hill in 1928 and was active in the Junior League but was also independent-minded. She was unable to attend her brother Mason's wedding in 1935 because she was sailing aboard a Swedish fully rigged ship in the grain trade.

Sam, Home from the West is the title of this image. He certainly looks like he was having an adventure before attending Harvard. Completing an advanced degree from the Harvard Engineering School in 1925, Sam became a utility executive in Newark, New Jersey. Too young for World War I and too old for World War II, he drove ambulances for the Red Cross and was an air raid warden on the home front.

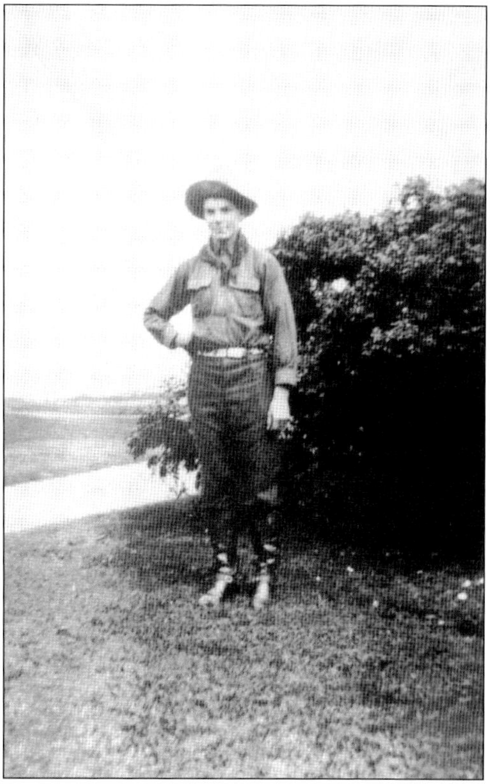

Mason, seen in front of the Nahant Dory Club, seems a little camera shy as he climbs aboard his Bug in 1921. Designed in 1906, the 18-foot Bug was the predecessor of the Star class of small sailboats and meant to be affordable to anyone who liked racing. At least 10 were made for the club by Richard T. Green of Chelsea, Massachusetts.

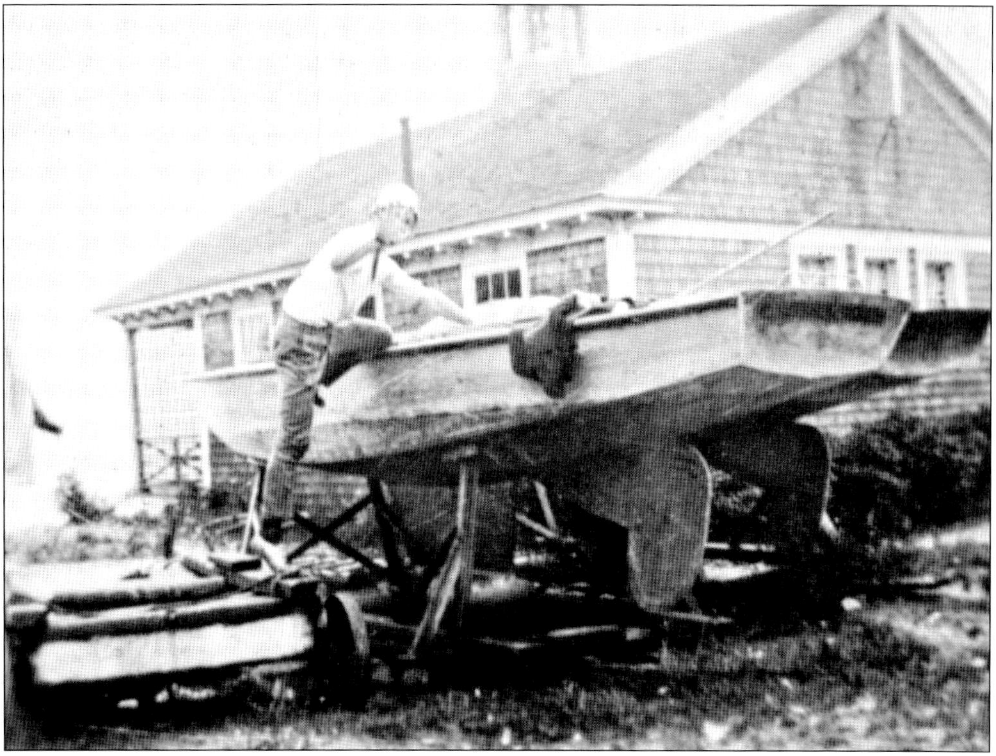

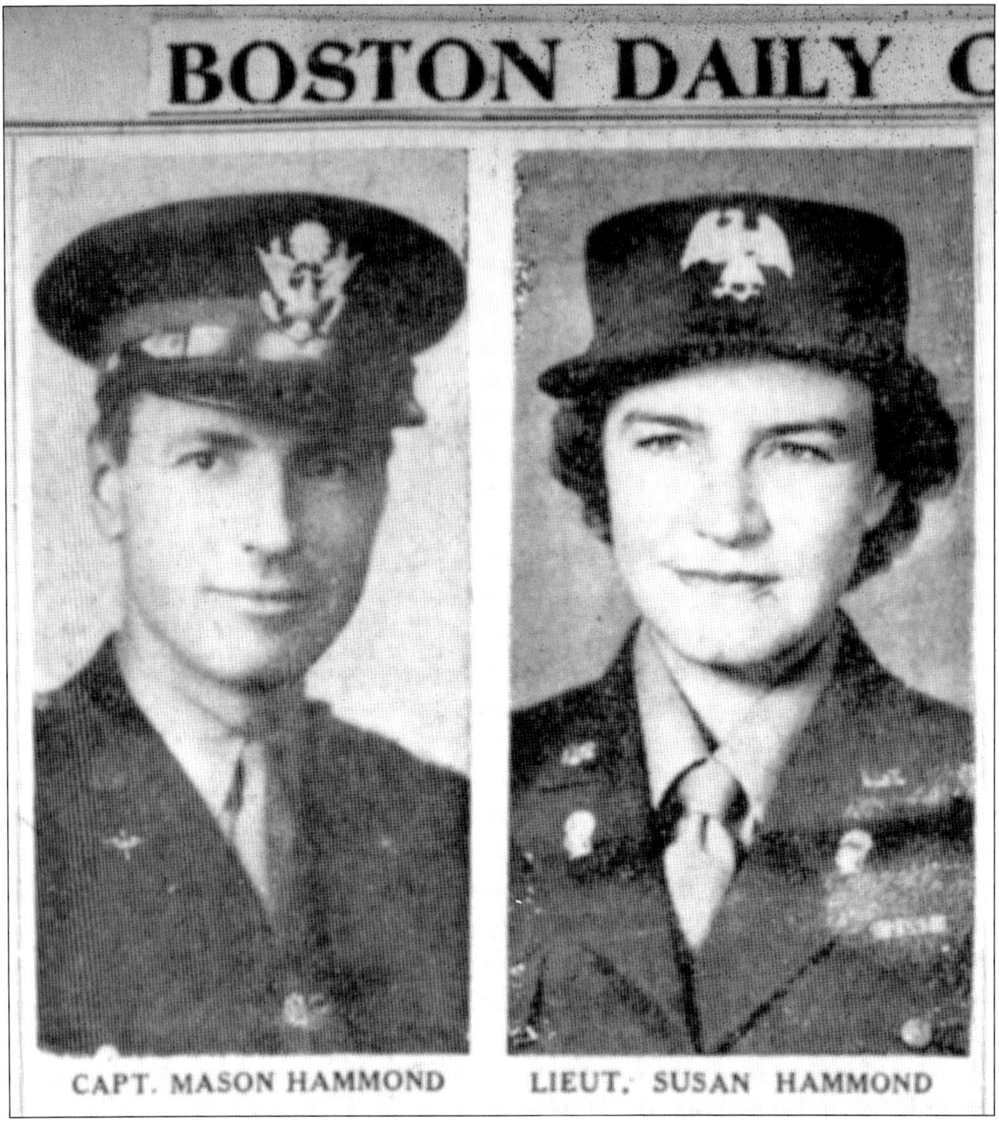

Susan Hammond was among the first women to drive ambulances in France and Belgium in 1940, evacuating nurses, women, and children from war zones during World War II. For this, she was awarded the Croix de Guerre with a star by the French government. In 1942, she enlisted in the Women's Army Corps. Lt. Susan Hammond served with distinction in Algiers and Italy. Lt. Col. Mason Hammond served as chief in the Allied Military Government section for Monuments, Fine Arts, and Archives (MFAA), seeing duty in Algeria, Italy, England, France, and Germany. Because of his deep knowledge of art and history, he and other Monuments Men were responsible for saving European patrimony from looting, destruction, and loss. He was awarded the Bronze Star and decorated by the governments of France, Holland, and Italy. He returned to his position at Harvard a greatly admired man.

Four

PEOPLE AND PLACES

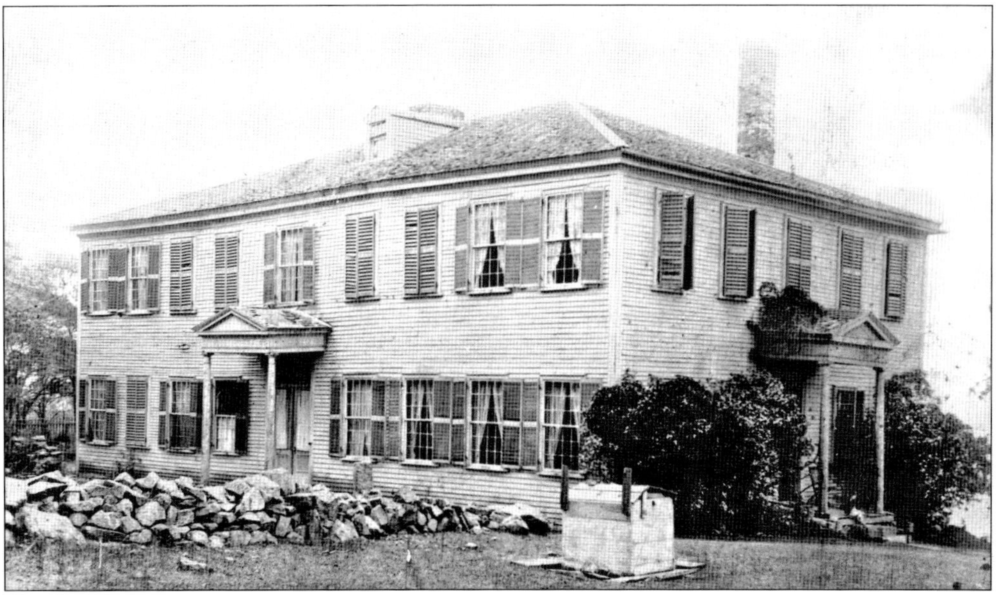

Overlooking Lynn harbor, the Old Castle was built around 1800 by Joseph Johnson of Lynn as a hotel. In 1840, it was sold to John Phillips, Boston's first mayor (1822) and father of Wendell Phillips (1811–1884), the outspoken abolitionist. It was demolished in 1903 by Edward E. Strout (1855–1915), who developed this area, which was to be called Castle Park. The street names (Castle, Phillips, and Wendell Roads) reflect this history.

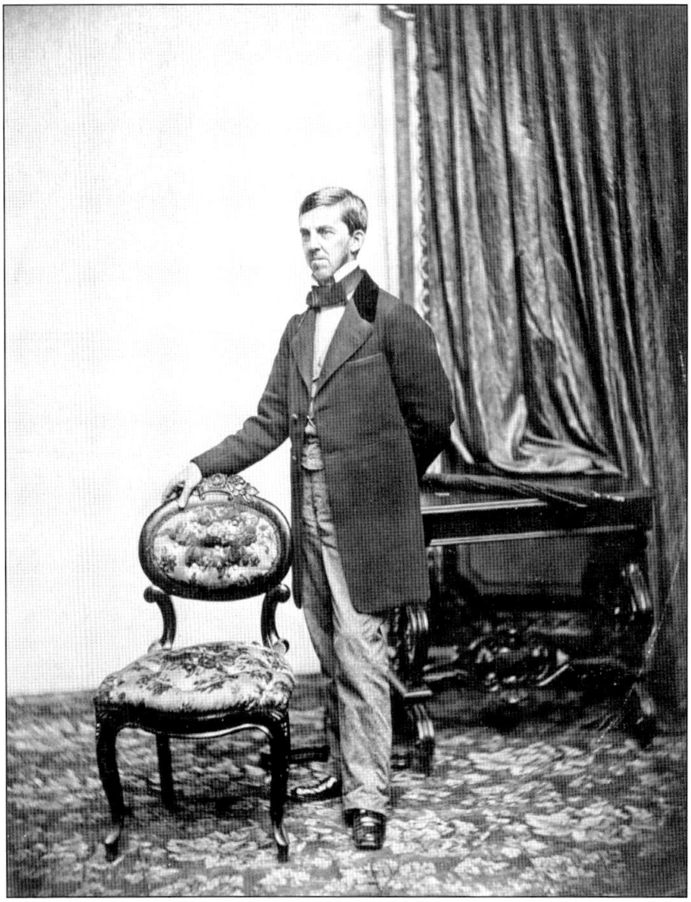

Oliver Wendell Holmes Sr. (1809–1894) was a Boston-based physician, professor, author, and Nahant summer resident. He earned his medical doctorate at the Harvard Medical School, taught there for many years, and in 1836, became its dean. In 1859, he perfected the handheld stereoscope, used for viewing two almost identical photographic images simultaneously to create a three-dimensional effect. This way of seeing nature, historic sights, and amusements was a widely popular form of home entertainment, allowing people to feel like they were there. Holmes deliberately did not patent this device and allowed Joseph L. Bates to acquire the patent.

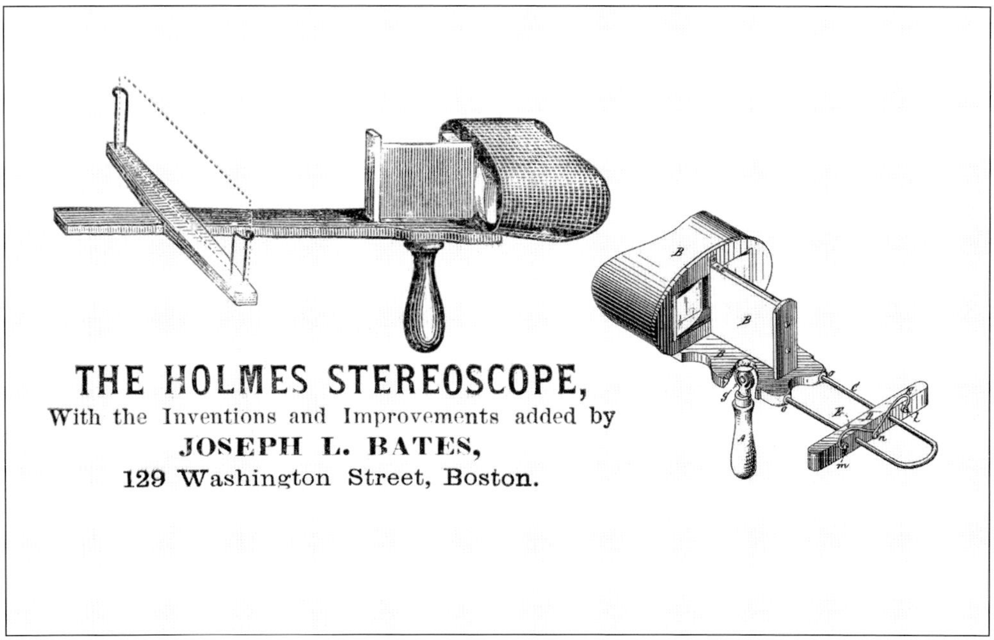

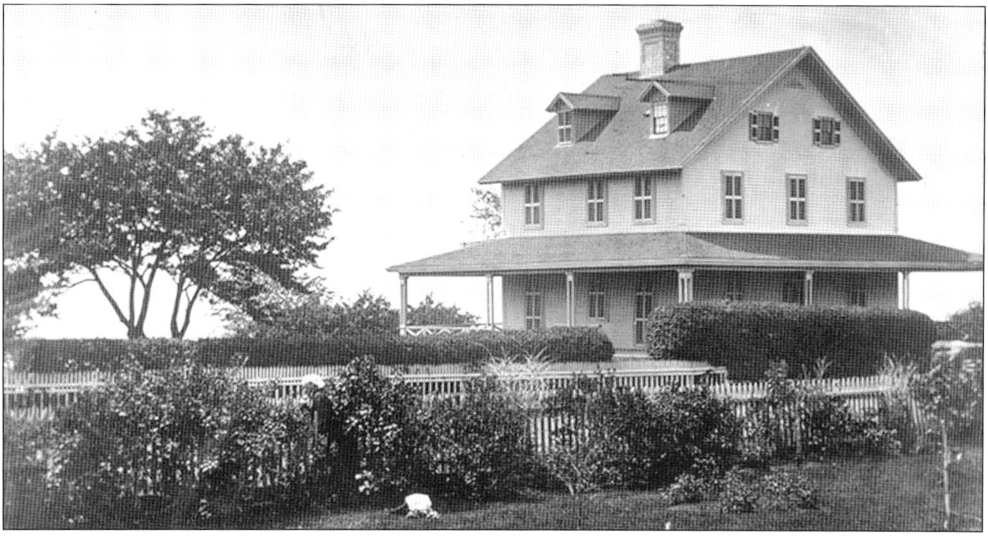

Oliver Wendell Holmes Sr. summered in Nahant from 1871 until 1878, renting the Charles Amory/Thomas Dwight house at 44 Cliff Street. Among his close neighbors were Henry Wadsworth Longfellow and Henry Cabot Lodge. As a humorist, his book *The Autocrat of the Breakfast-Table* was admired for its wit and sagacity.

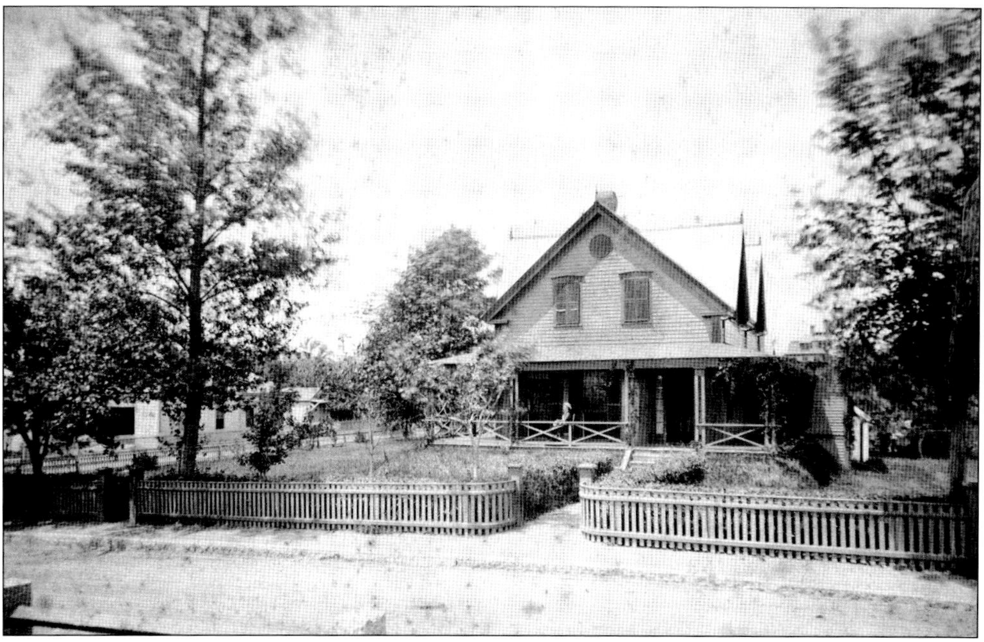

This Gothic Revival cottage at 16 Pleasant Street was built in 1850 by Charles Benjamin Johnson, who was known as "Charlie Lamplighter." He was responsible for the lighting and maintenance of all the gas street lamps in town. The figure sitting on the porch (now removed) is thought to be his wife, Annie Johnson, an artist and the poetess of Nahant.

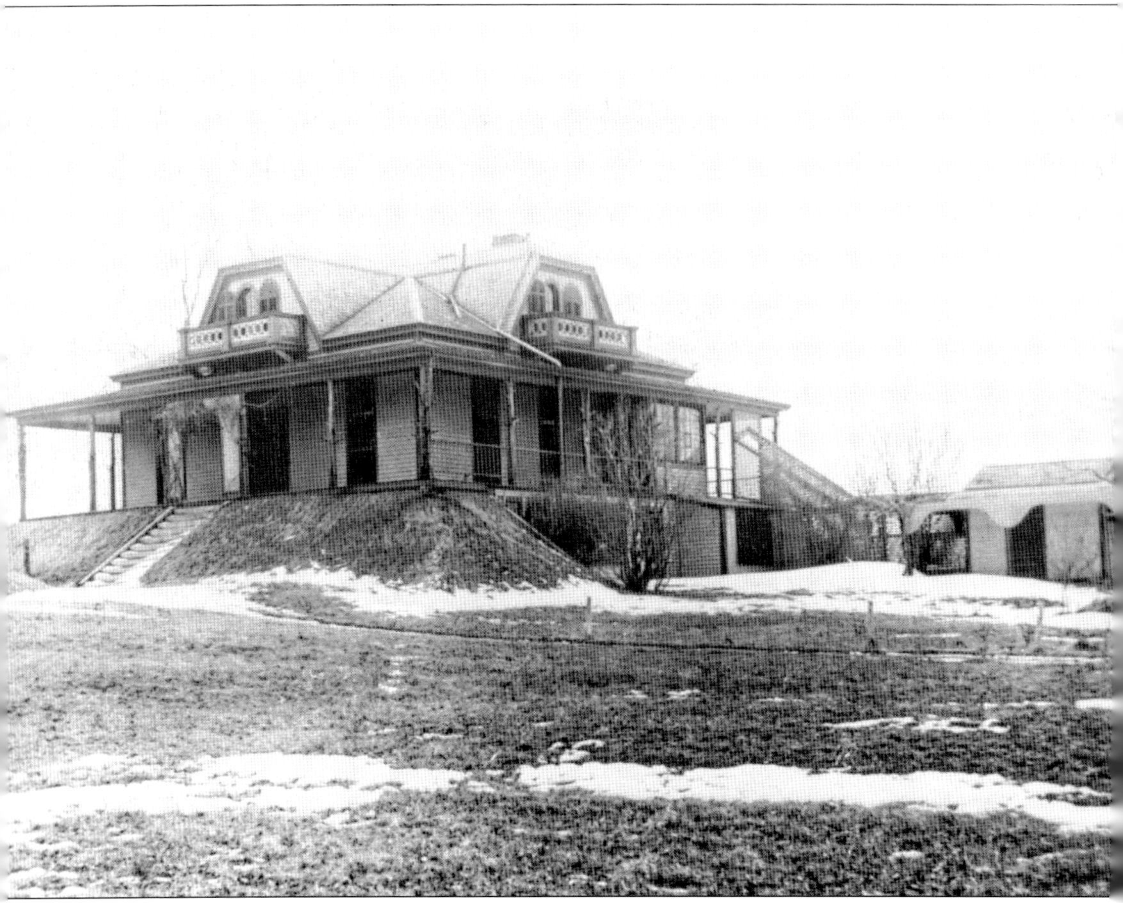

Gen. John C. Frémont (1813–1890), called "the Pathfinder of the West," ran for US president and lost to James Buchanan in 1856. In 1863, he and his dynamic wife, Jessie Benton Frémont (1824–1902), bought the Edward B. Phillips house at 171 Willow Road. While the general was mostly away, seeking his fame and fortune, Jessie and their daughter Elizabeth summered here for several years. Jessie Frémont, daughter of Missouri senator Thomas Hart Benton, knew politics and the art of persuasion. She requested from the town that Willow Road, then just a cart path, be constructed in front of the house from Cliff Street to Summer Street. It was granted, and she paid for all of it, including the road around to Tudor Wharf.

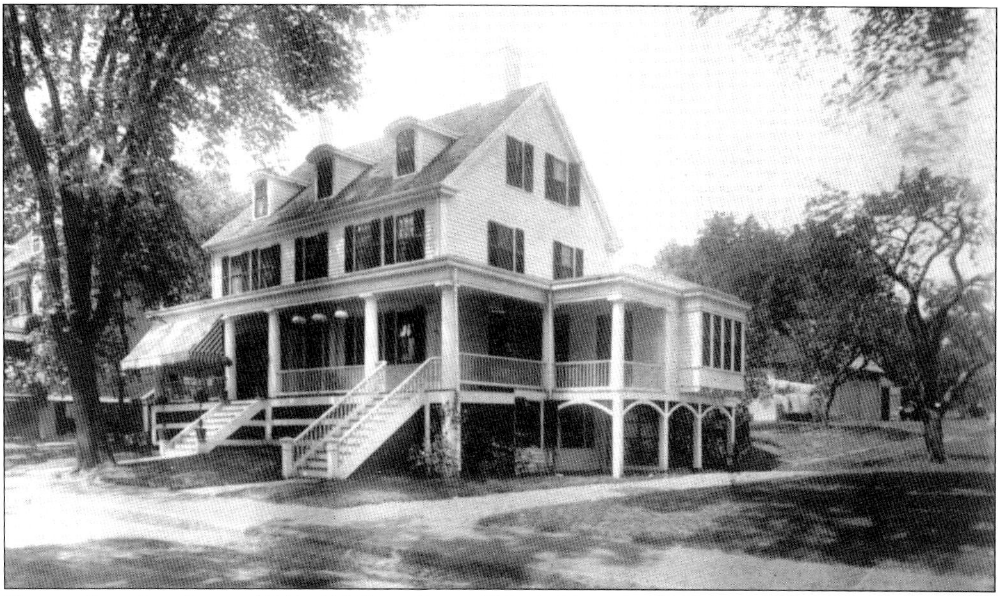

Harriet Beecher Stowe (1811–1896), author of *Uncle Tom's Cabin*, was a frequent visitor in the 1870s and 1880s. She stayed with her daughter Georgina and son-in-law Henry F. Allen, who rented seasonally at 298 Nahant Road. In a letter dated July 26, 1884, she writes, "We have concluded to go to Nahant next week." (The letter was a gift to the Nahant Historical Society by Anne and David Bromer.)

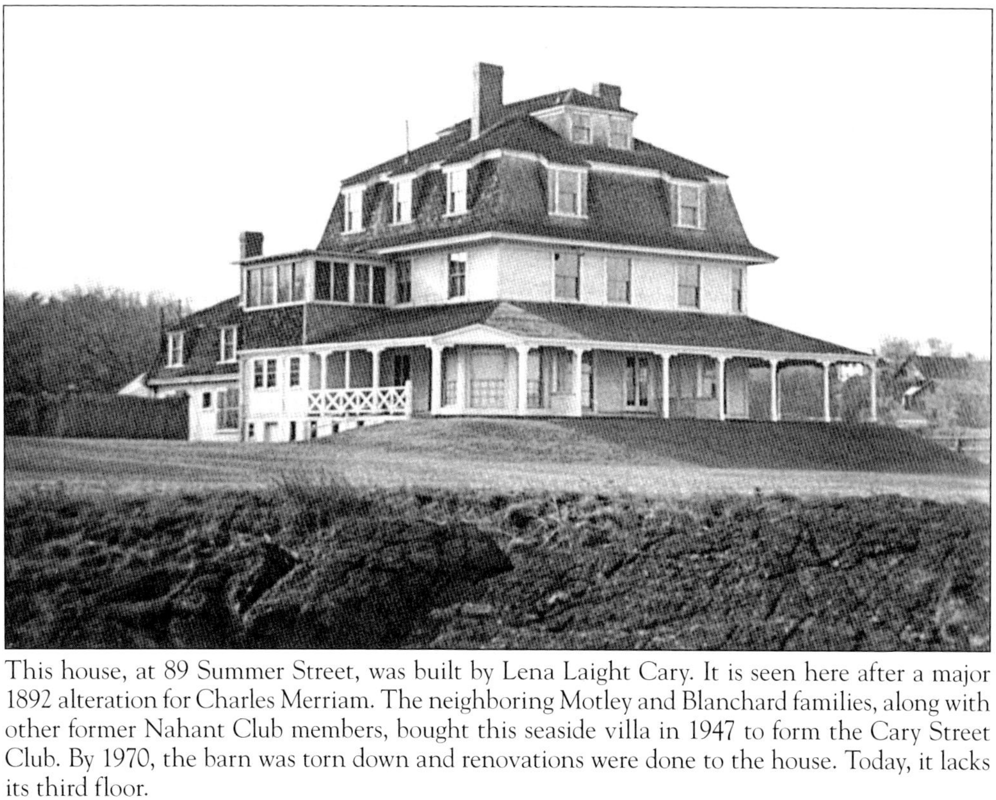

This house, at 89 Summer Street, was built by Lena Laight Cary. It is seen here after a major 1892 alteration for Charles Merriam. The neighboring Motley and Blanchard families, along with other former Nahant Club members, bought this seaside villa in 1947 to form the Cary Street Club. By 1970, the barn was torn down and renovations were done to the house. Today, it lacks its third floor.

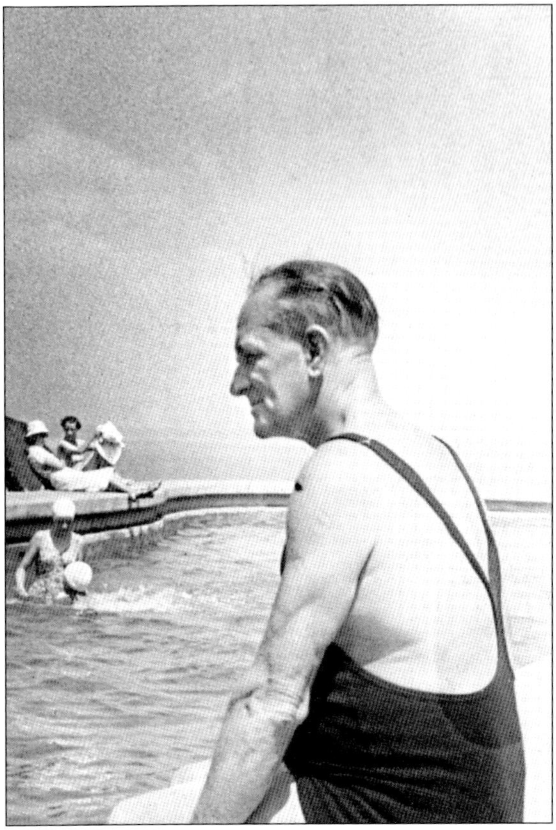

A later owner of the Charles Merriam house was Richard Harte, who had a seawater swimming pool built into the rocks in front of the house in 1927. George Emerson, pictured here in 1937, was the swimming instructor for the earlier Water Carnivals at Forty Steps Beach and continued teaching the children of Nahant at the Hartes' pool under the auspices of the Nahant Club.

This Tudor Revival house at 78 Maolis Road was built by J.T. Wilson in 1893 for the architect George Foster Shepley (1860–1903). It is unknown if Shepley designed it. He worked in the firm of H.H. Richardson, one of the greatest architects of the period. Following Richardson's death, Shepley took over the firm under the name Shepley, Rutan, and Coolidge and completed Richardson's design for the portico of Trinity Church, Boston.

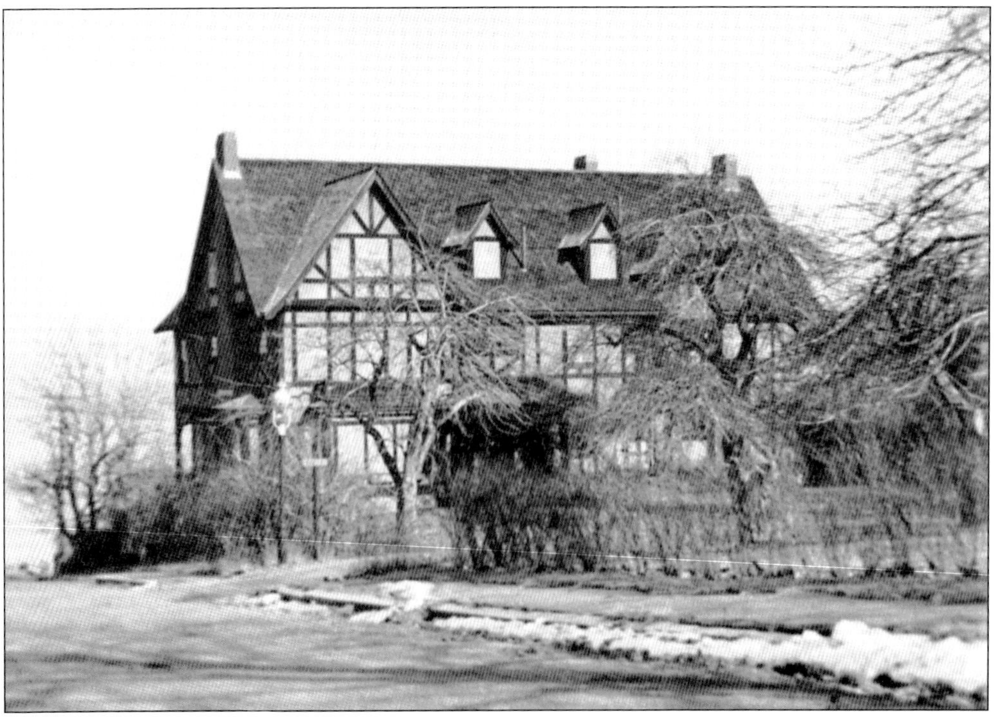

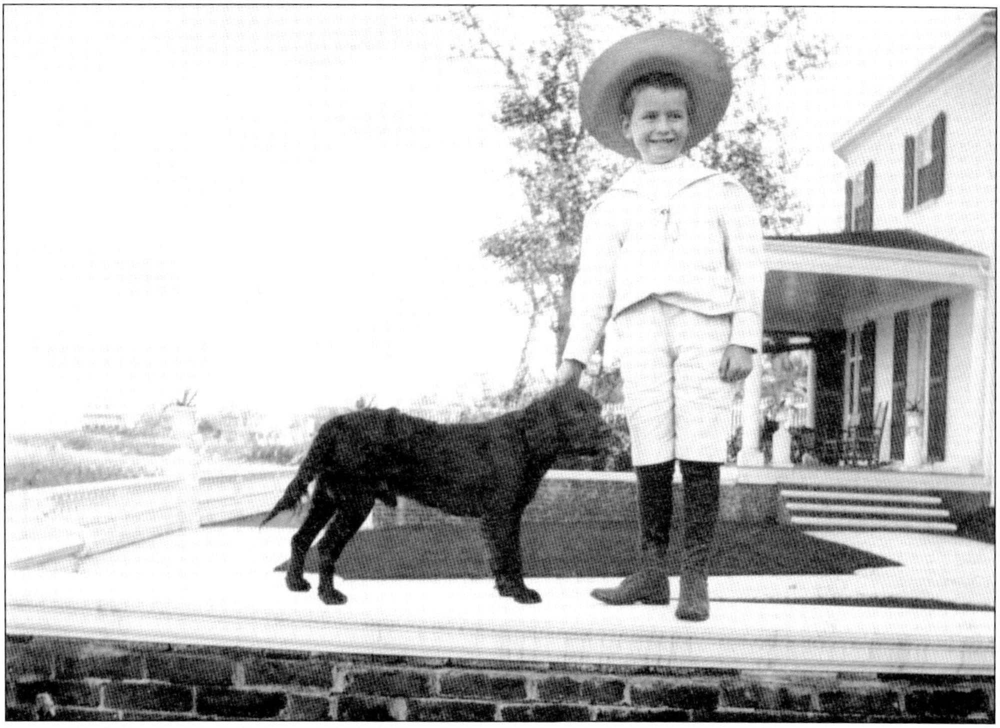

Samuel Eliot Guild Jr. (1892–1977), later a Boston investment counselor, is pictured with his dog Don in 1901 on the seaside terrace of Maolis (66 Ocean Street), the family summer home. It was built by J.T. Wilson in 1893 on the grounds of the former Maolis Gardens, created by Frederic Tudor. On the left in the distance is the Charles Merriam house, which became the Cary Street Club.

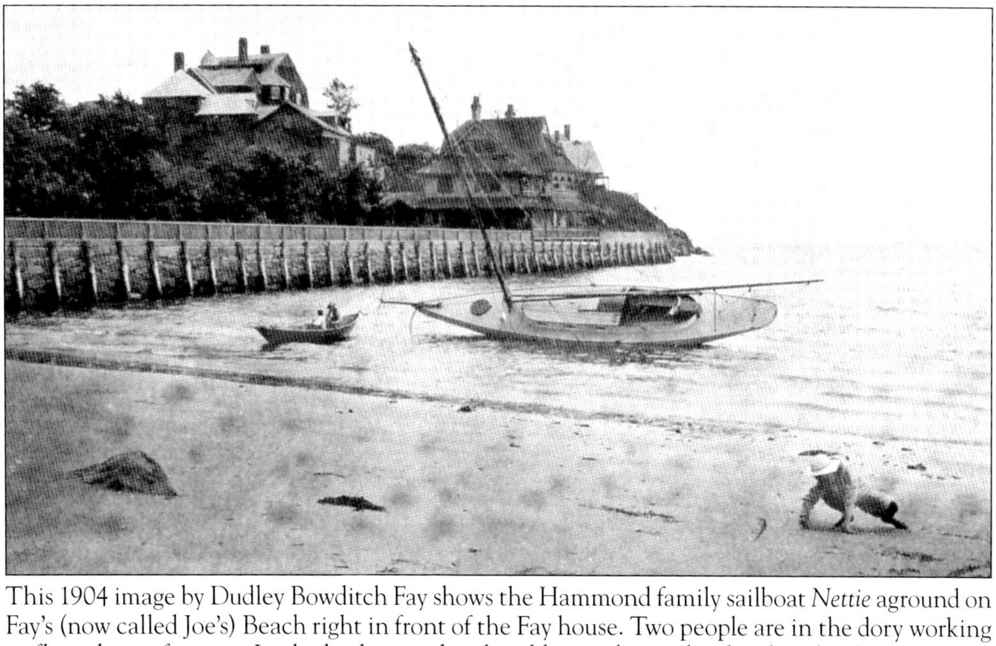

This 1904 image by Dudley Bowditch Fay shows the Hammond family sailboat *Nettie* aground on Fay's (now called Joe's) Beach right in front of the Fay house. Two people are in the dory working to float the craft again. In the background is the old steamboat wharf with Wharf Cottage and other houses on Swallow Cave Point. (Courtesy Fay/Garfield family.)

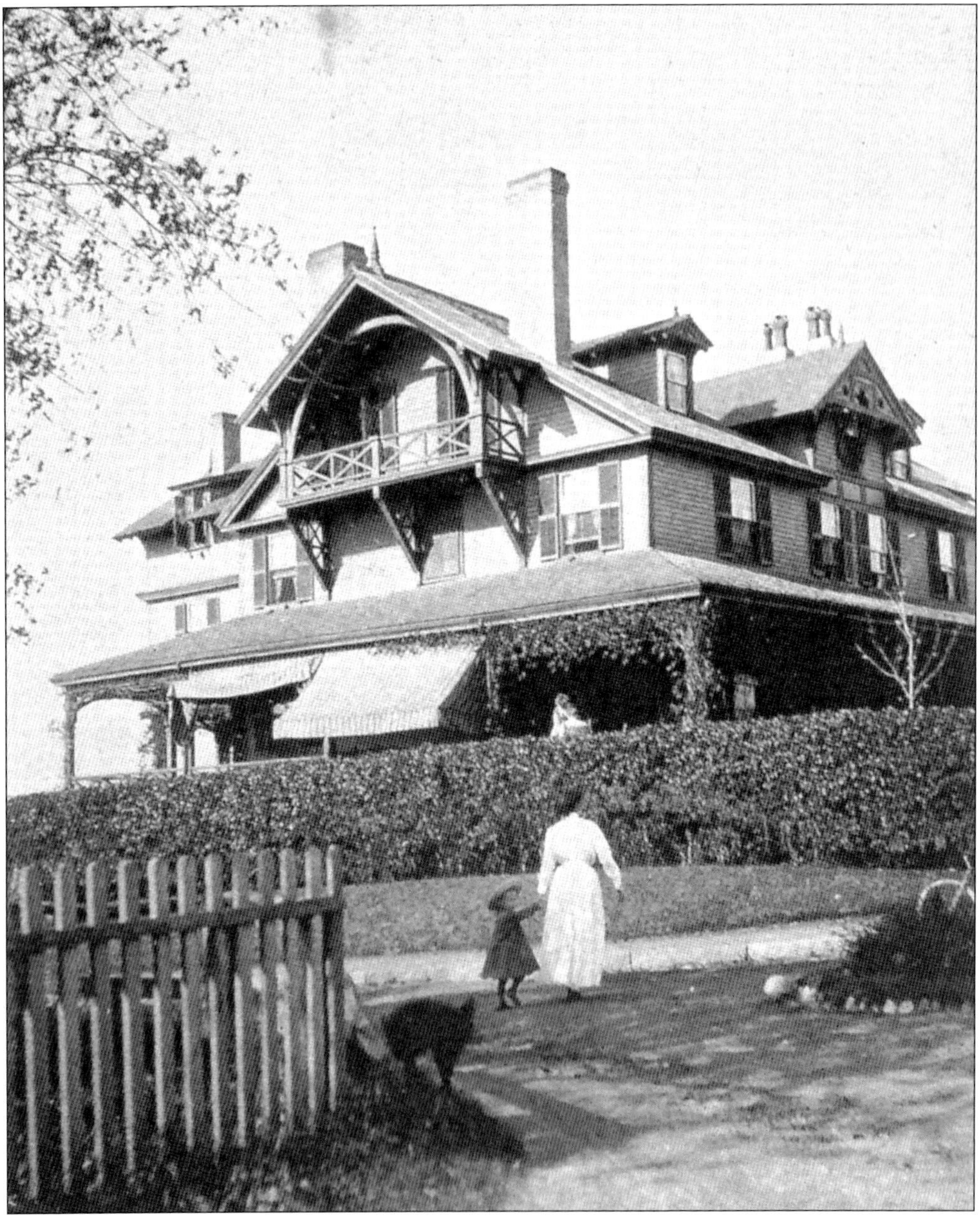

This house at 33 Vernon Street began as the Nahant House hotel, built by Cornelius Coolidge in the 1820s. It was a competitor of the Nahant Hotel at East Point because of its proximity to the wharf, but when the Nahant Hotel expanded in the 1830s, it was less so. It was sold to brothers George and Francis Peabody of Salem in 1837 and significantly remodeled into a family house. George became sole owner in 1847 and summered here until his death in 1892. Dudley Bowditch Fay (1860–1921) and his wife, Katharine Gray Fay (1860–1958), then bought it in the same year. Their seven children enjoyed the large summer house and beach. This 1903 image by Dudley Fay, an aspiring photographer, shows the stylish cottage it became. Unfortunately, it was destroyed by fire in 1958. (Courtesy Fay/Garfield family).

Arthur Dudley Fay (1896–1971) is watching the 1912 Nahant Dory Club Labor Day regatta. After a career in teaching, he built his home at 15 Vernon Street in 1958. Fay stated, "I've always been interested in steamers since I was a small boy in Nahant and watched the Maine boats go by." In retirement, he became a volunteer steamship historian at the Peabody Museum in Salem. (Courtesy Fay/Garfield family.)

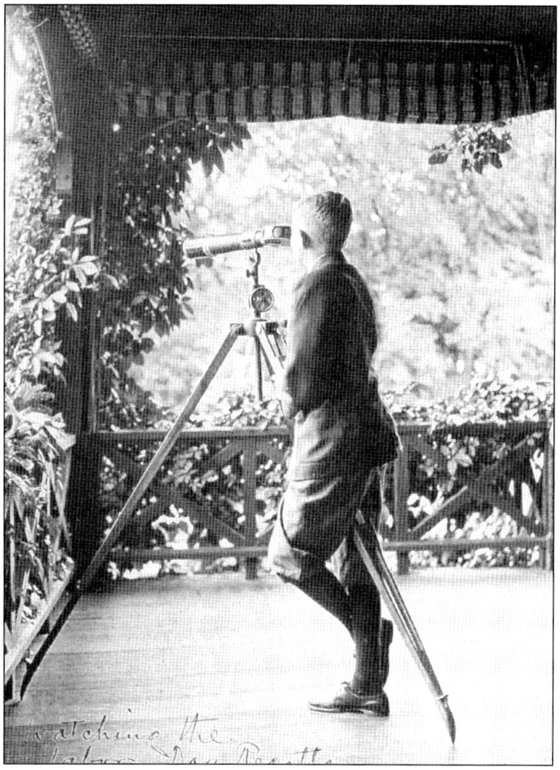

This real-photo postcard, dated August 16, 1908, shows the modest Russell cottage probably at Bass Point. The message reads in part, "As the cat and myself were the only ones round we had to make our appearance." Photographs were taken and printed on postcard stock for a very personalized greeting.

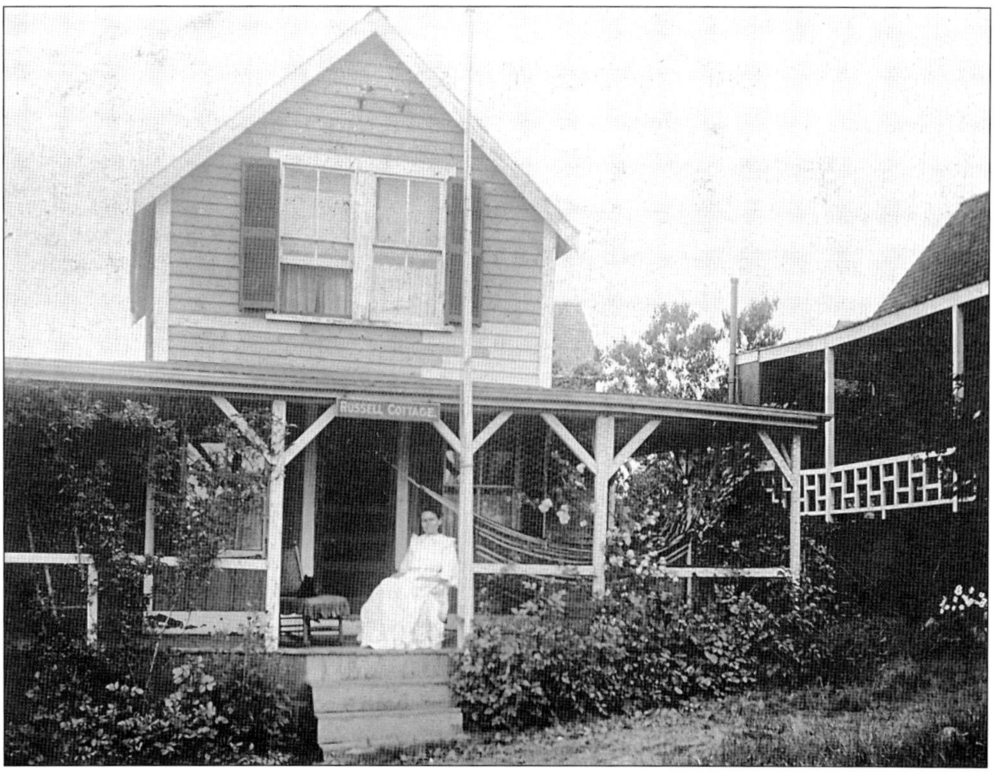

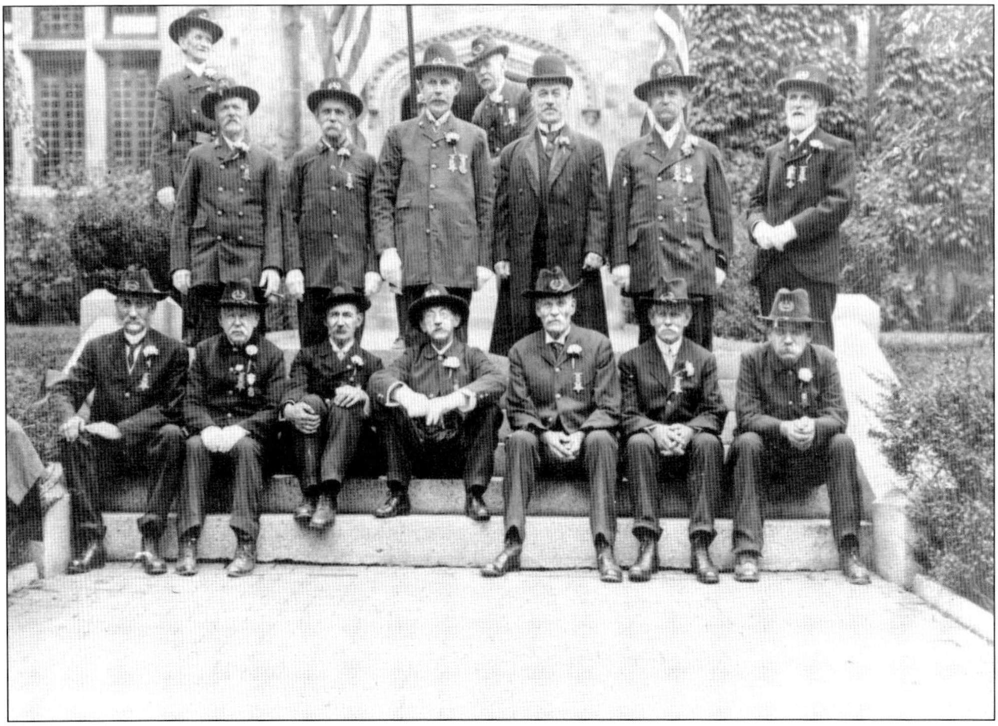

This group of Civil War veterans from Lynn and Nahant poses in front of the Nahant Library on Memorial Day 1910. Only a few Nahant veterans remained. They are Thomas J. Cusick (first row, second from right), Augustus A. Barnes (second row, third from left), Edmond B. Johnson (second row, far right, with a white beard), and Welcome J. Johnson (at back in front of the arch).

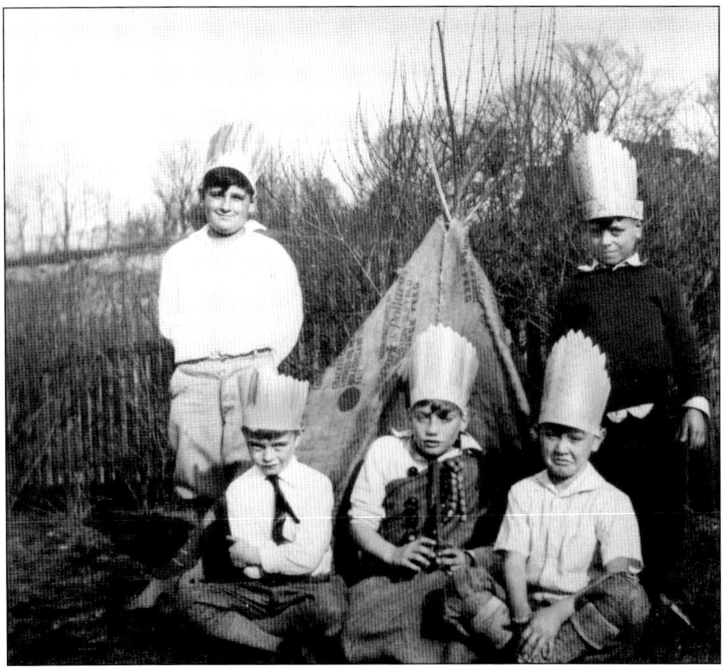

In the late 1920s, third graders on the grounds of the J.T. Wilson school presented a demonstration of their knowledge of Native American lore. Seated from left to right are a dubious Jack Cadigan, Tom Burke, and a downright unhappy John Foley; standing on the left is Sam Cavallaro, with Carmen Solimine on the right.

Nahant joined the Metropolitan Water District in 1900, and this standpipe (reserve water supply) was constructed in 1902. Built of steel plates, it stood 90 feet high with a diameter of 30 feet and had a capacity of 365,000 gallons. It was located on High Street behind the police station. After the very cold 1918 winter, five tons of ice were removed and distributed locally. It was removed in 1957.

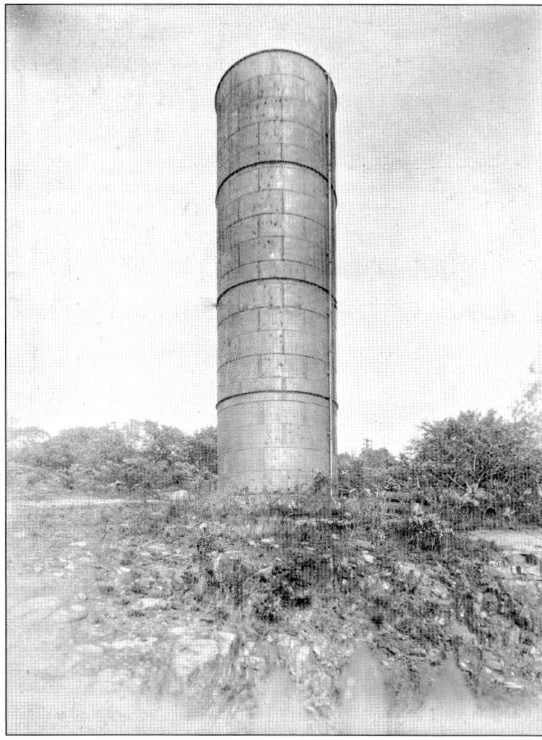

The George H. Green album, documenting town infrastructure, was created in the early 1930s. This image shows the location where the Metropolitan Water District supply line entered Nahant at the beginning of the causeway. It is protected by fencing and a simple gate. Through the scenic copse of trees can be seen the 1902 state bathhouse.

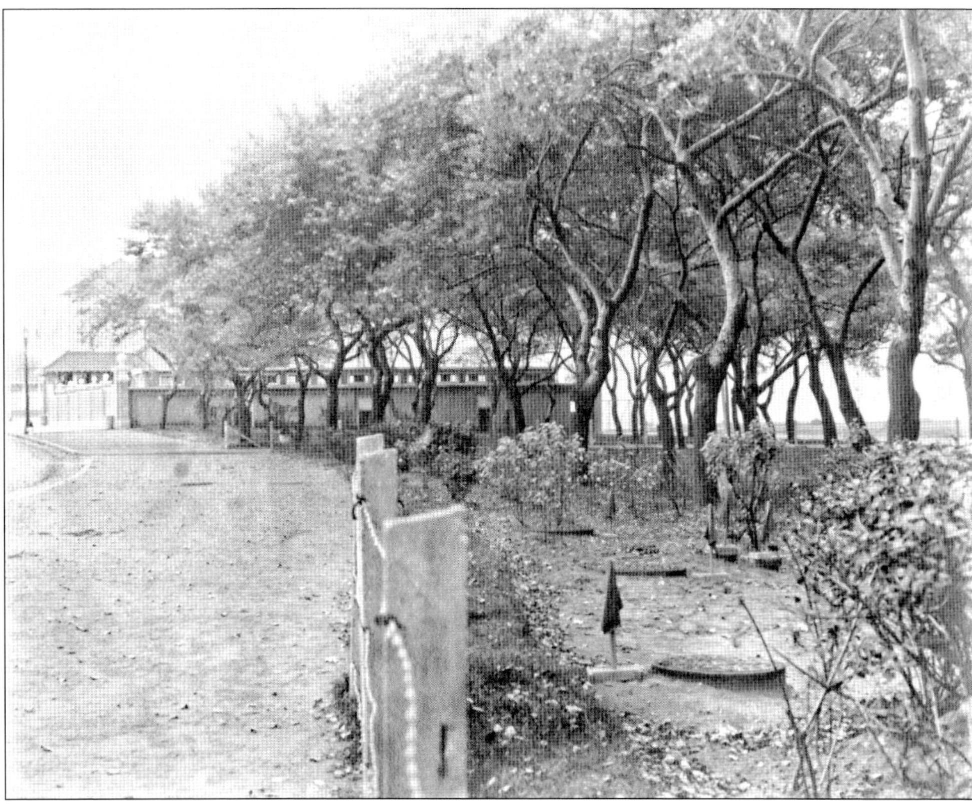

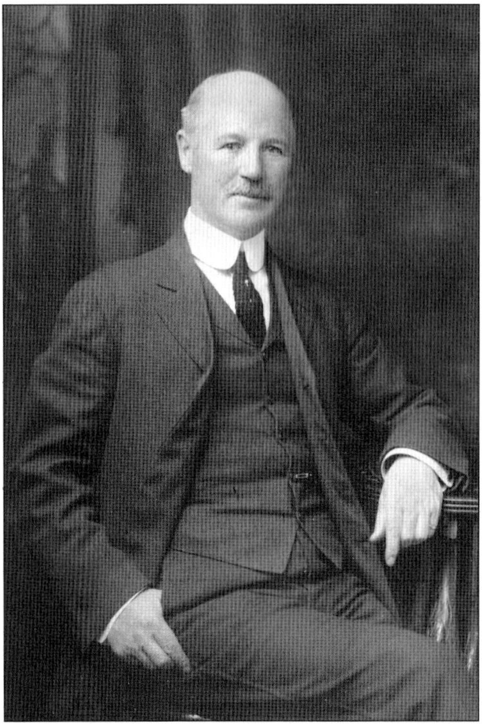

Thomas Roland (1862–1929) came to Nahant in 1883 from England, where he was an undergardener at Hampton Court Palace. Here, he began as a private gardener for Anna Moering's estate at 40 High Street. In 1891, Roland established commercial greenhouses behind his house at 33 Summer Street in the area that is now Christopher Drive. From 1908 until 1917, he was the town forester and helped plant Greenlawn Cemetery. To this day, the Massachusetts Horticultural Society annually awards the Thomas Roland Medal for exceptional skill. The image below shows the interior of the service building of his 20 Nahant greenhouses in December 1929, when his funeral was held there. It was filled with music, his pet birds flying free, and of course, beautiful plant and flower displays.

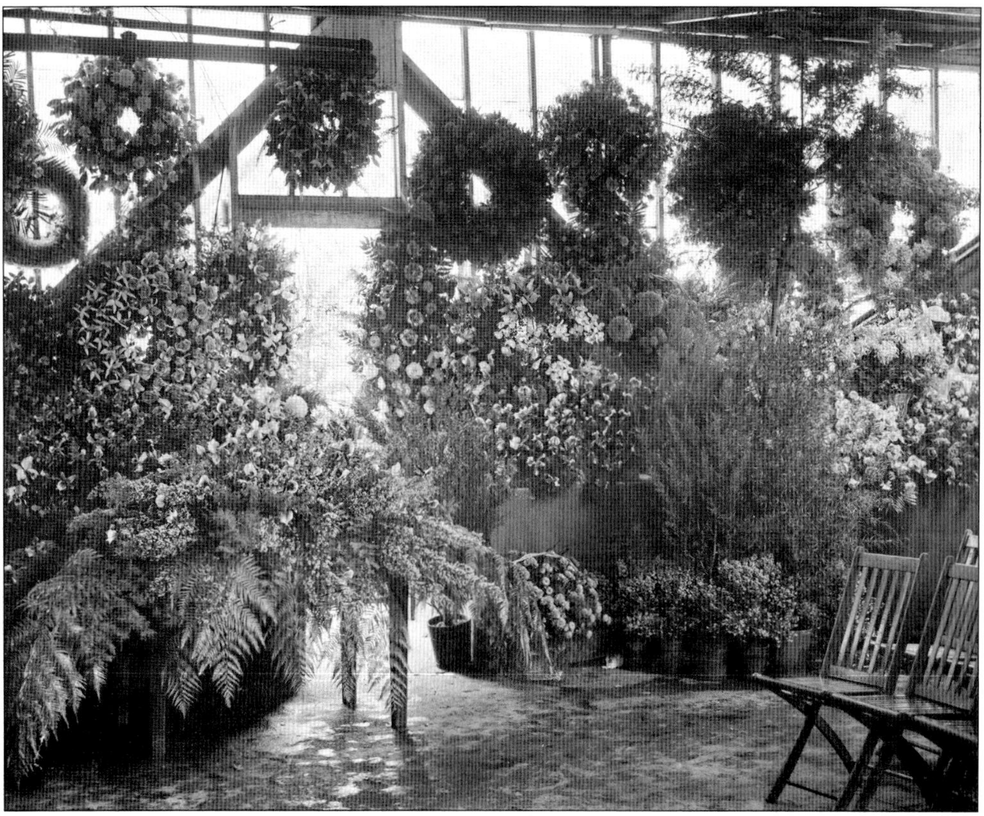

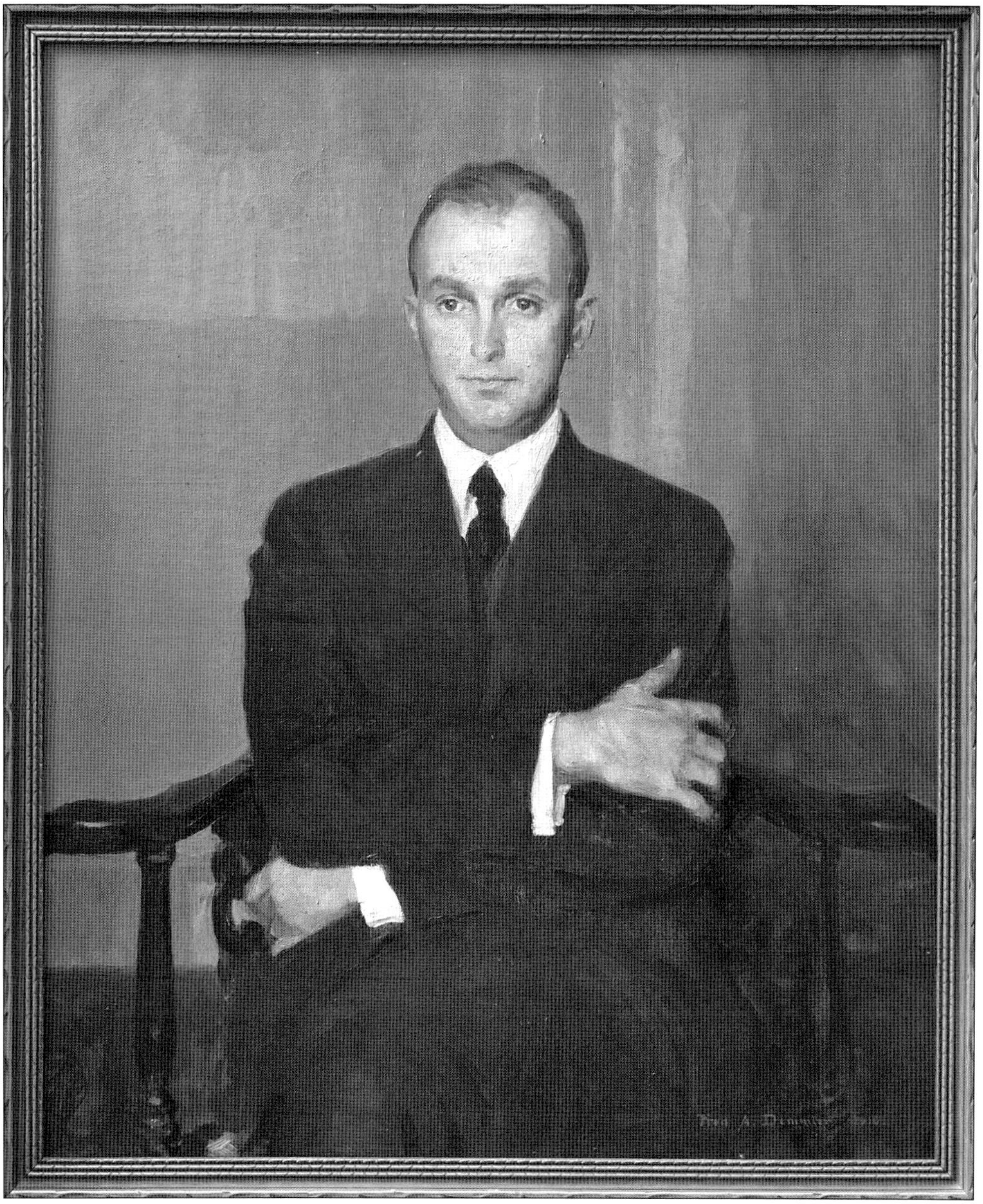

Lucien Price (1883–1964) was on the staff of the *Boston Transcript* from 1907 to 1914 and thereafter worked for the *Boston Globe* as an editorial writer and a columnist under the byline of "Uncle Dudley." He summered in Nahant, on and off, from 1922 to 1963, renting rooms in various locations, including 329 Nahant Road in 1931, 11 Wendell Road in 1923 and 1934, and at the Edgehill Inn. Price authored *All Souls*, a novel in eight volumes set in the small town of Seableak, which was closely modeled on Nahant. He was a gay man living openly, as far as was possible in this time period. Frederick Demmler (1888–1918), the artist of this 1916 oil portrait of Price, was his life partner. Unfortunately, Demmler's potential was cut short when he was killed in action at the end of World War I.

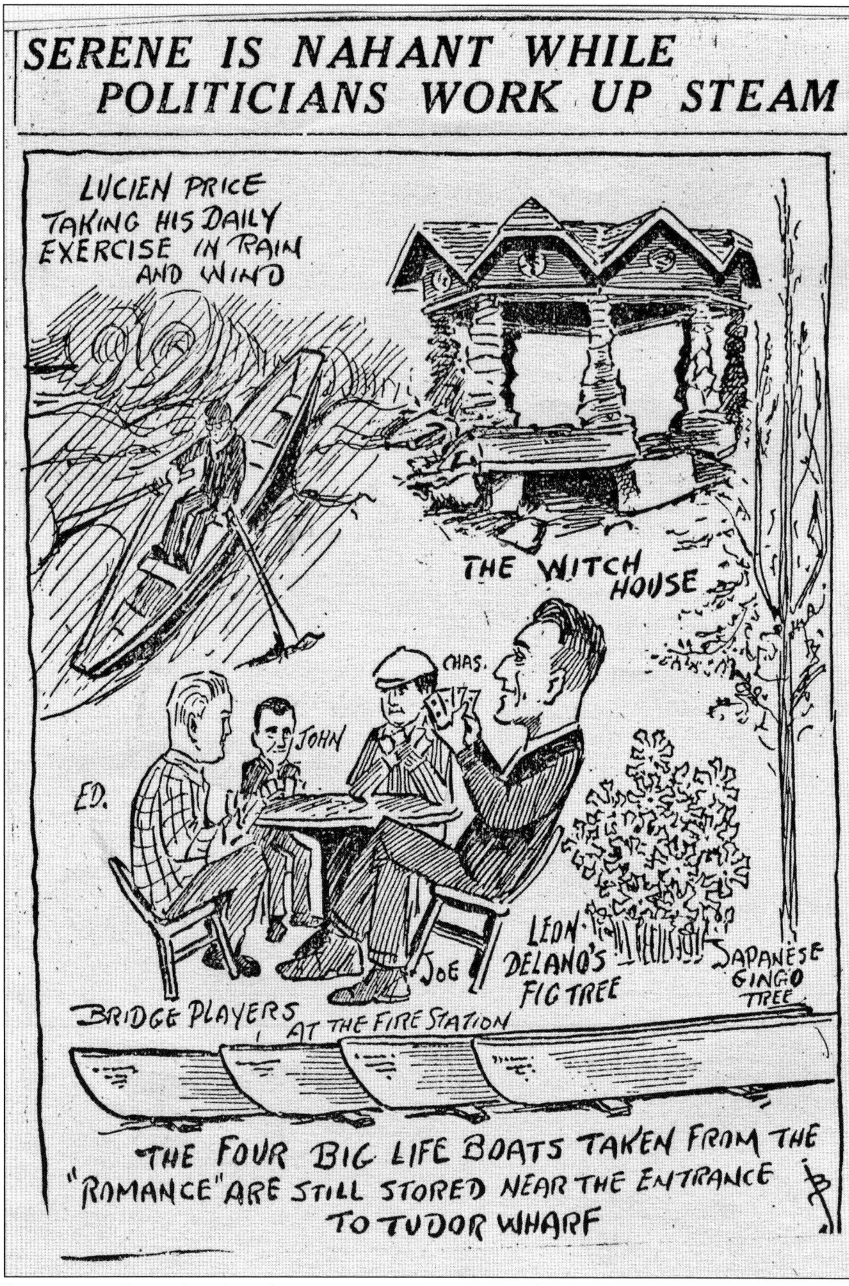

This illustration, from the October 29, 1936, *Lynn Item*, depicts some of the sights in Nahant. In the upper left is Lucien Price during his regular exercise of vigorous rowing in one of Captain Kemp's dories, rented at Tudor Wharf. To the amusement of some, Price would sunbathe in the nude while out in a dory. The lifeboats (at the bottom) were from the SS *Romance*, an excursion steamer that collided with the SS *New York* near the Graves Lighted Whistle Buoy 1A at 7:05 p.m. on September 9, 1936, in heavy fog. There was no loss of life, but much from the *Romance* washed or was brought to shore at Nahant. The captain, Adelburt C. Wickens, was the brother of George W. Wickens, who resided at 74 Castle Road, and was well-known in Nahant. The Witch House was an eccentric structure built on the grounds of Maolis Gardens for Frederic Tudor.

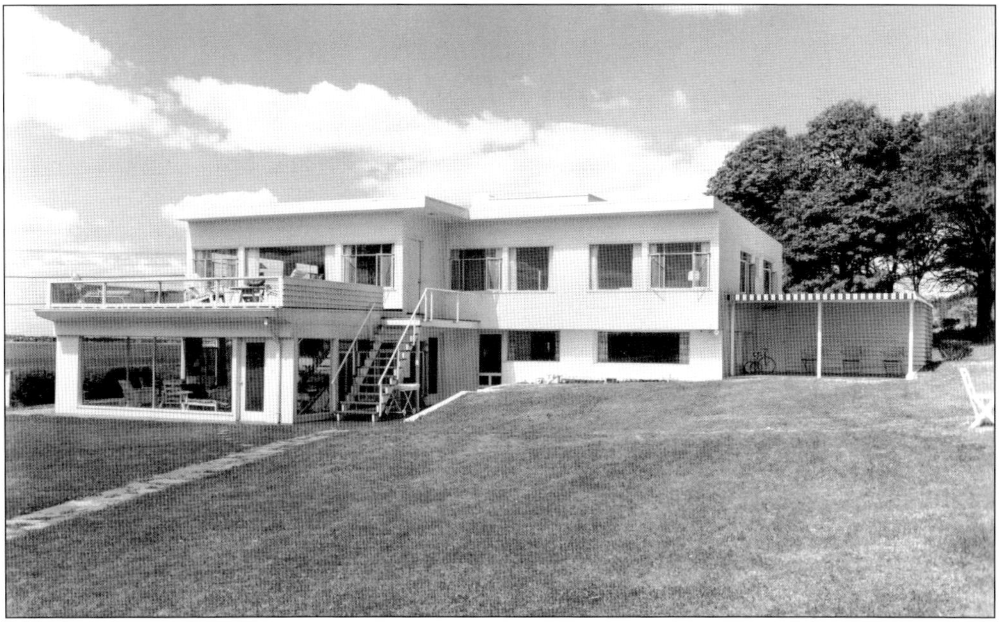

Walter W. Welch, a Boston businessman, commissioned the architectural firm of Royal Barry Wills Associates to design a house at 52 Nahant Road. It was constructed in 1945 with a lower addition and terrace above in 1949. Adjacent to Short Beach, it had a commanding view of Nahant Bay. Its clean modernist design is enhanced by the expansive lawn. The interior photograph shows the high-style late-1940s design by William Leavens and Company. Through this living room window can be seen the northwest coast of Big Nahant. Taken down in 1999, it was replaced by several newer houses. Seen here are the interior and exterior of the views of the Walter Welch Esq. house. (Both photographs by Arthur C. Haskell, courtesy Royal Barry Wills Associates Archives at Historic New England.)

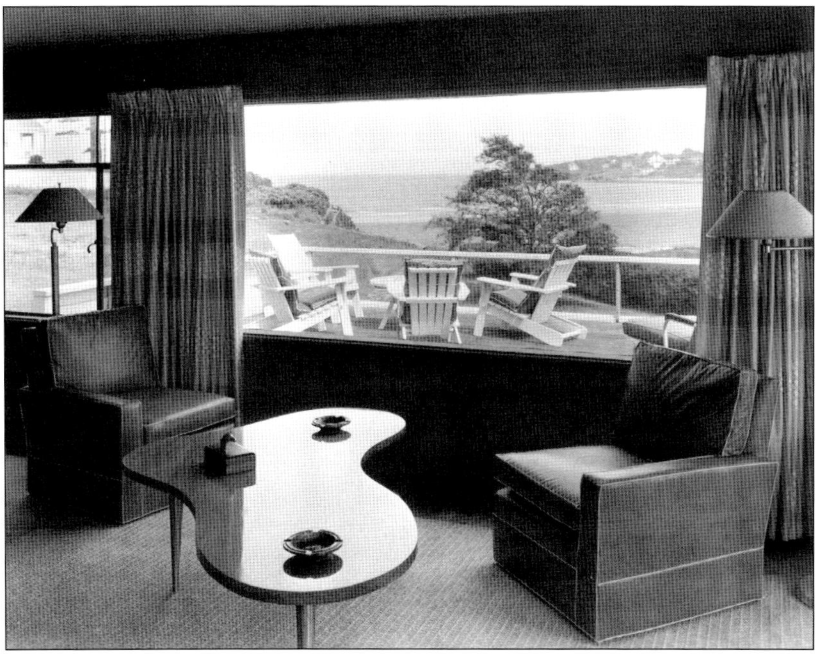

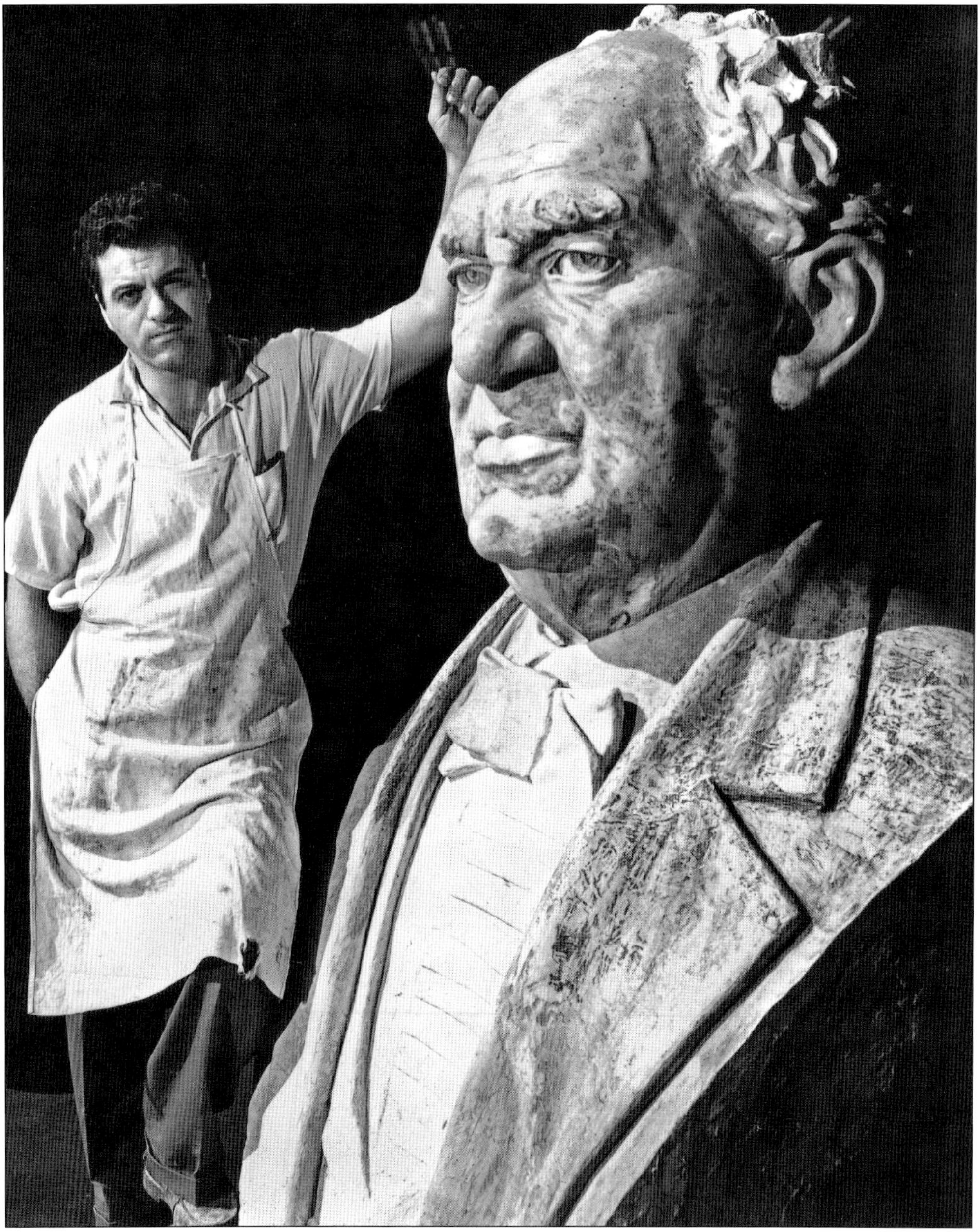

Reno Pisano (1923–), born in Lynn, is a noted sculptor. He is seen here at work on a large-scale bust of P.T. Barnum. It was commissioned for the annual Barnum Festival parade in Bridgeport, Connecticut, and was the centerpiece of the 1966 event. Pisano was a founding faculty member of the Montserrat College of Art in Beverly, Massachusetts. Works of his located in Lynn include the bronze relief sculptures of Frederick Douglass (the African American social reformer), Mary Baker Eddy (founder of the Christian Science religion), and Jan Matzeliger (an African American inventor of shoe machinery). He donated *Tectonic Eclipse*, a five-by-five-foot granite sculpture, to the town of Nahant. It is now installed in front of the public library. In loving memory of his wife, Mary Votano Pisano, he carved the headstone for their burial plot at Greenlawn Cemetery.

Five

SEASIDE

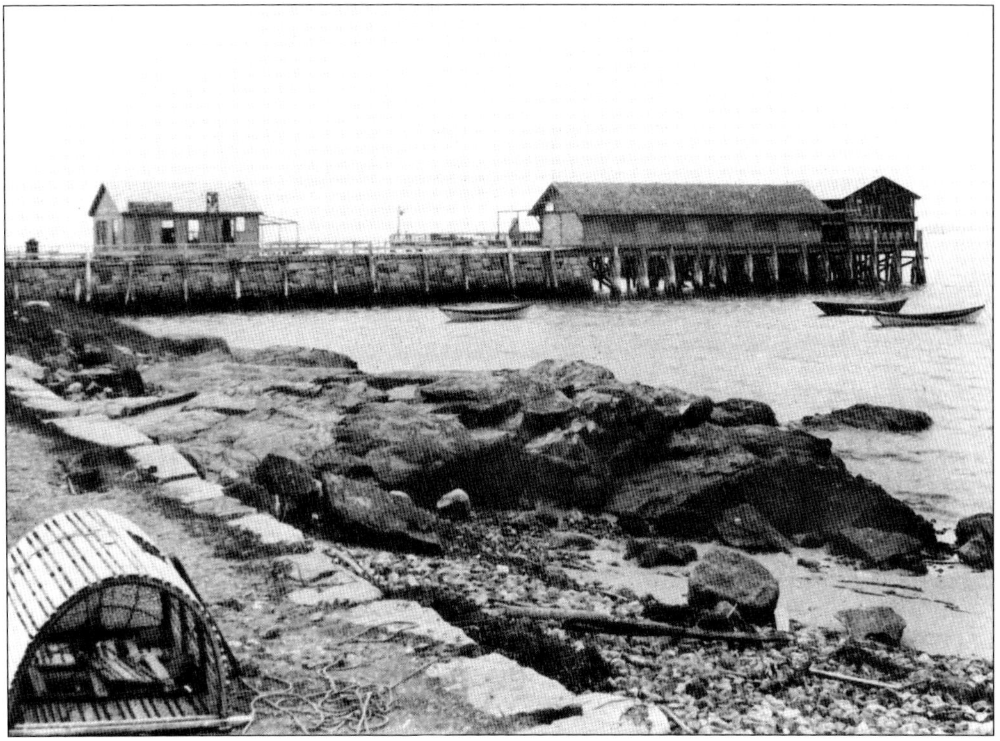

After Frederic Tudor's passing in 1864, his wife, Euphemia Tudor, rebuilt Central Wharf, and she extended it in 1875. The executors of her estate gave it to the town in 1884. This pre-1900 image of the renamed Tudor Wharf shows three structures. On the left is a store, in the middle is the current building, and on the right is a coal bunker to supply the steamships with fuel.

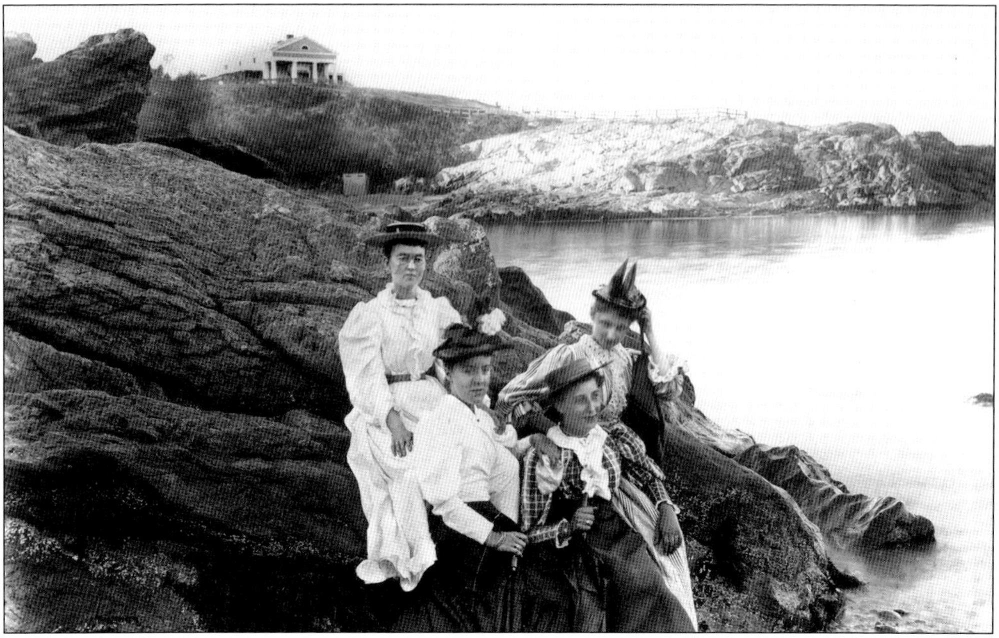

Fashion has always been a concern even while exploring a rocky headland. This c. 1894 image, captured by Harry Wilson in a glass-plate slide, features (from left to right) Alice Wilson, Carrie Parsons, Edith Johnson Wilson, and Georgiana Wilson near Castle Rock. Harry Wilson was a long-serving town selectman and played on the town baseball team as catcher when it competed against the summer people's Nahant Club.

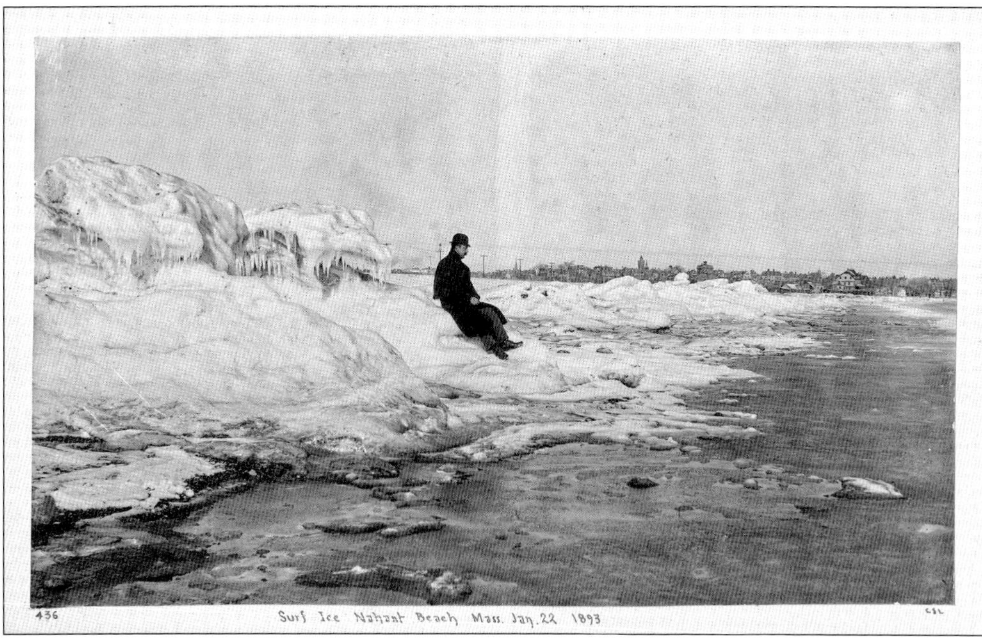

This dramatic winter scene documents the piling up of surf ice on Long Beach during an extended cold period. This lone figure seems unconcerned as he contemplates the freezing ocean water on January 22, 1893. Behind this man are the electric poles on the causeway, and to the right is the spire of the 1880 St. Stephen's Episcopal Church in Lynn.

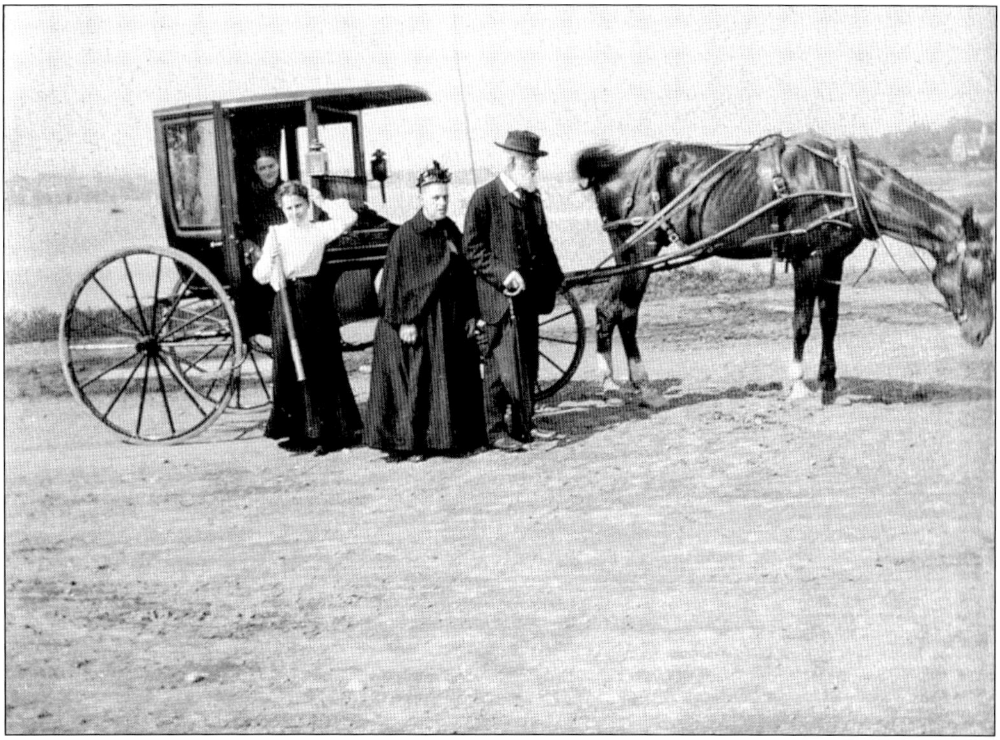

Edmund Buxton Johnson (1832–1914), a Civil War veteran, and his wife, Mary Cheney Johnson (1838–1909), have alighted from their carriage and seem to be starting off on a walk at Short Beach. They resided at 1 Central Street. This and the next image are from the Bertha Johnson family albums in the collection of the Nahant Historical Society.

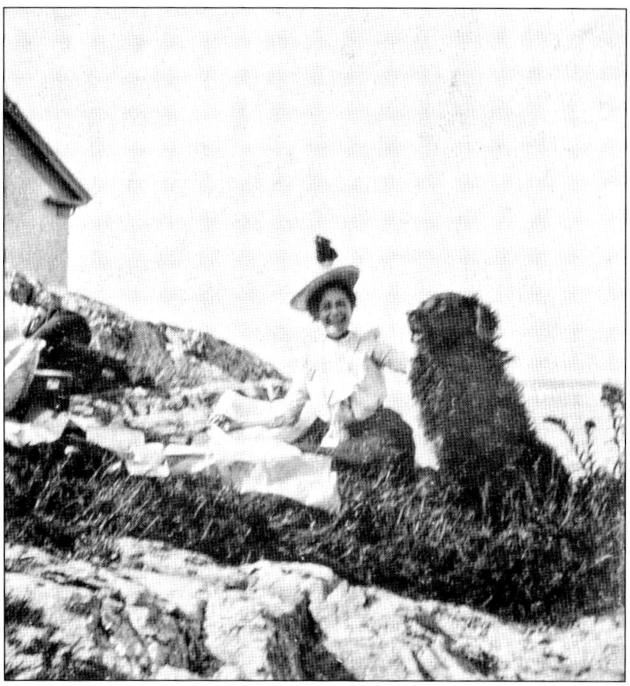

One of the Johnson women is enjoying a luncheon outing on Egg Rock. Could this dog be the famous Milo? He moved to Egg Rock with the first lighthouse keeper, George Taylor, and his family in 1855. He became famous after the story of Milo's rescue of one of the Taylor children was reported in 1856. The English artist Sir Edwin Landseer painted Milo and the child in the iconic image entitled *Saved*.

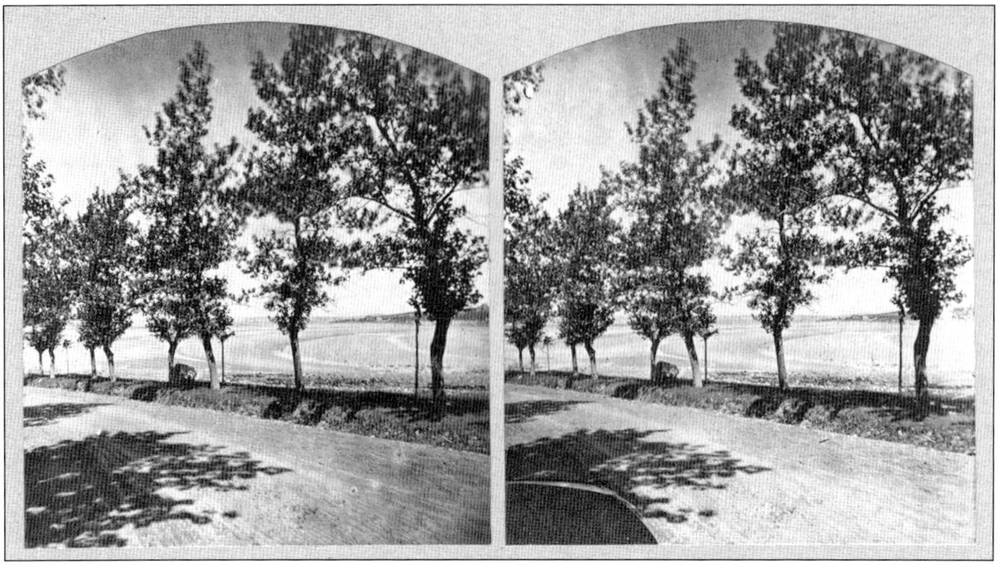

This undated stereoscopic card is titled *The Beach Between Great Nahant and Little Nahant (Short Beach)*. It shows the sweeping curve of the beach from the Big Nahant end toward Little Nahant. This beach is formed of fine sand and is very shallow, making it a prime location for swimming and walking. The construction of this card suggests that it may have been homemade.

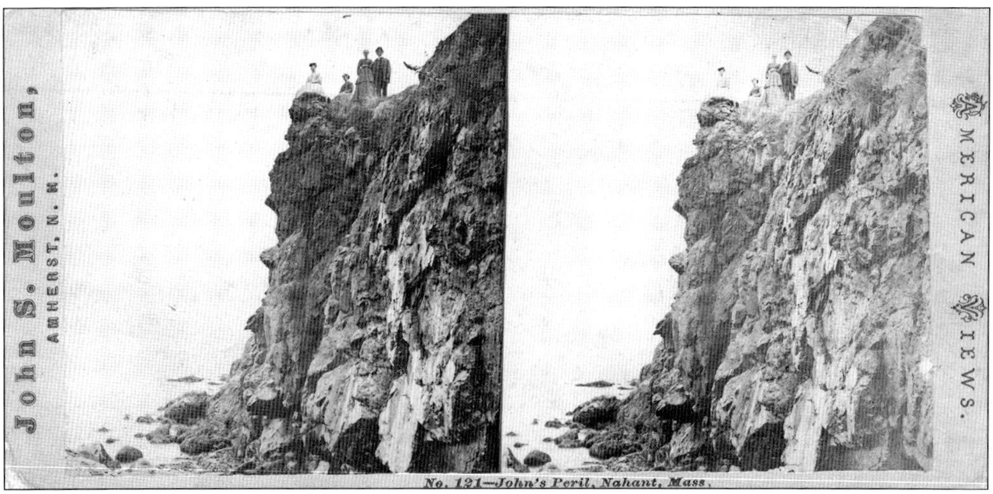

John's Peril, on Nahant's north side, is the cliff descending vertically at the end of what is now High Street. It was so named because, before this area was developed in the 1930s, John Breed came too close with his oxcart and lost control. He was able to extricate himself and the animals, but the cart and contents went into the sea.

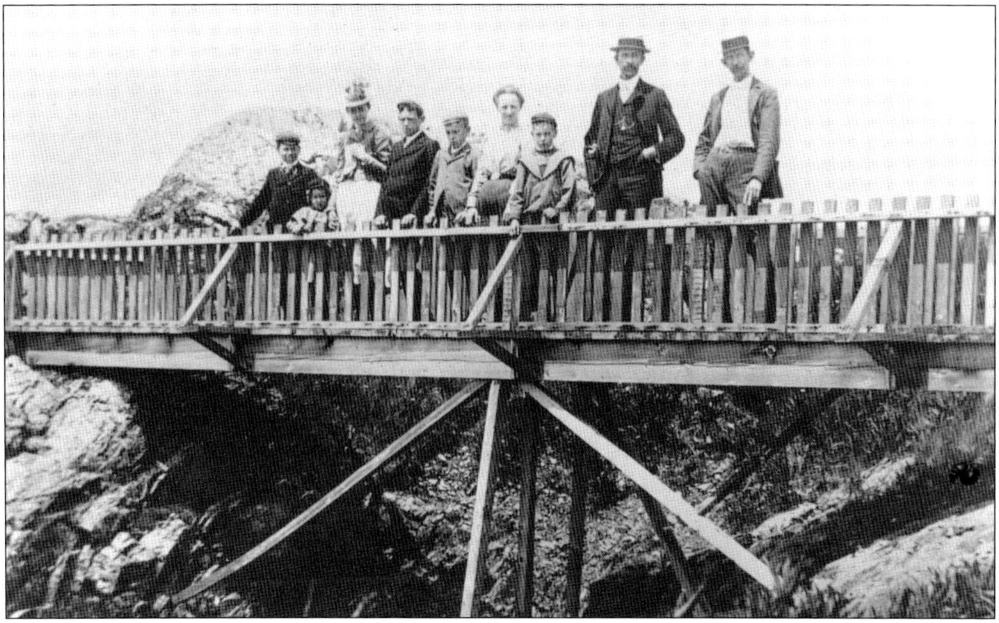

The well-dressed Bruce family, enjoying a day out, were captured by a daring photographer. This wooden bridge (called the Trestle) was part of the Cliff Walk at East Point. It spanned the chasm over Natural Bridge just east of Pulpit Rock. Henry Cabot Lodge allowed public access to this path around his estate so that all could appreciate the drama of the site.

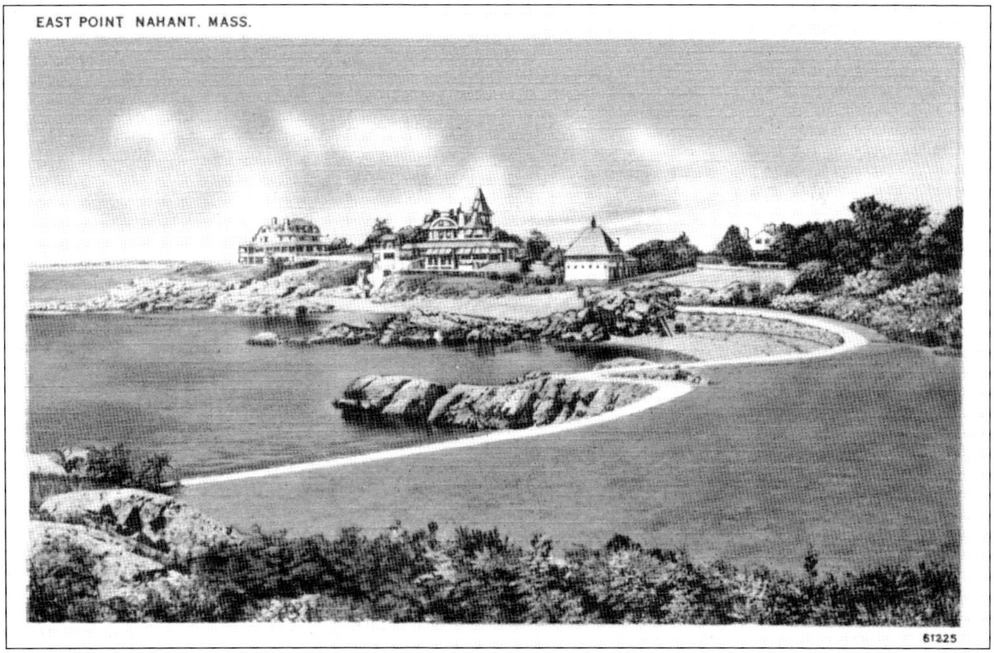

Looking over the beach on the Lodge/James estate, the Ralph and Charlotte Lowell compound is in the center and the Sprague house on the left. Ralph Lowell (1890–1978) bought this property in 1927. He cofounded the WGBH public broadcasting group in 1951. Charlotte's message on this 1966 postcard reads, in part, "found this card at the village store . . . it was taken about 45 years ago."

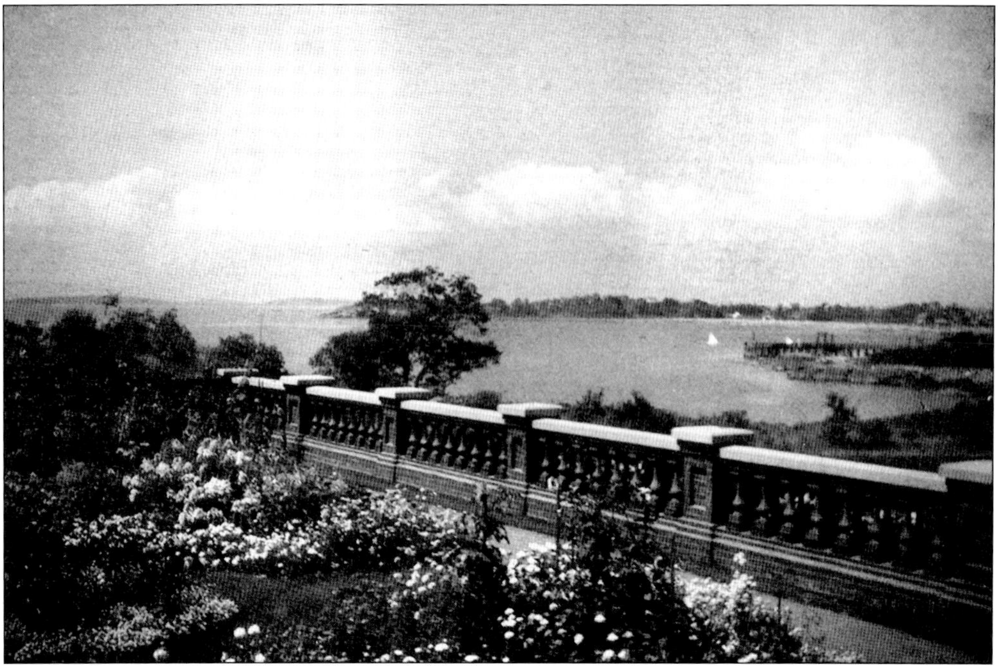

This August 17, 1905, image by Dudley Bowditch Fay captures the delight of the terrace at Snakehill. This is the new house of George and Laura Blanchard Duncan at 51 Cliff Street following the disastrous fire of 1896. The well-designed garden is a counterpoint to the expansive vista to Tudor Wharf, Bailey's Hill, and the open Atlantic. (Courtesy Fay/Garfield family.)

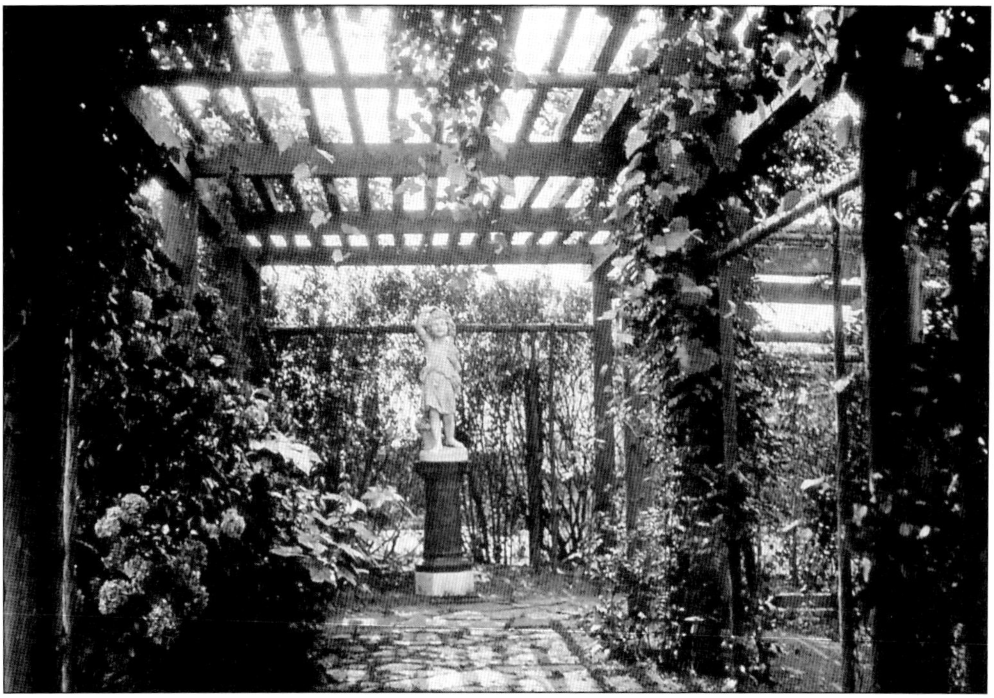

Dudley Fay artfully shot the intimacy of the vine-covered pergola of Snakehill in the summer of 1915. It was a shady retreat from the sun-drenched garden. (Courtesy Fay/Garfield family.)

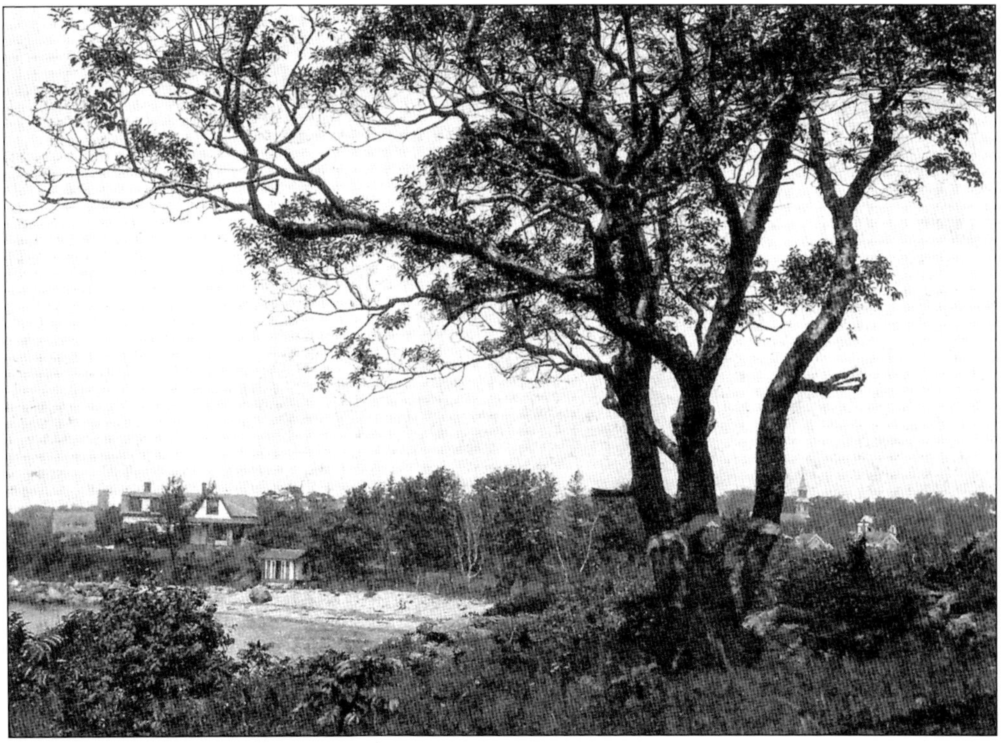

Dudley Fay shot this well-composed image in the summer of 1915. His view is from the site of Longfellow's house and looks down across Curlew (Longfellow's) Beach to the General Fremont cottage. The town water standpipe is visible in the distant far left. To the right of the tree is the Village Church steeple. (Courtesy Fay/Garfield family.)

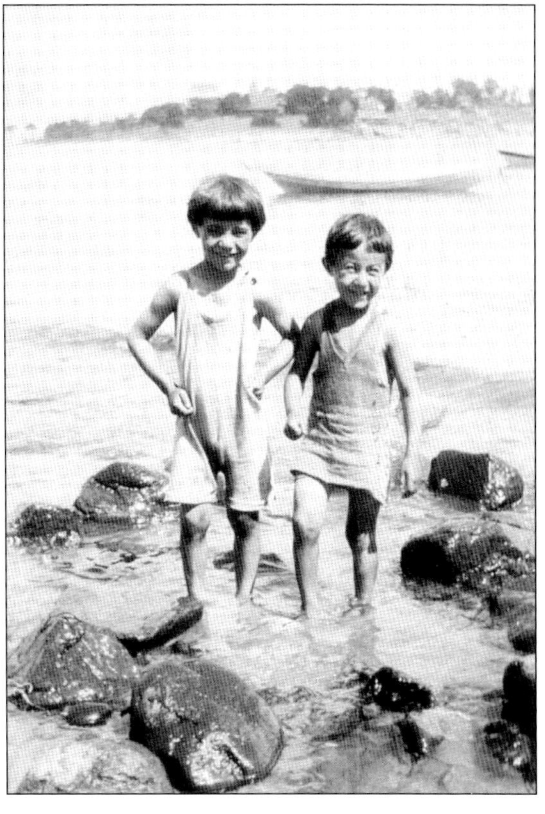

Brothers D. Frank (left) and Tom Famulari are enjoying a day at Short Beach in 1924. Frank became a family dentist and served on the town school committee. Tom ran the Central Café in Lynn and enjoyed skiing well into his 80s. On Little Nahant, in the background, is the Hotel Nahant, and to the right is the Howe estate. Fishing dories are moored just offshore.

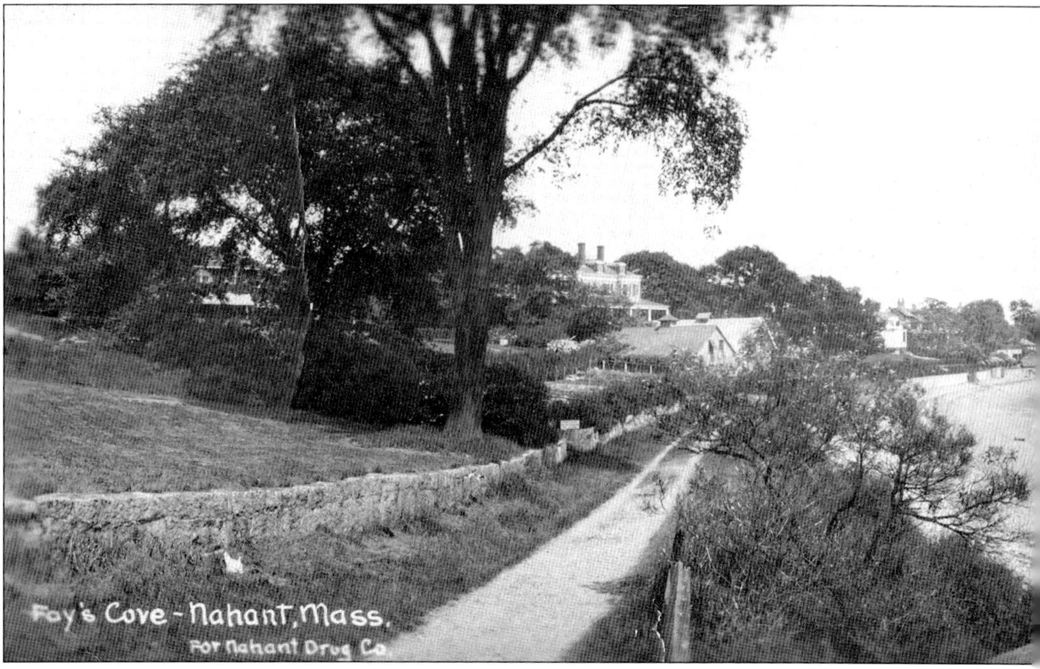

This panoramic photograph, titled *Fay's Cove*, was published for the Nahant Drug Company in the 1920s. It shows the long sweep of Joe's Beach with a road just above. The houses to the left are on Vernon Street, and at the end is the old steamboat wharf and Swallow's Cave Point. This stone wharf was the original water access to the Nahant Hotel and the rest of town. On the

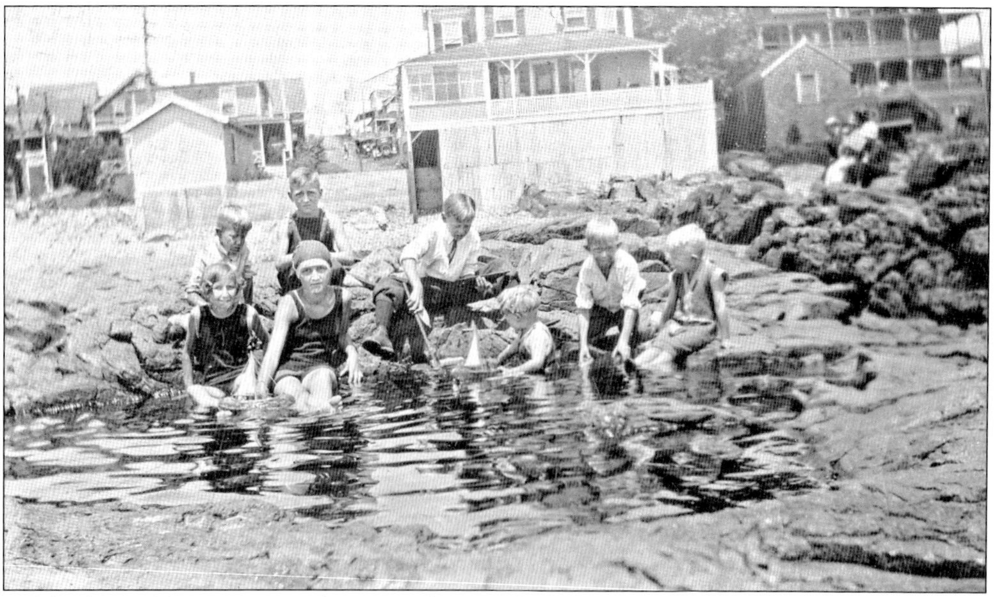

Unlike the wealthy summer residents, people of modest means rented smaller cottages. The Deegan family stayed at Cambridge Cottage on Bass Point Road, seen in the background in July 1925. This delightful image documents the joys of summer. This family and their friends are enjoying bathing in a refreshing tide pool and playing with their model boats near Lewis Beach at Bass Point.

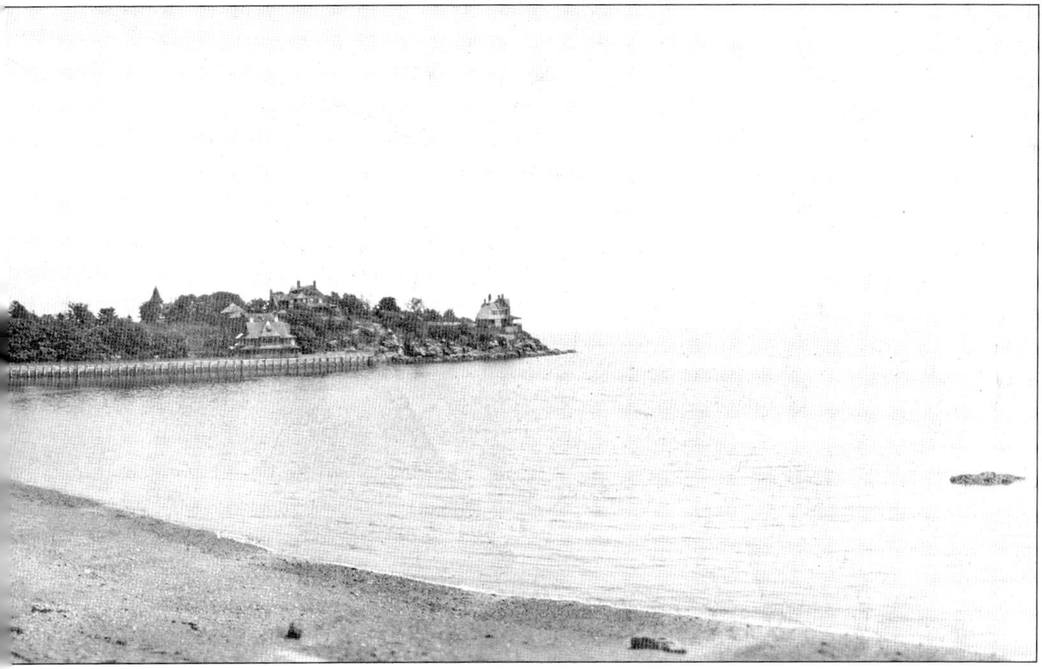

wharf is Wharf Cottage, built for John E. Lodge in 1879. Just to the left, through the trees, is the tower of the Knyvet W. Sears house of 1874. To the right is the Samuel Eliot Guild house, and at the end is the Sprague/Lowell house. These last two, along with other nearby buildings, were removed in the late 1930s to make way for Harmon Elliott's new house, Cas-el-ot.

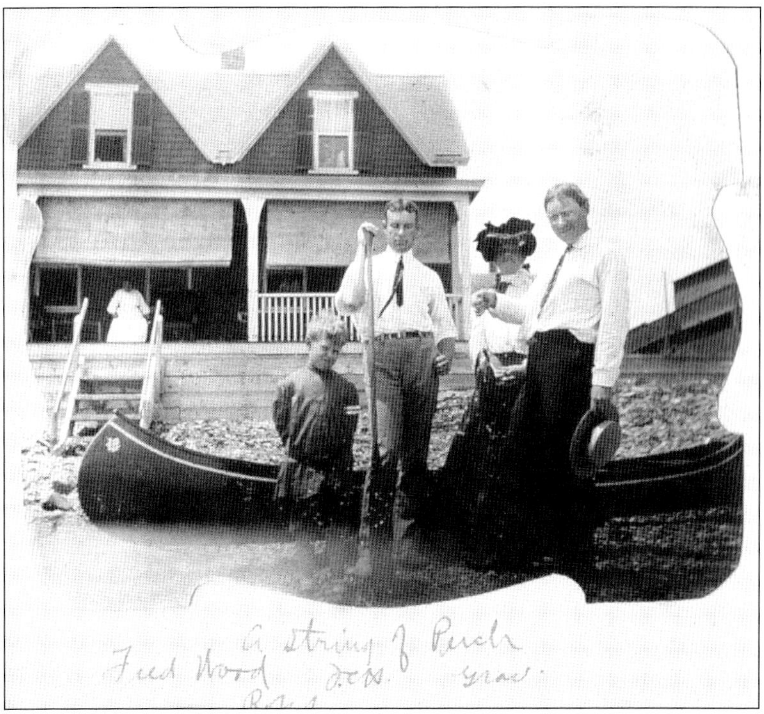

These formally dressed sport fishermen show off their catch after returning to Pond Beach in their canoe. The beach was so named because just beyond the berm of rocks and houses is Bear Pond. The cottage in the background is located at 75 Willow Road. This group will eat well tonight.

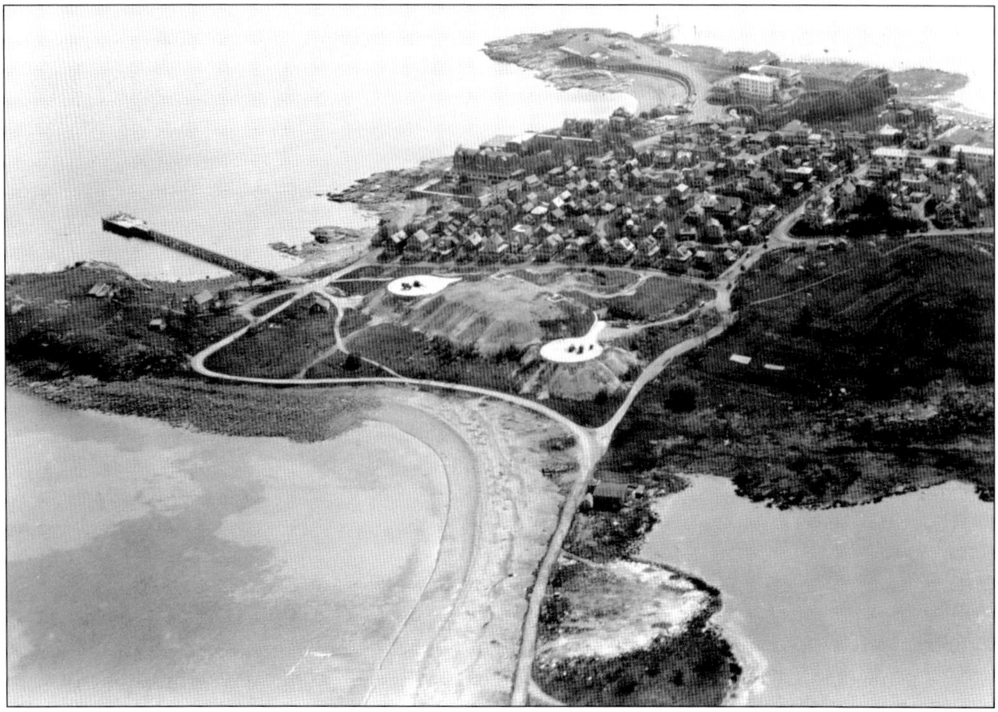

This May 1924 aerial view shows Bailey's Hill and Bass Point. Bear Pond is in the right foreground, and in the middle distance are the gun emplacements and military pier of Fort Ruckman. At the top right is the ferry pier that gave holiday-makers access to the Bass Point amusements and small cottages. To the extreme right is the Bass Point House hotel next to the Scenic Coaster.

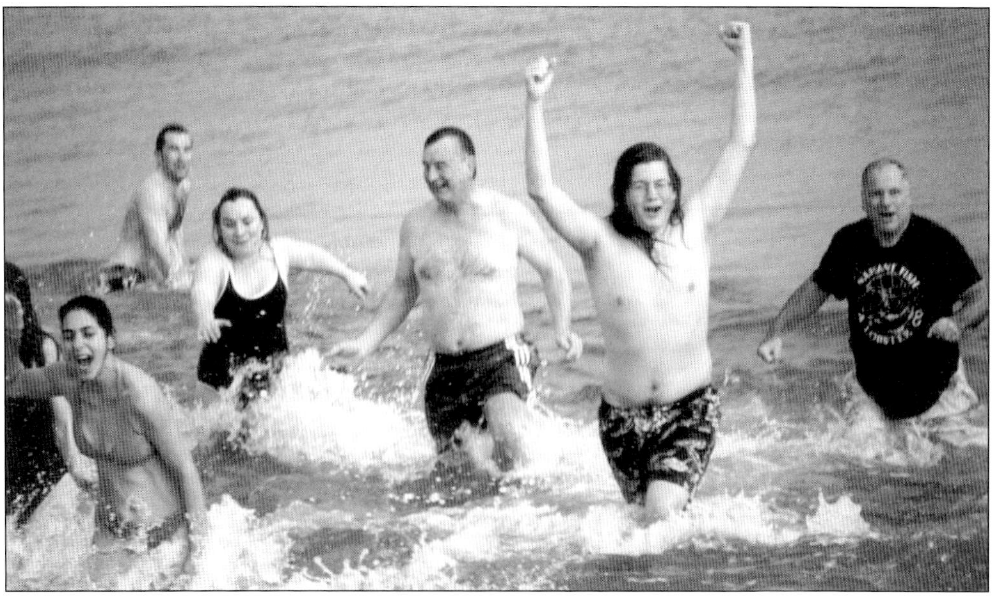

In 2003, John Welsh organized a New Year's Day ocean plunge. Now a tradition, it continues and grows larger every year. The Nahant Sea Serpents make their quick escape from the frigid water in 2010. Owen Welsh runs out with his arms raised in triumph, with Carl Jenkins to the right. These days, an open fire, hot drinks, and a cheering crowd greet the exhilarated revelers.

Six

AT WORK

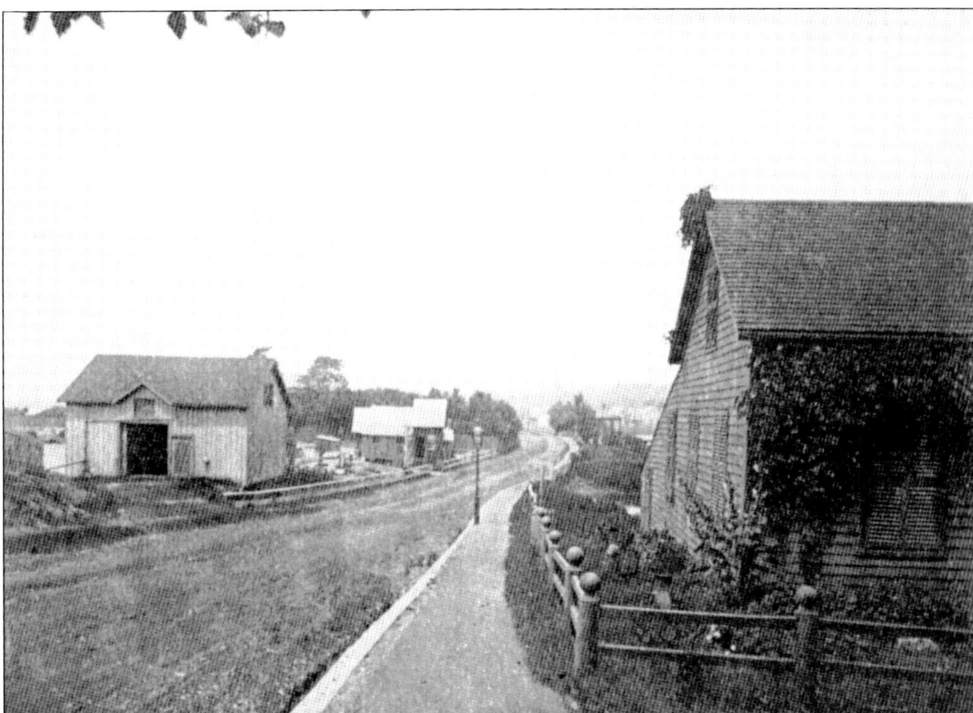

This 1879 view down Willow Road shows, on the left, Henry Wadsworth Longfellow's barn and, further on, a seasonal cobbler's shop perched on the rocky shore of Curlew Beach. The cottage to the right is no longer extant. In a letter to Thomas Gold Appleton, Longfellow writes on July 14, 1872, "We have asphalt sidewalks, running on one side of each street like . . . a bit of black ribbon."

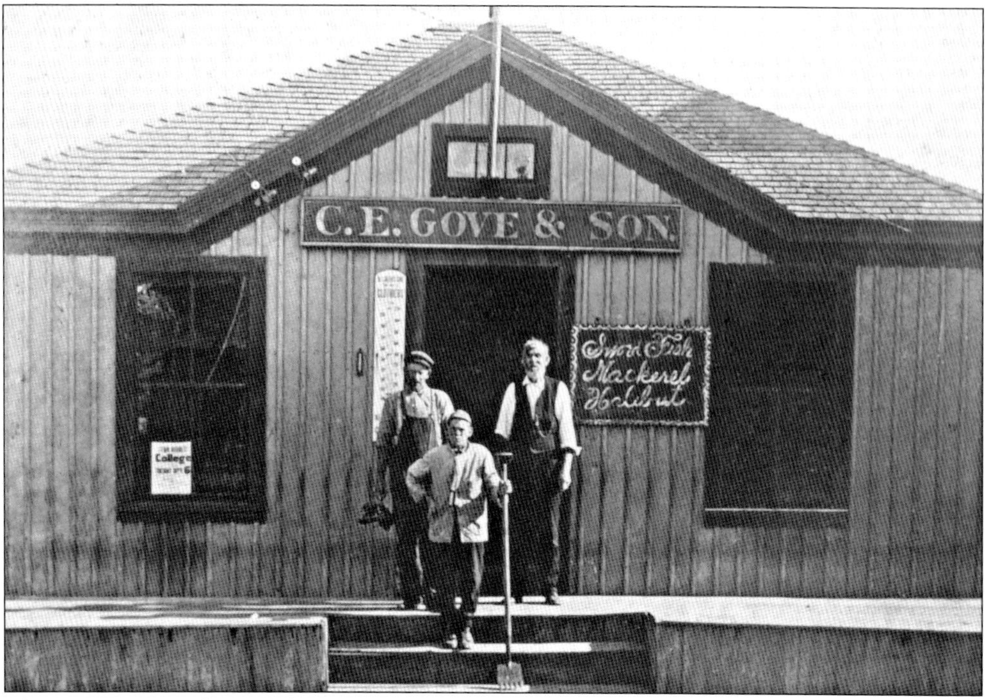

The C.E. Gove and Son fish market was a fixture on Tudor Beach facing Emerald Road. Seen in front, on the step, is Charles A. Gove Jr. In back are Frank A. Gove Sr. (left) and his father, Charles E. Gove, who died in 1920 at the age of 82. The building was moved in 1924 to 78 Willow Road, and the land was sold for housing.

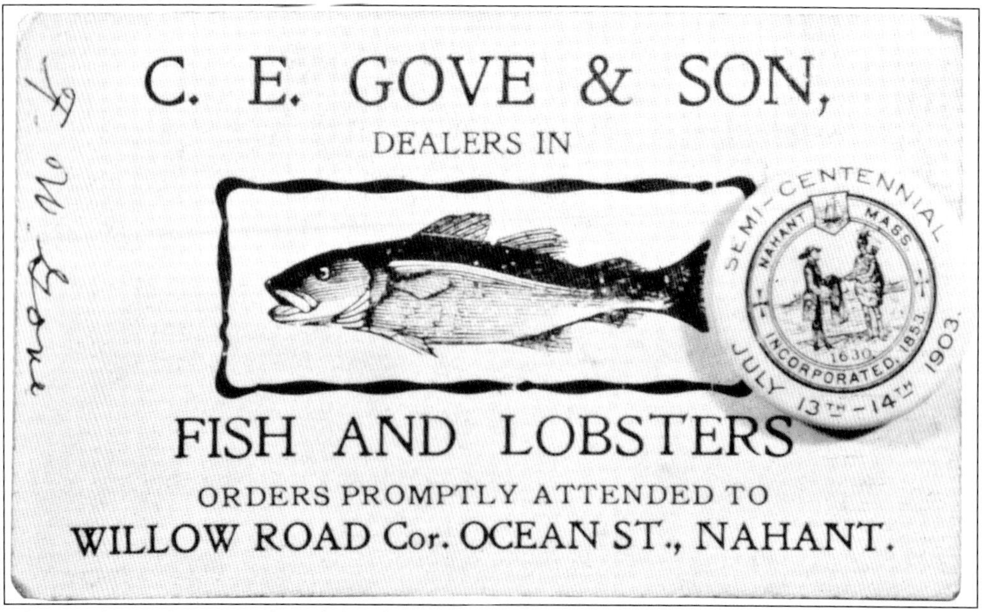

This trade card was produced for the C.E. Gove and Son fish market during the Nahant semicentennial year of 1903. Charles E. Gove was a policeman in 1871, and for many years until his death, he was the treasurer of the Nahant Mutual Benefit Association. This private group gave money to assist bereaved families after the passing of a member.

Henry Cabot Lodge (1850–1924) summered in Nahant most of his life. He served in the Massachusetts House of Representatives (1880–1882), the US House of Representatives (1887–1893), and the US Senate (1893–1924). He also served as the Nahant town moderator (1908–1921) and was a big presence in town.

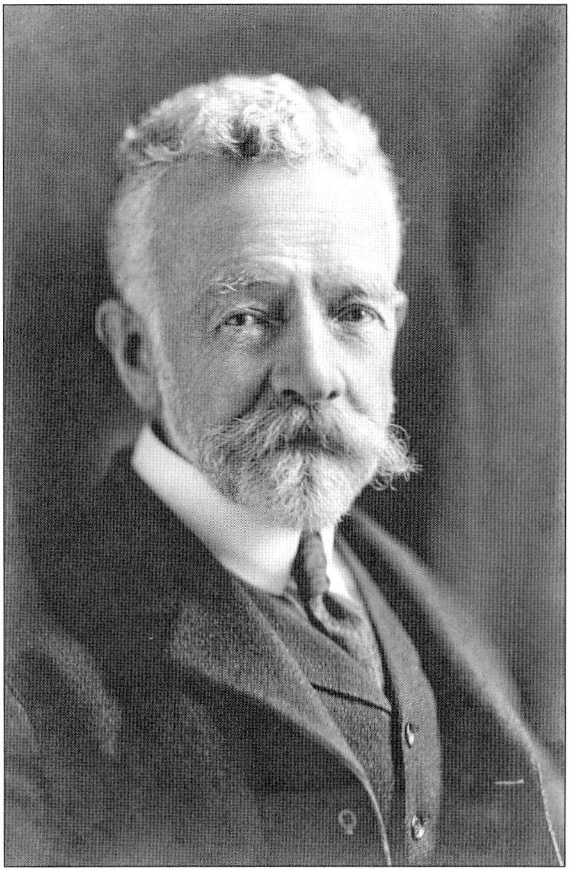

While at Harvard (1868–1872), Henry Cabot Lodge acted in the Hasty Pudding theatricals. On the left, he is portraying Lady Macbeth, and on the right, he is fair Imogen in Shakespeare's *Cymbeline*. These Harvard student productions began in 1844 and continue annually as fully staged farces with great humor and are still heavily subscribed.

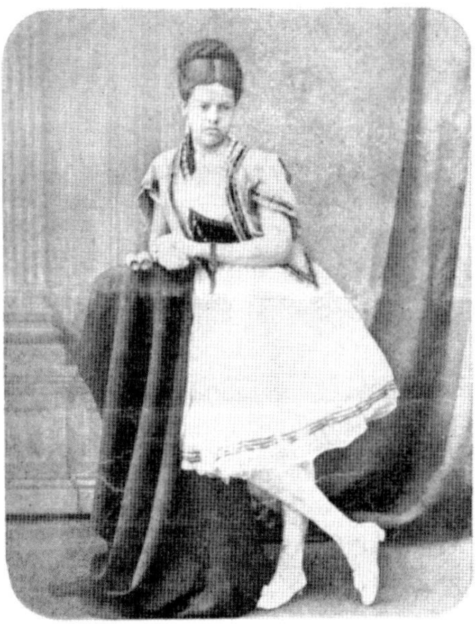

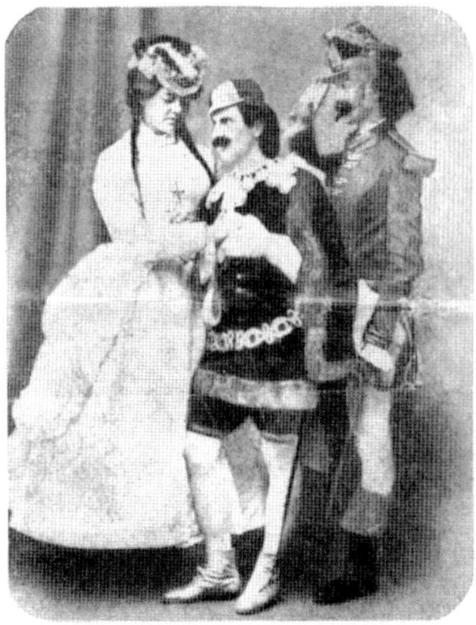

AN ACCOMPLISHED ACTRESS. Lodge played female roles in Harvard theatricals—Lady Macbeth (*left*) and Fair Imogen in a Hasty Pudding show. He loved theater so much that he paid for chance to act bit parts in Boston operas.

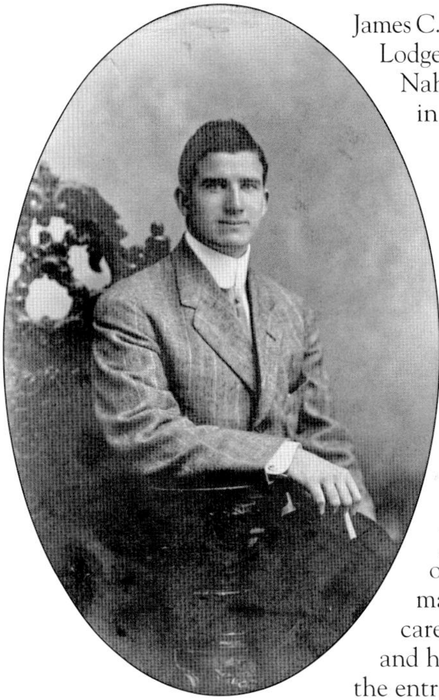

James C. Tierney (1891–1972), born in Nahant, was Henry Cabot Lodge's chauffeur for many years. He got to spend summers in Nahant but accompanied the senator back to Washington in the winter. He was the uncle of Louise Tierney Titus.

Third from the left, leaning on a rake, is Willard D. Johnson (1867–1938) with a grounds crew at the estate of Henry Cabot Lodge. Johnson came to Nahant in 1882, marrying Hessie Baxter in 1890. In 1912, he became the caretaker of the estate, where he remained for 26 years. He and his family lived happily in the caretaker's cottage near the entrance gate.

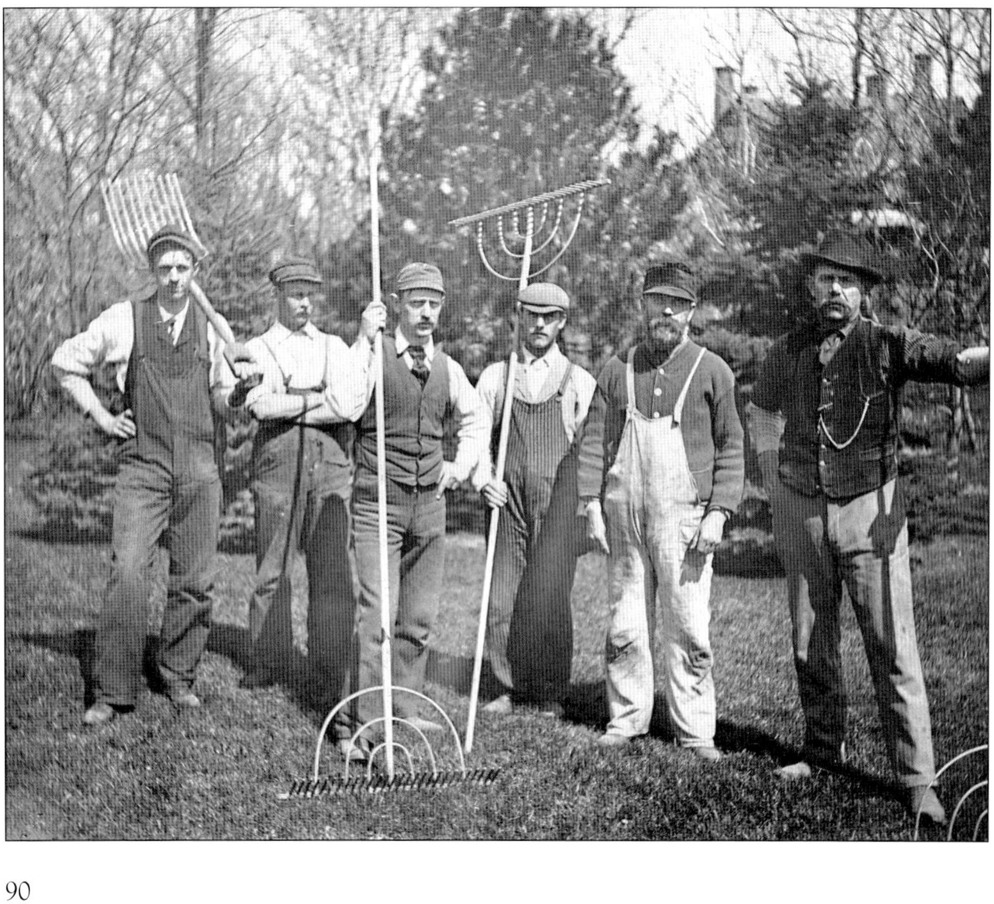

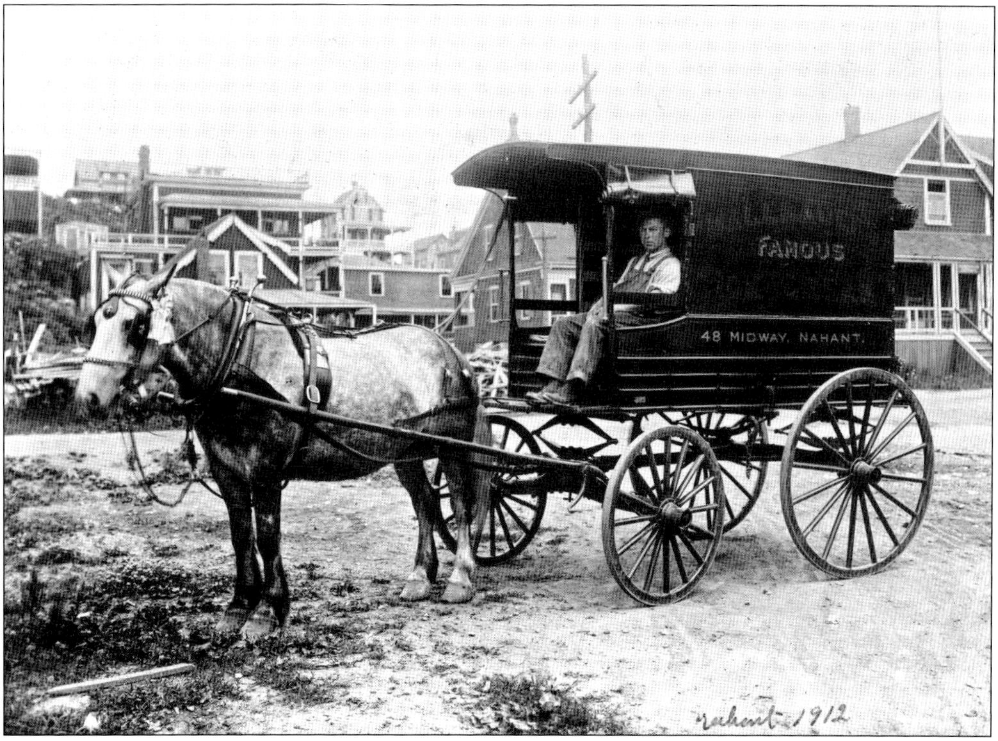

William G. Hallbauer of Lynn developed his recipe for ice cream using a high-butterfat-content cream in the early 1900s. He established a shop on the Midway at Bass Point. Here a relative, Walter Hallbauer, makes a delivery in 1912 with Bass Point cottages in the background. In the late 1920s, William partnered with Howard Johnson. This recipe spurred on the empire of Howard Johnson restaurants.

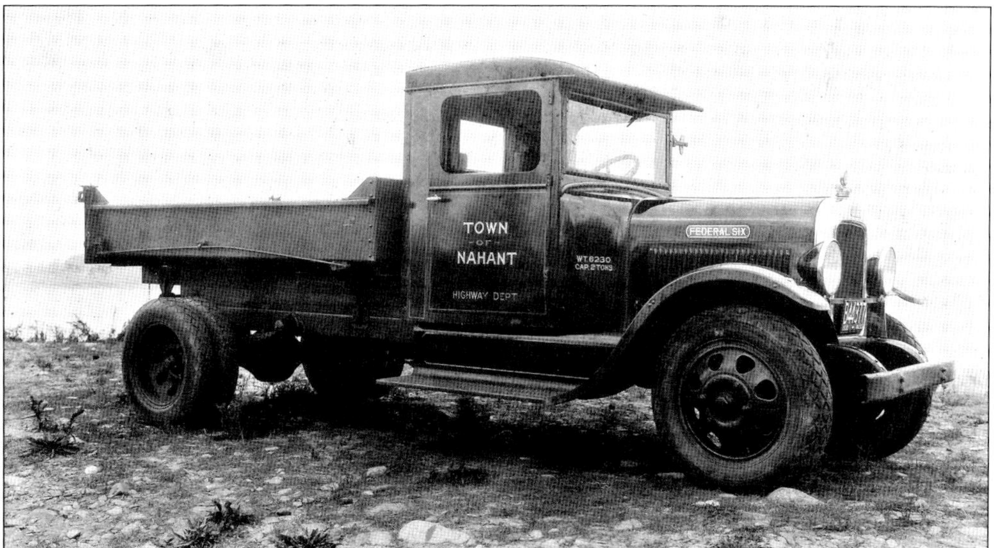

George H. Green, a commercial photographer who lived at 175 Little Nahant Road, documented the town infrastructure in the 1930s. This highway department truck is posed against Nahant Bay with part of Little Nahant visible at the rear of the truck. It carries a license plate dated 1930.

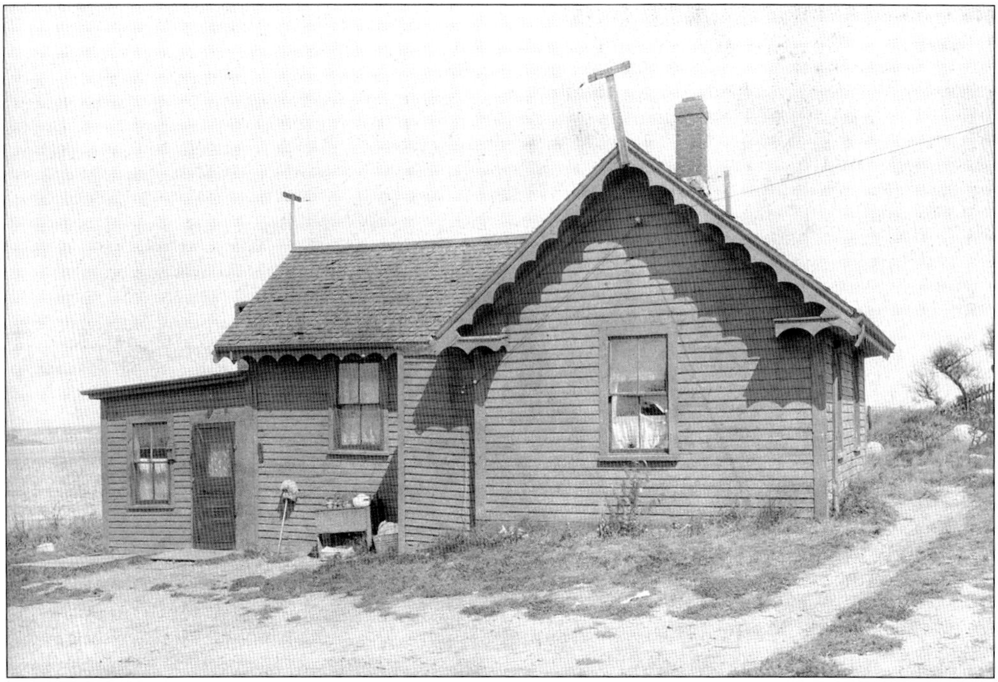

The "little brown house in the Pit" (190 Nahant Road) was the home of the Timmins family and later the Cirafice family and was adjacent to the Pit. Used by the highway department, the Pit was in the vicinity of the current Greystone Road, near Nahant Road. The area was thus named because stone was mined and worked here, including the stone for the Ellingwood Chapel.

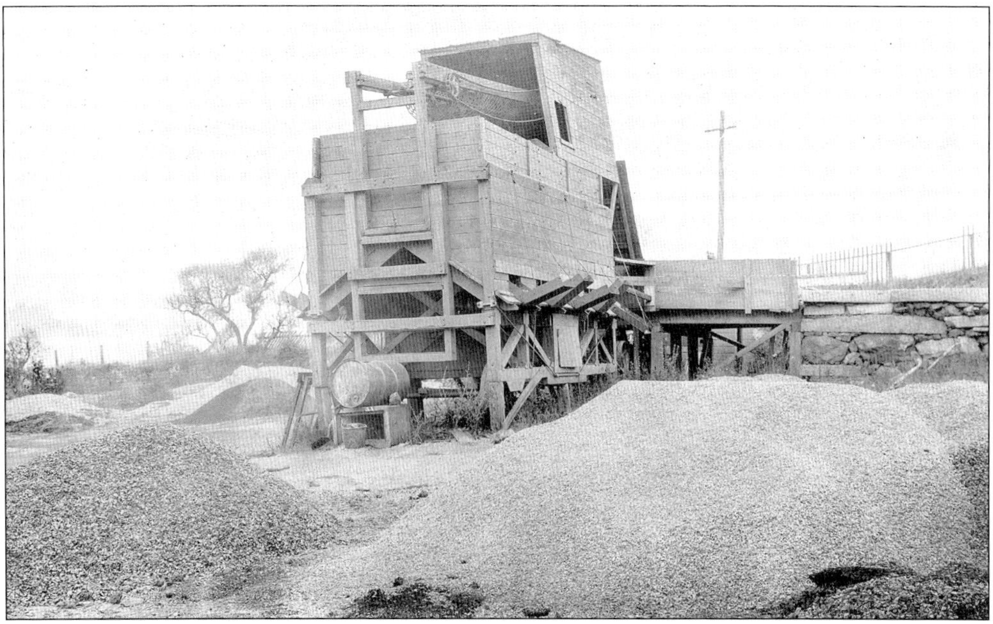

In the Pit also was the stone crusher. The highway department had to prepare the gravel to build and repair the roads. Seen on the ground around the crusher are piles of various grades of gravel to be used for different purposes, including making concrete. To the right is a stone retaining wall that can still be seen in winter.

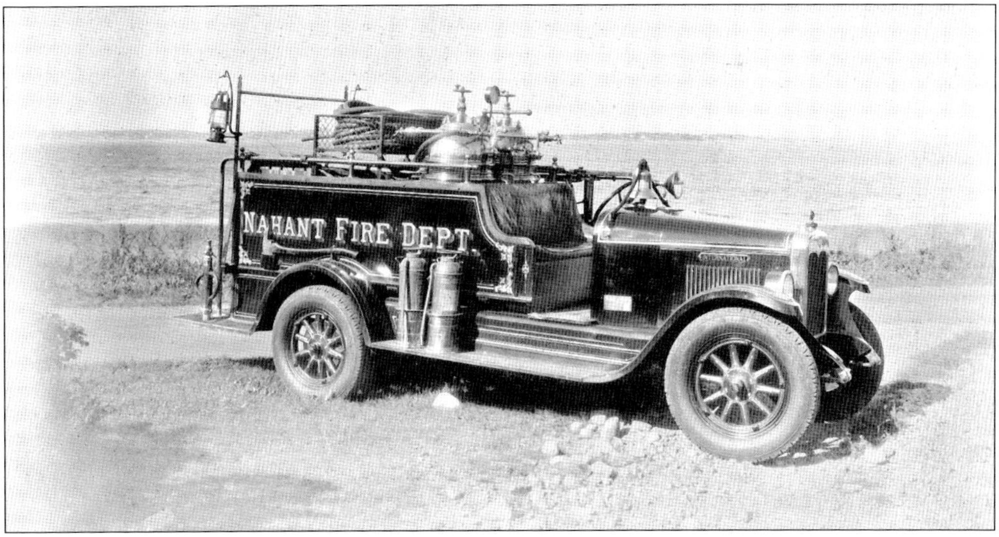

This International Chemical fire engine is proudly posed on Marginal Road with Swampscott and Marblehead in the distance. The chemicals are in the tanks visible behind the seat. Sulfuric acid combined with bicarbonate of soda produces carbon dioxide, which, propelled onto a fire, smothers it without the use of water. The last of this type of engine was produced in 1934.

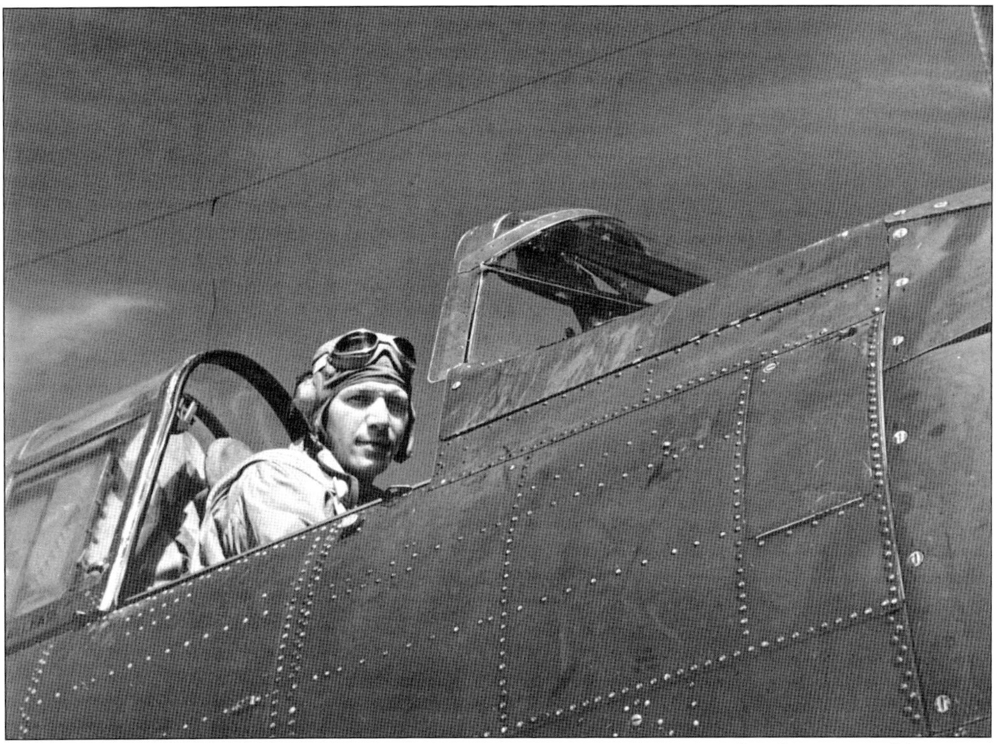

Arthur Lithgow Devens (1908–1995), a US Navy lieutenant commander during World War II, was a pilot in the Alaska campaign. Air warfare was key to fighting the Japanese occupation of several Aleutian Islands. Pilots needed great skill to fly in the dangerous weather conditions in this vast archipelago. He and his wife, Necie, who operated a gift shop in the post office block, lived at 11 Valley Road.

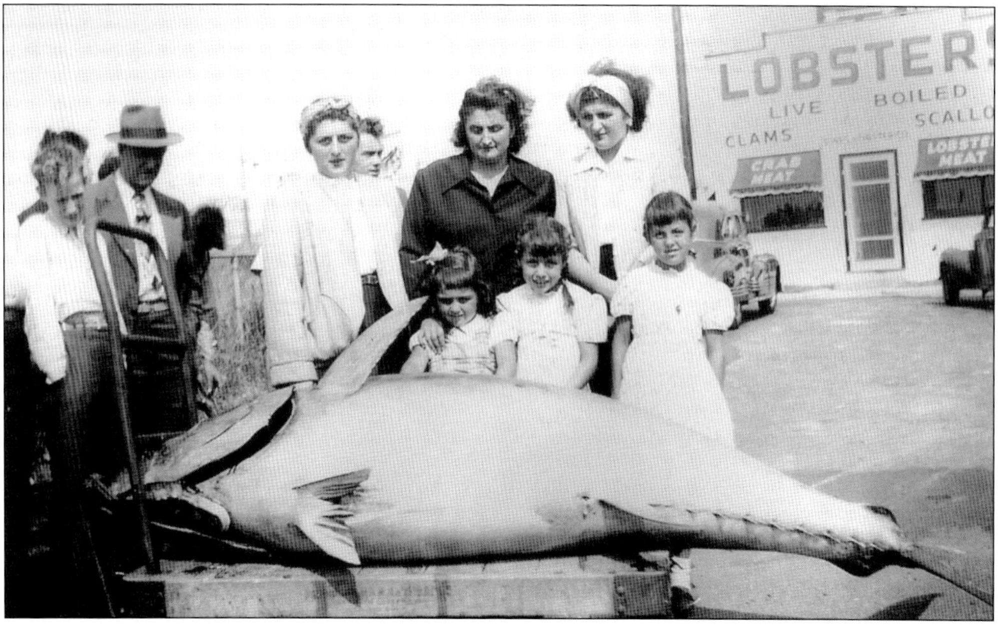

Large fish are still caught in Nahant Bay. This tuna was brought to shore by Charles Carnabuci and presented to his cousin Cosimo Carnabuci. Some of the extended family admire the catch in an undated photograph taken at Short Beach. To the right is Nathan Sherber's fish café and shop near 157 Nahant Road. These families lived in the three houses on Antigo Way.

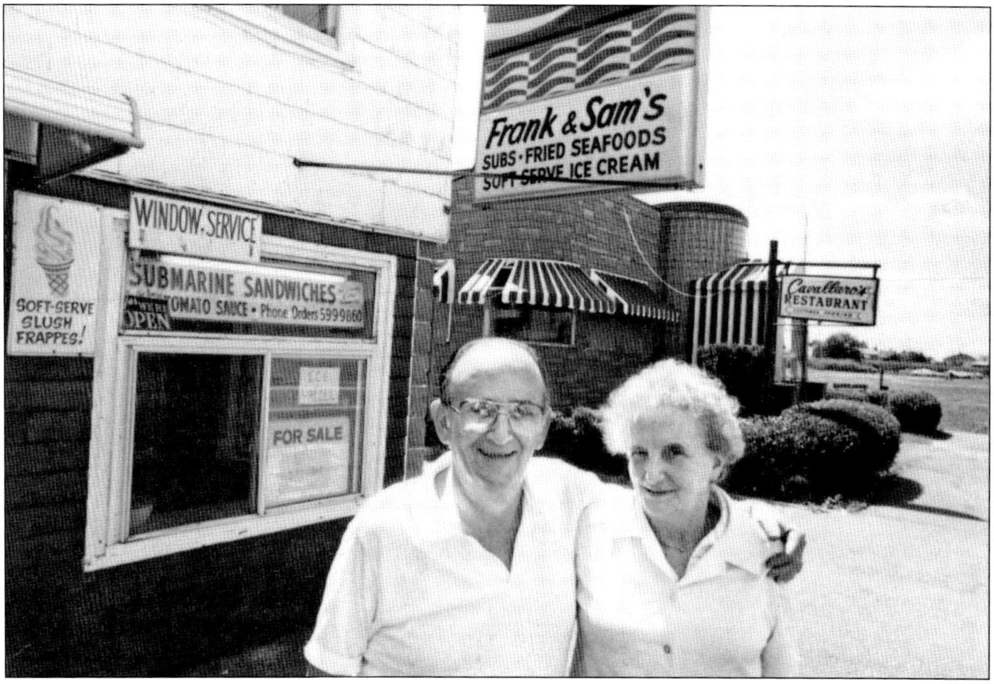

Salvatore "Sam" and Isabelle Cavallaro are happy to pose in front of their sandwich shop, Frank and Sam's, at 141 Nahant Road, across from Short Beach, in the 1980s. This extended family ran a series of restaurants here beginning in 1921. In the background is their larger establishment, which, by 1938, was called the 400 Club. It burned in 1981.

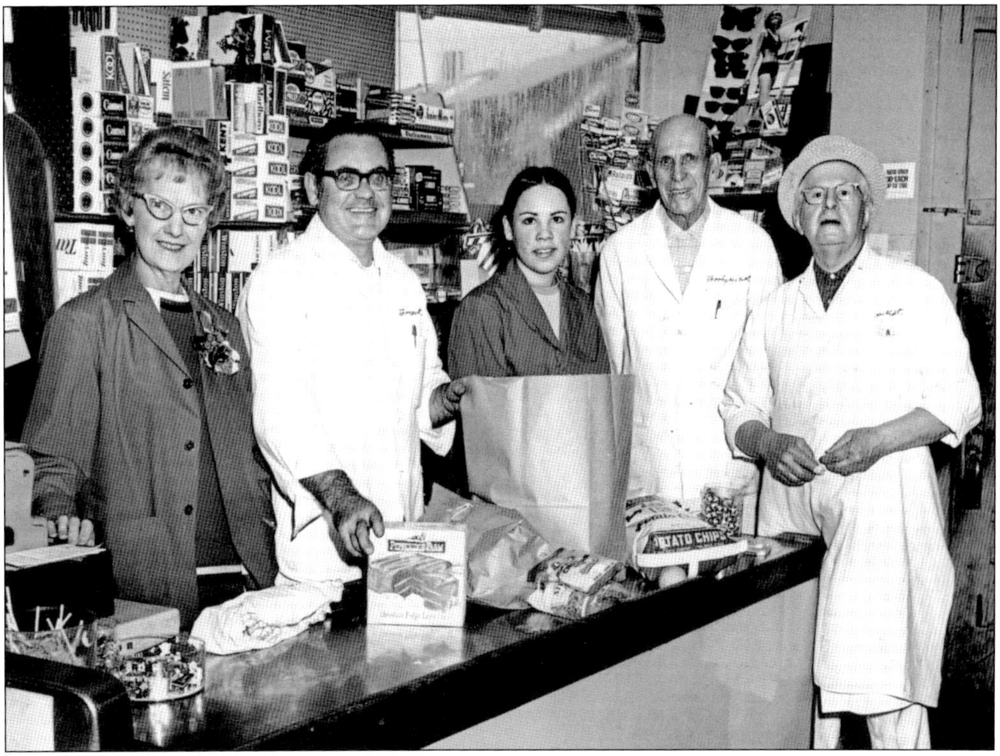

Foody's Market, at 37 Emerald Road, was located at the intersection of Ocean Street and Willow Road. In the 1950s, it was staffed by, from left to right, cashier Clara Stevens, owner Eddy Foody, clerk Judy Bonner, and in the meat and fish department, Andrew Murray Croft and Ed Bishop. It was a full-service grocery store that also delivered. It has now been converted into a house.

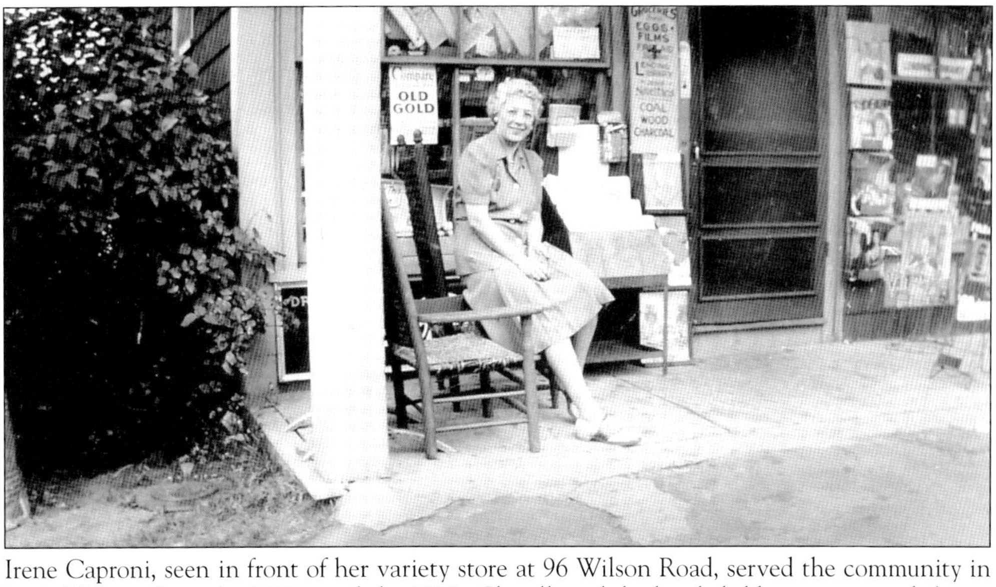

Irene Caproni, seen in front of her variety store at 96 Wilson Road, served the community in Little Nahant from the 1950s until the 1970s. She allowed the local children to run a tab (up to one dollar) to buy penny candy and other treats that she kept well stocked. She is remembered as a mentor to some of them for her ability to listen and advise if asked.

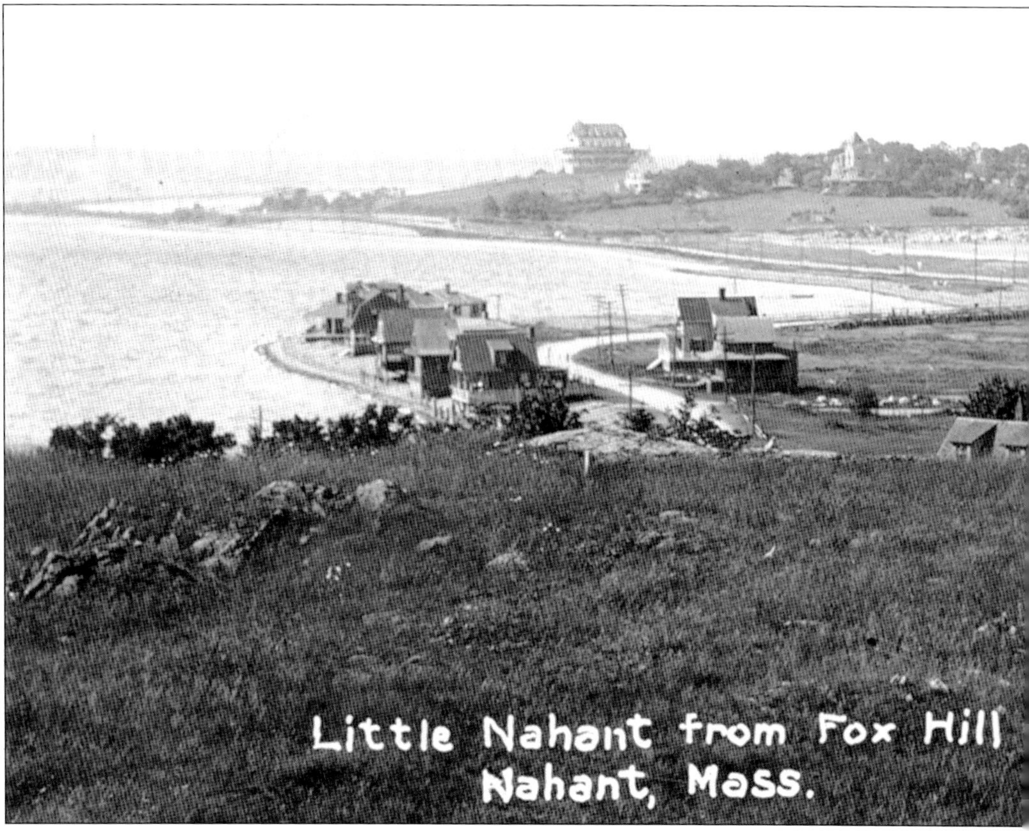

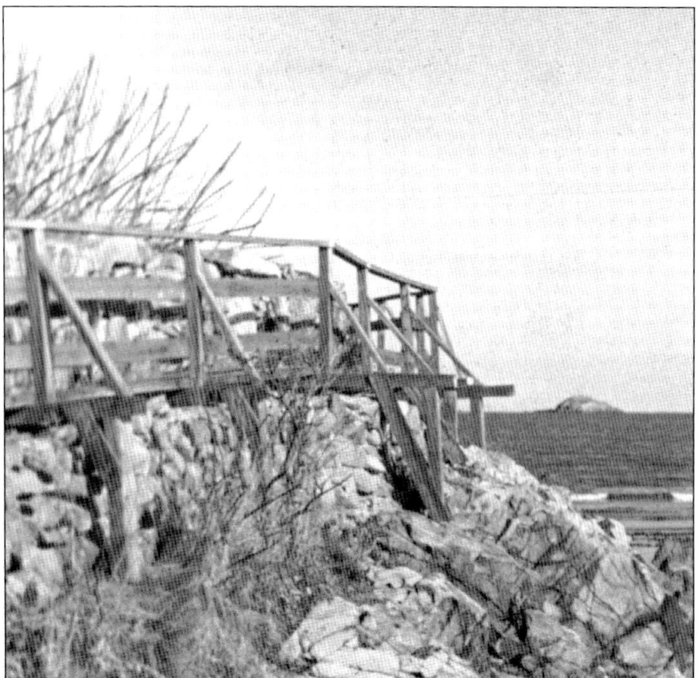

The boardwalk at Little Nahant extended from Short Beach to the foot of Mills Terrace. It was built and maintained by the town initially but later taken over by the Little Nahant Improvement Society. Constructed on the water side of the seawalls, it was independent of them and posed no risk of damage. This view is toward the open ocean with Egg Rock in the distance.

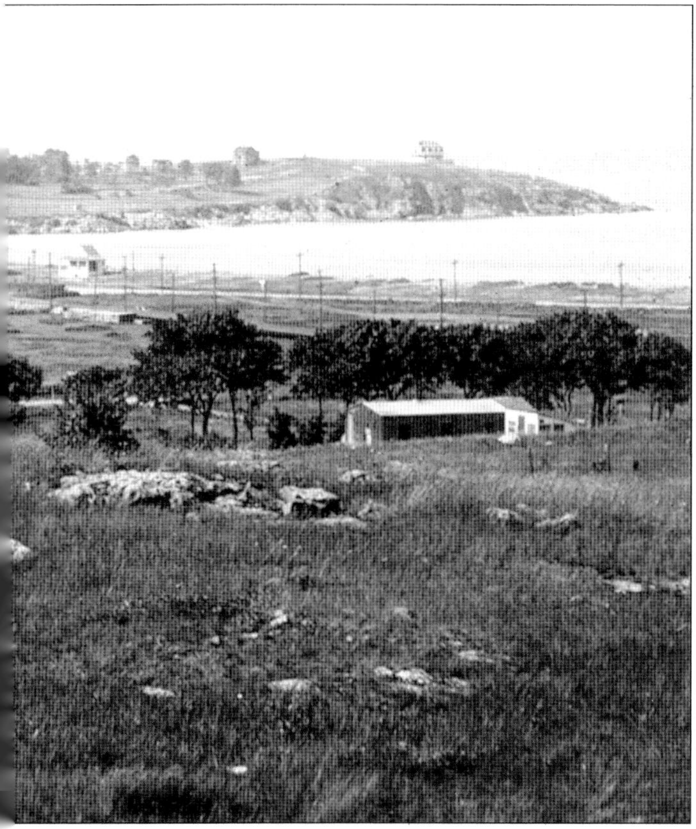

In 1905, a syndicate of Lynn businessmen, including J.T. Lenox, E.E. Strout, and F.E. Baker, purchased 23 acres of land on Little Nahant from Sallie Simmons. Building lots of 5,000 and 10,000 square feet were laid out, including streets. Water lines and electricity were provided. The Lynn Gas and Electric Company brought electricity to most of Nahant by the mid-1890s and gas by 1908. In this panoramic view from just after 1905, the whole of Little Nahant is visible beyond the Nahant Life Saving Station at Short Beach. The preexisting Hotel Nahant can be seen on the left, and just to the right is the Howe estate. A few of the lots had been sold and built on but not many.

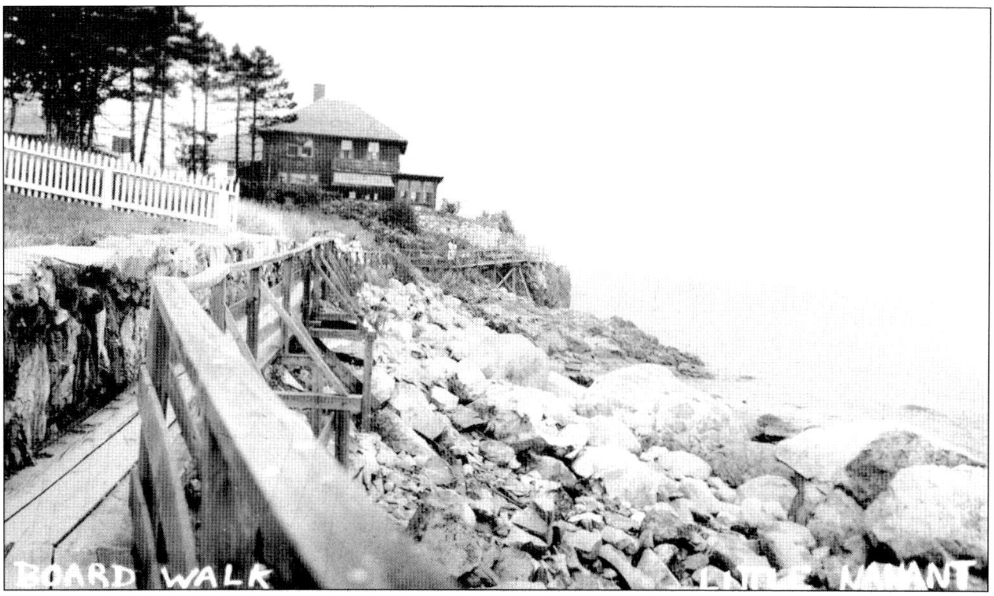

In constant use both summer and winter, the boardwalk provided a shortcut to schools, beaches, and public transportation. This image, also looking out to the ocean but from on the boardwalk itself, shows the house located at 29 Mills Terrace. It was occupied by the Bee family and later by Doris and Henry Fickbohm in the 1950s and 1960s.

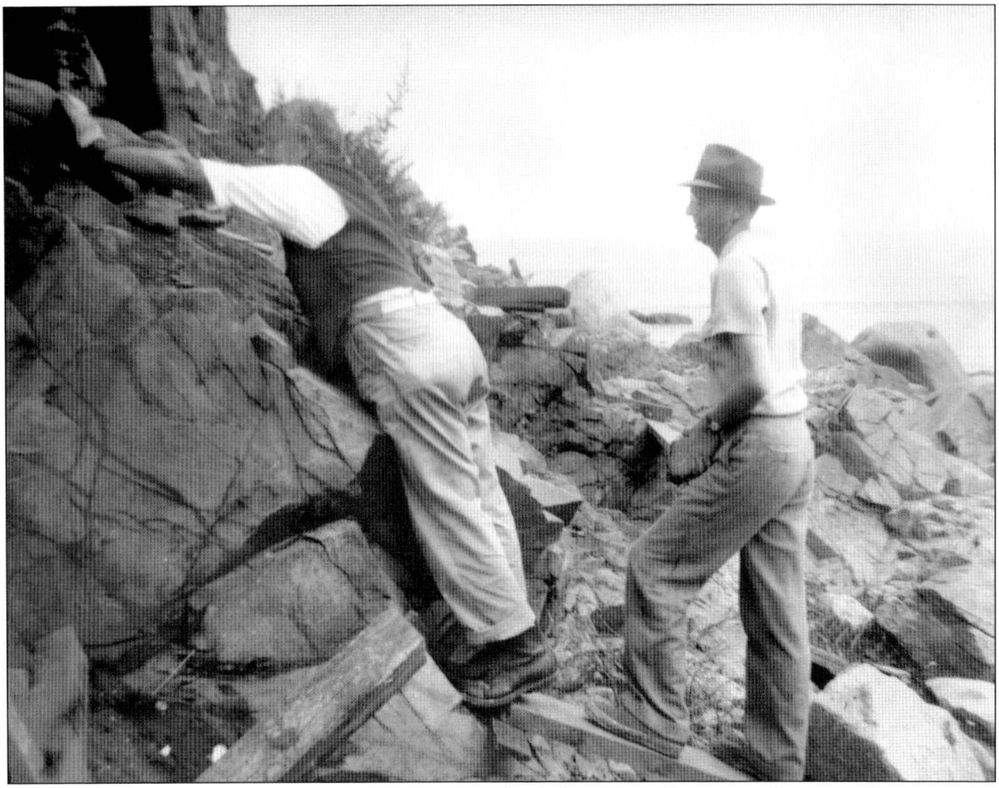

The image above shows Howard Nichols on the left and Fred Manter busy working on the constantly needed repair of the boardwalk in 1953. The open Atlantic is in the distance. The image below looks toward Short Beach as the boardwalk passes in front of the Welch property, located at 52 Nahant Road, adjoining the beach. It had been maintained by money collected from Little Nahant residents but became deteriorated and was finally demolished in the 1960s. Everyone who remembers this walkway greatly misses the experience of strolling above the rocks and crashing surf.

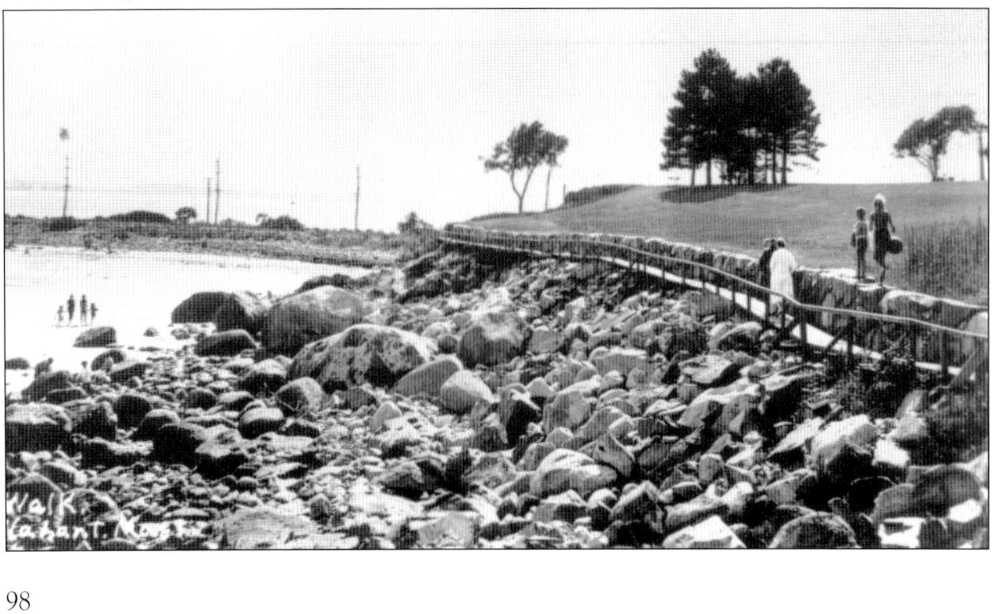

Seven

Civic Life

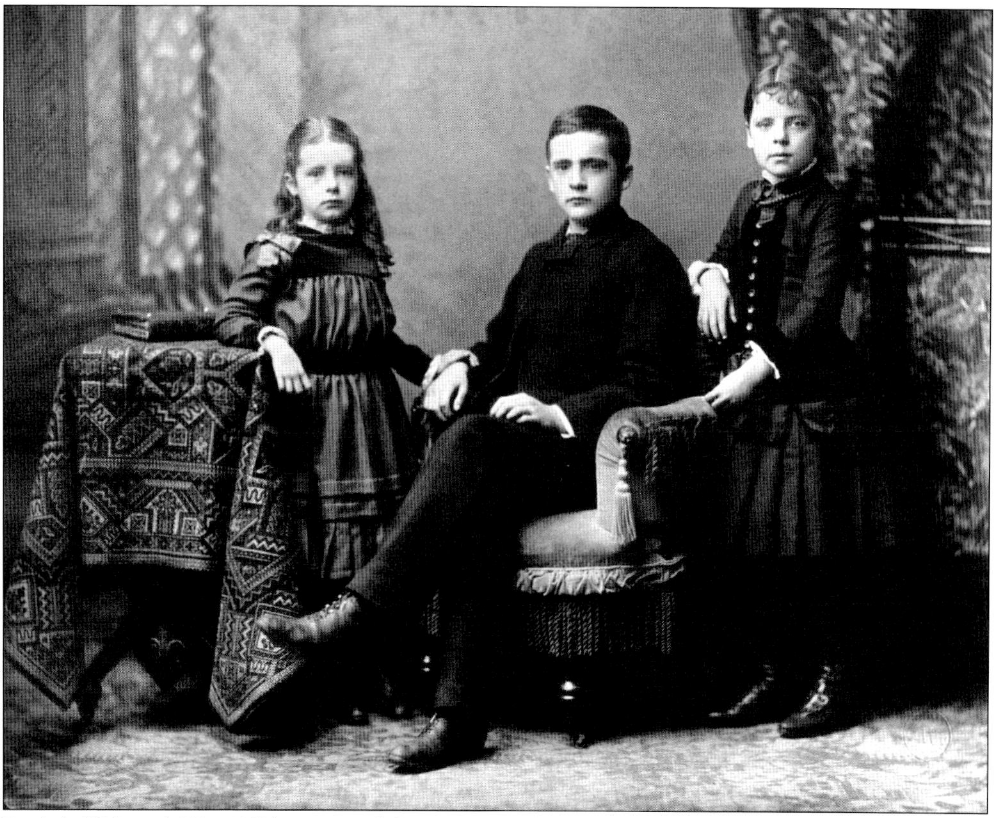

Fred A. Wilson (1871–1950) poses with his sisters Nellie (left) and Abby around 1886. Fred, an 1891 MIT graduate, joined his father's contracting firm of J.T. Wilson and Son. A dedicated resident, he was town moderator for 31 years. His 1928 book *Some Annals of Nahant* was a groundbreaking history of Nahant and remains a fundamental research tool today.

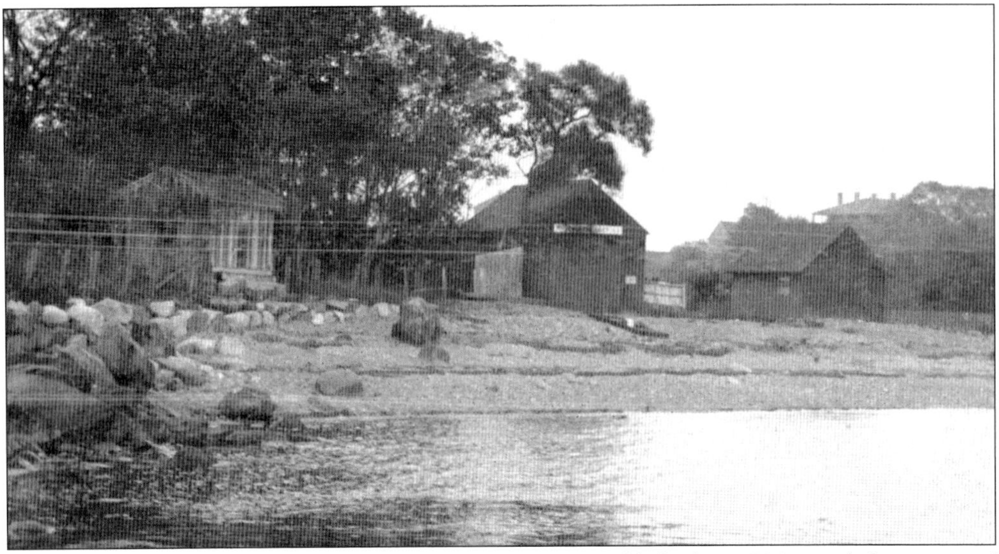

The all-volunteer Massachusetts Humane Society was established in 1786 to aid the rescue of ships and sailors. In the late 1800s, the Nahant branch was located in this building on Curlew (Longfellow's) Beach. In 1911, it was relocated to 171 Willow Road, and it was later converted into a house. (Courtesy F.A. Wilson family collection.)

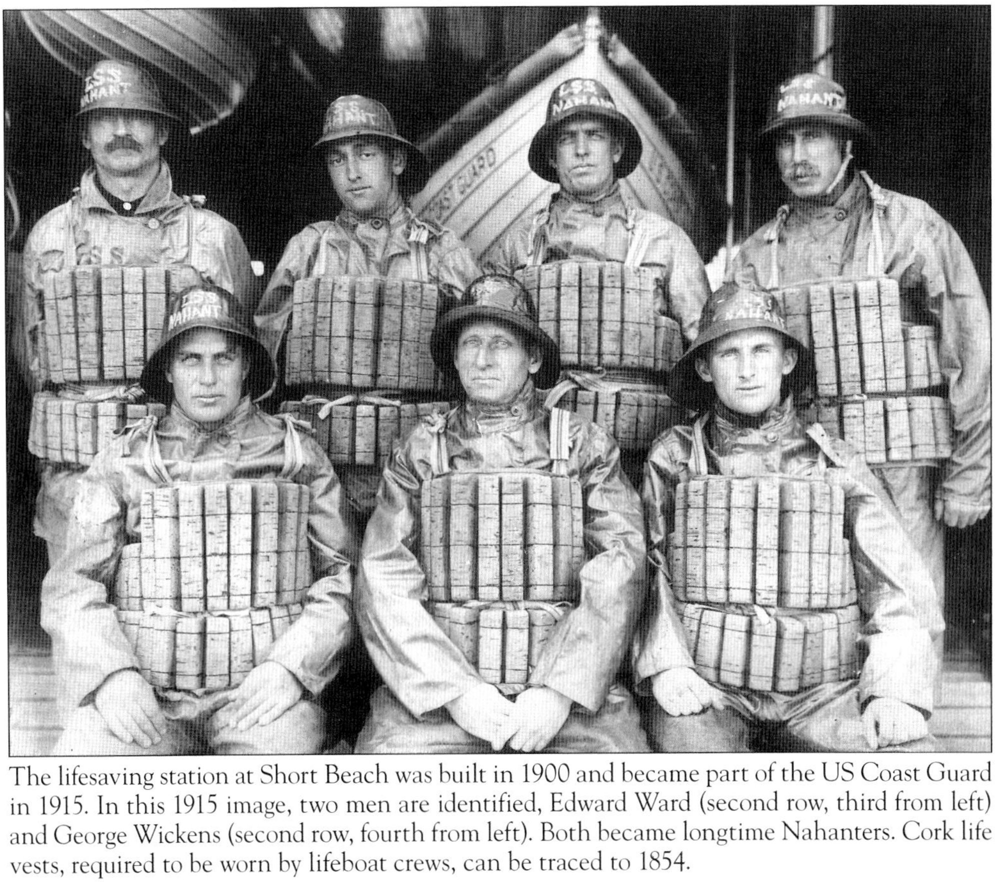

The lifesaving station at Short Beach was built in 1900 and became part of the US Coast Guard in 1915. In this 1915 image, two men are identified, Edward Ward (second row, third from left) and George Wickens (second row, fourth from left). Both became longtime Nahanters. Cork life vests, required to be worn by lifeboat crews, can be traced to 1854.

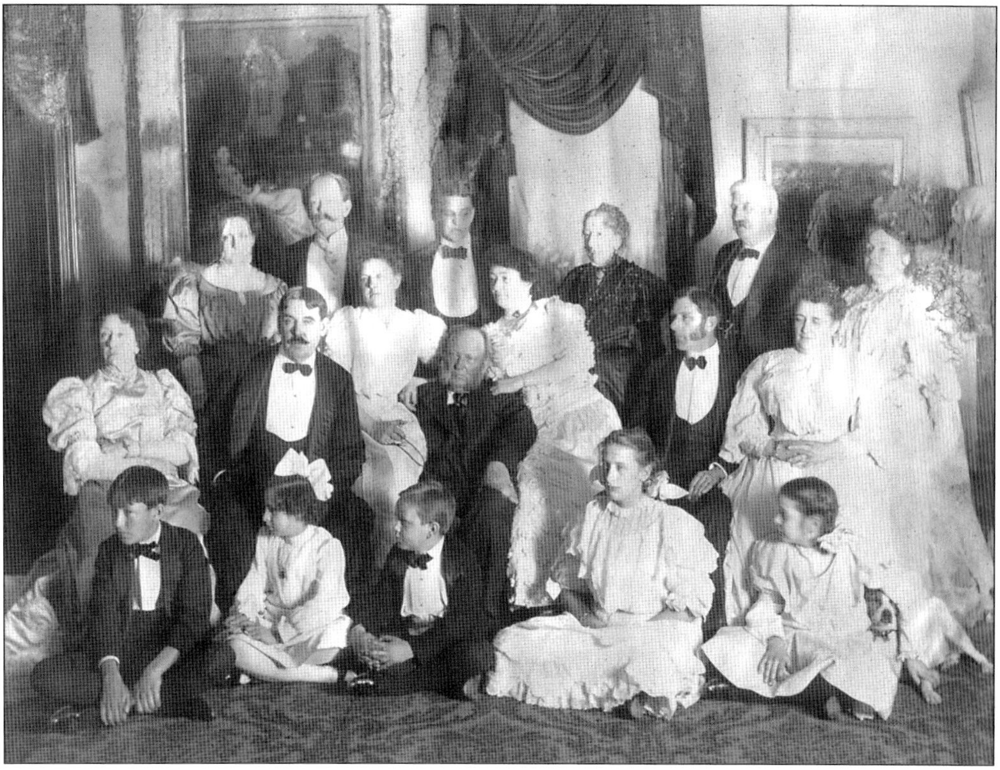

Francis H. Johnson (1838–1918) is seen in the center of his family in 1905. Born in Nahant, he lived in Cambridge but summered in Nahant at 63 Willow Road. As a real estate investor, he developed Willow Road between Bear Pond and Ocean Street into house lots. His wife, Ida Tremaine Johnson, seated to the extreme right, presented the town with the arched stone entrance gate to Greenlawn Cemetery in 1919.

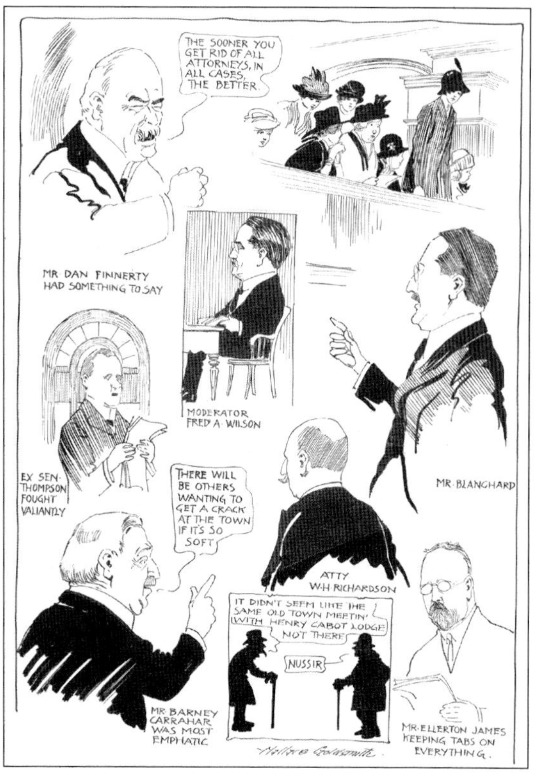

This political cartoon of the 1917 town meeting certainly captures the spirit of the frequently contentious issues. Prohibition was on the agenda. It lost by 15 votes, allowing residents to retire to their homes for a much-deserved cocktail. Henry Cabot Lodge, town moderator, was absent, so Fred Wilson stepped in. The men pictured were active and often outspoken citizens. Note that women had to sit in the upper gallery.

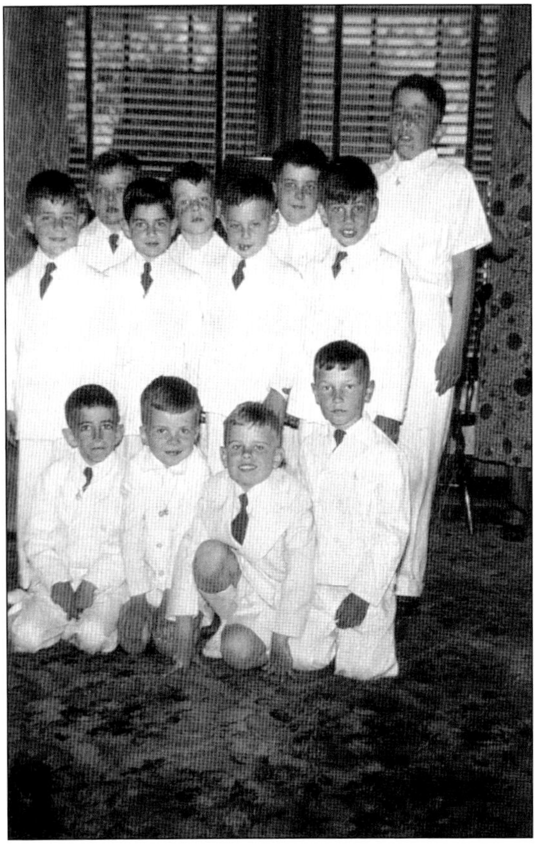

In May 1950, this group of young Nahanters gathered after receiving their First Holy Communion at St. Thomas Aquinas Church. From left to right are (first row) Alan Genosi, Stephen Robinson, Gerry Titus, and Paul Sciaba; (second row) Charles "Chuck" Cody, Ronny LeGault, Michael Richardson, and Manny Bongiorno; (third row) Richard Hanson, Peter Renaghan, Thomas Rogers, and John Floccher. Bridget Sciaba chaperoned.

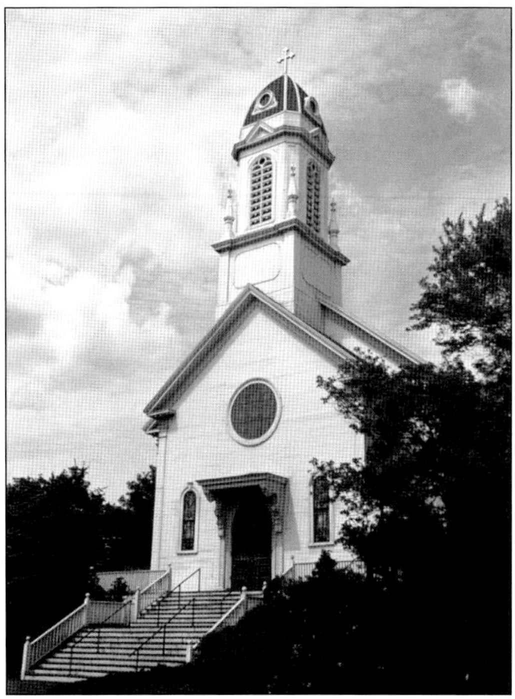

By the late 19th century, the Catholic population was increasing, and there was a need for a church in town. Located at 248 Nahant Road, St. Thomas Aquinas Church was built in 1872, with the tower added in 1874. In 1901, the building was raised up to provide a basement. This c. 1953 image shows it before it was torn down and replaced in 1966.

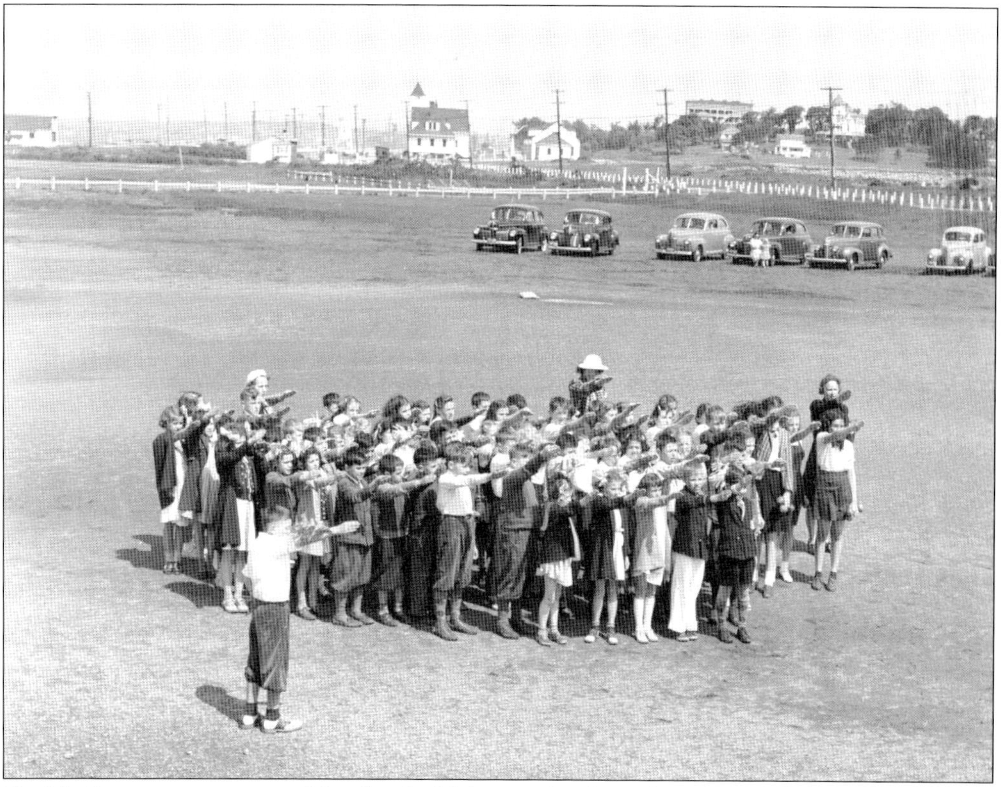

Health Day was an event in May for the Nahant schools in the 1930s into the 1940s. It was a program of "physical examination, corrective work, and instruction in health." This 1941 photograph shows students and teachers gathered in the Lowlands playground saluting the flag. This style of salute was changed after it became strongly associated with Nazi Germany.

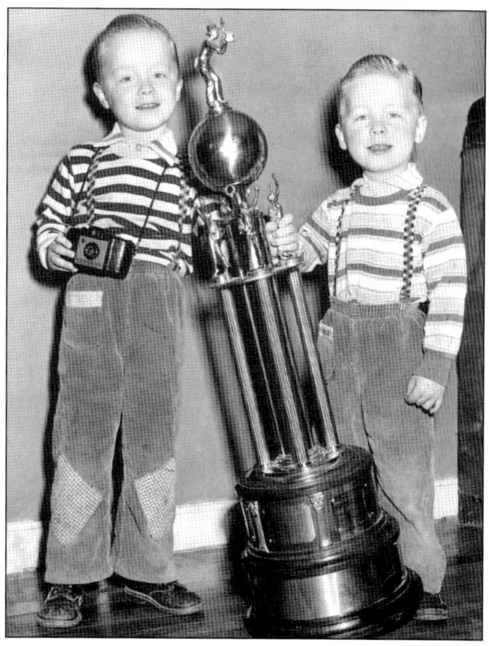

Brothers Ken (left) and David Oxton pose in 1959 with the Edwin T. Ramsdell Memorial Trophy won by their father, Roland P. Oxton (1911–1984). "Rollie," a photographer for the *Boston Herald American*, received this honor five times between 1949 and 1974. It is given annually by the Boston Press Photographers Association for Spot News. He also shared in the Pulitzer Prize for coverage of the Blizzard of 1978.

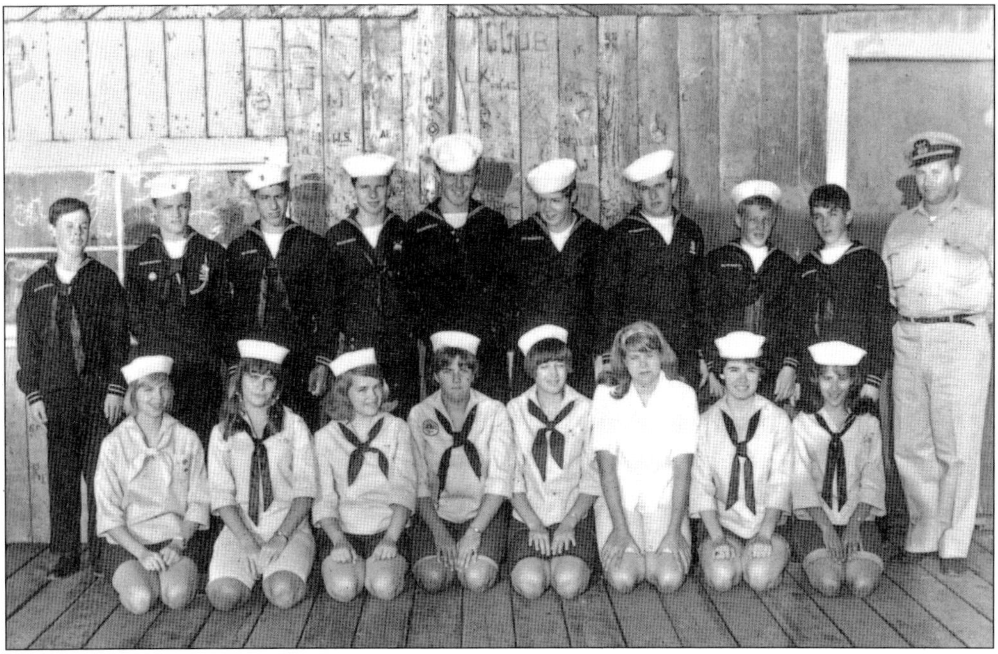

The Sea Scouts joined with the Boy Scouts of America in 1917, and the Mariners became a part of the Girl Scouts in 1934. Both groups had the mission to develop young people's skills in all water-related activities. These two active Nahant programs gather at Tudor Wharf in this 1960s-era photograph.

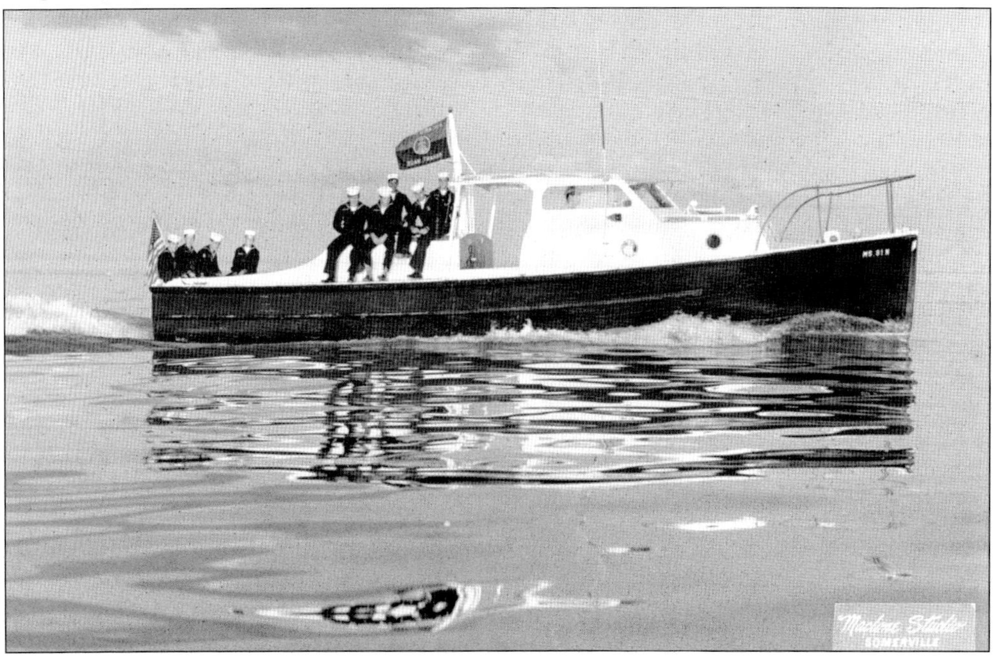

On a summer day in the 1960s, the Nahant Sea Scout vessel *Polaris* left Nahant for an extended training cruise to Provincetown with leader and skipper Maynard Nelson at the wheel. The Scouts are, from left to right, (in the stern) Mark Cullinan, Rick Hosker, Kevin Donahue, and Steve Lehto; (seated amidships) Wally Bunker, Warren Edwards, John Moleti, Phil Baldwin, and Bill Johnson.

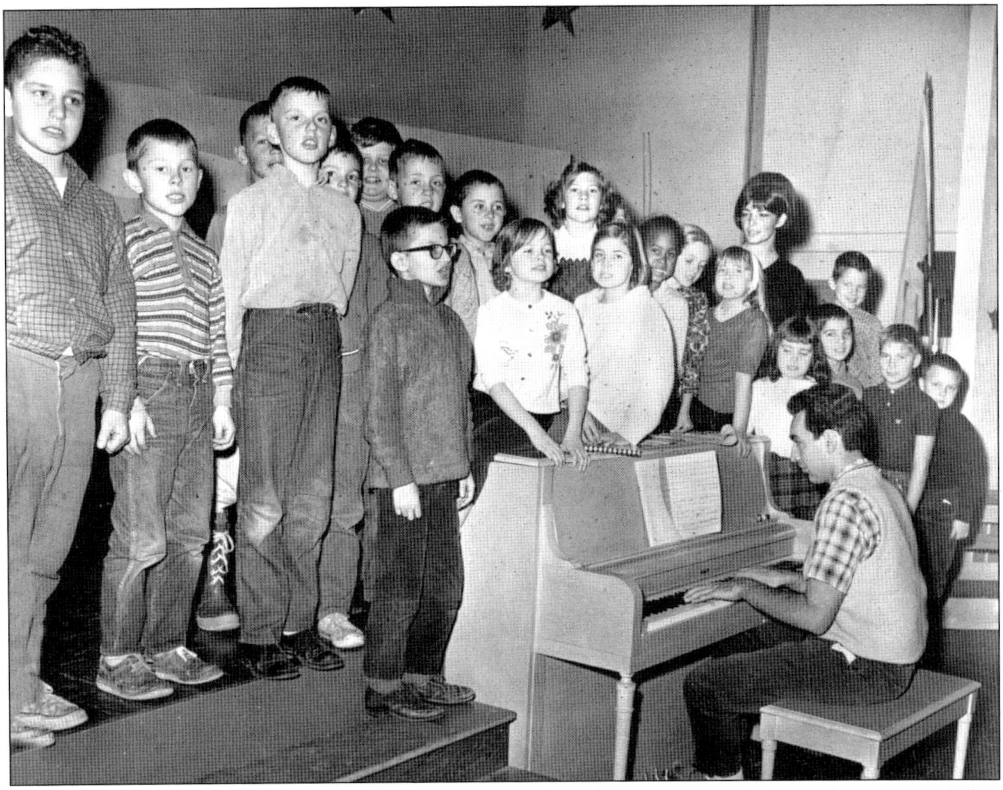

Victor DalPozzal, seated at the piano, was the Nahant Schools music supervisor for 34 years. This chorus in training was documented in 1964 during "Mr. D's" first year of service. Some Nahanters will recognize themselves and their classmates, and some may even remember what songs they were rehearsing. In the 1970s, he also directed four musicals for the local Peninsula Players.

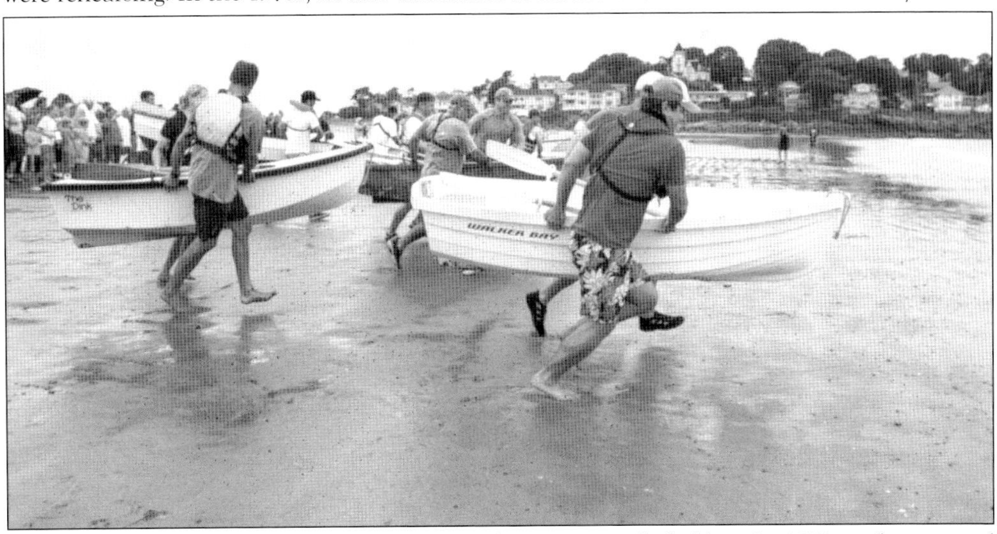

The Grand Pram Race, established by Bob Risch, was originally held in the 1970s and continued for several years, raising funds for local organizations. This Roland Oxton image shows Gail Davis running her pram across Short Beach. The race, an amusing and farcical event, was brought back in 2014 by the nonprofit group 01908. Note the Welch house at the end of the beach.

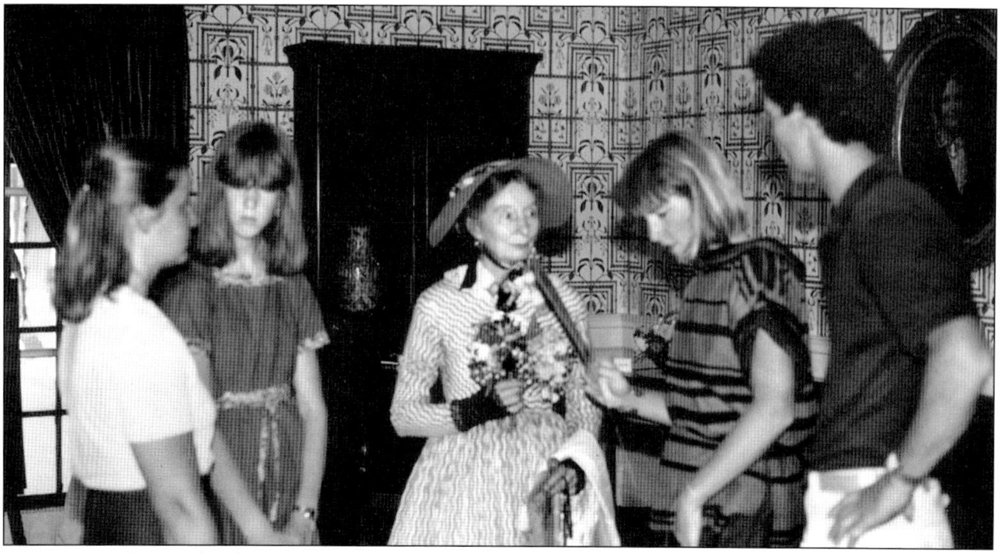

In 1983, Tasha Tudor (1915–2008), the great-granddaughter of Frederic Tudor (the "Ice King"), visited the Nahant Historical Society, then located in the former Tudor summer home. She and some of her family were guests at the opening of an exhibit about Frederic Tudor's life in Nahant. Tasha, an acclaimed children's author and illustrator, is wearing her great-grandmother's gown and bonnet.

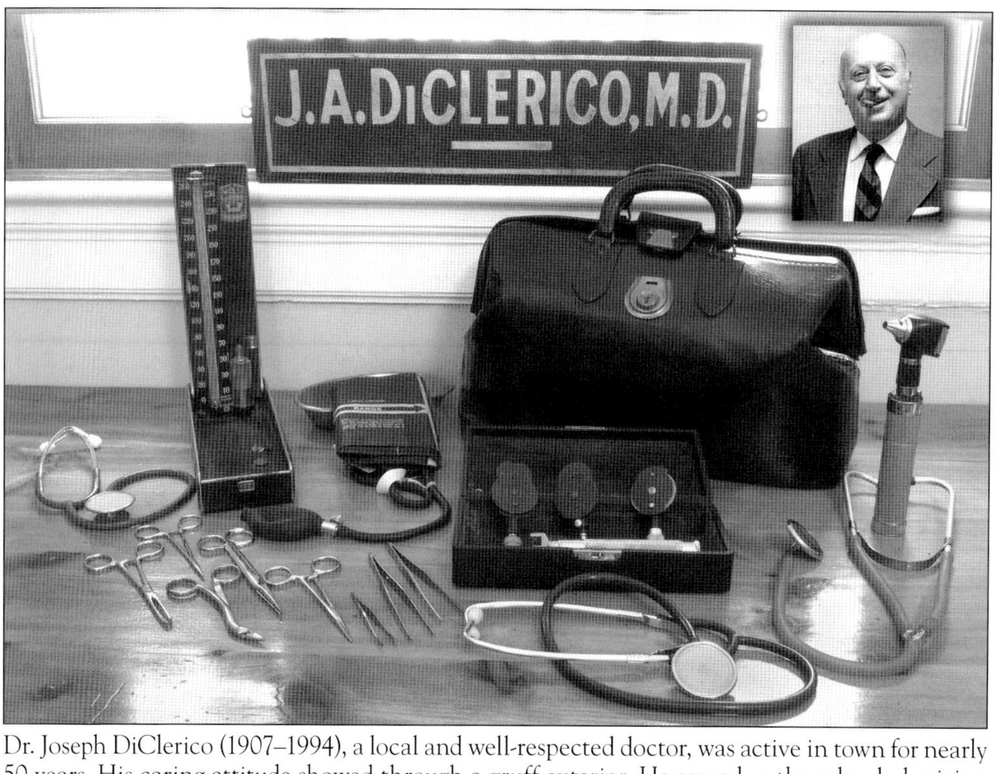

Dr. Joseph DiClerico (1907–1994), a local and well-respected doctor, was active in town for nearly 50 years. His caring attitude showed through a gruff exterior. He served as the school physician from 1940 to 1985. The DiClerico Award is given annually to a sixth-grade student who excels in science. (Courtesy Robert Wilson.)

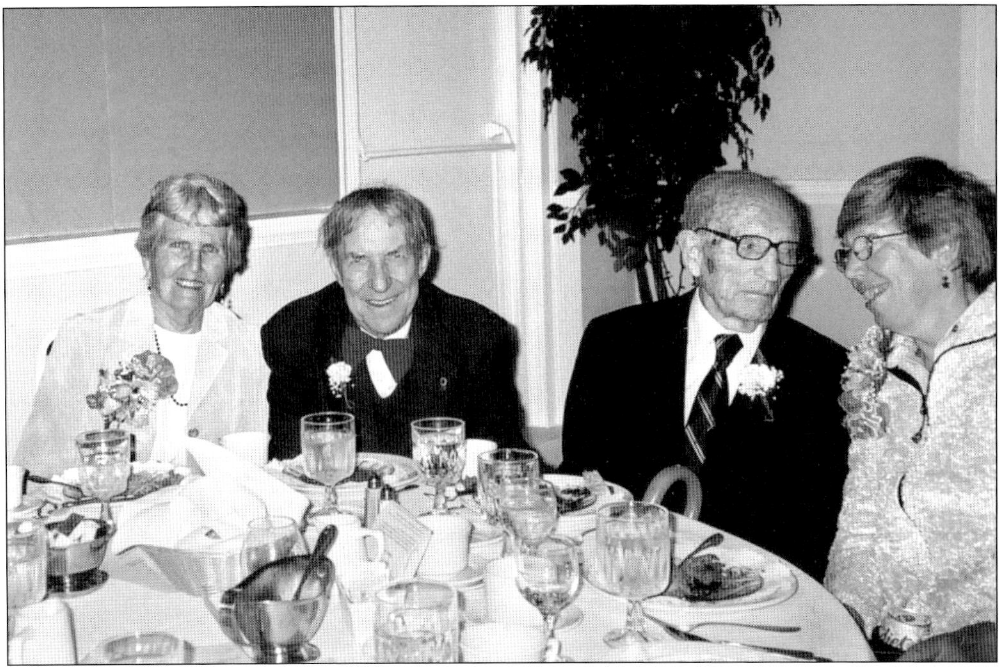

Harriet and Bob Steeves are seen here in 2005 at the Lions Club Lifetime Achievement Award Banquet. To the right are Dr. Charles Schepens and Ellen Steeves. Bob received this award for 30 years as a town selectman and other public service. Harriet served as town clerk from 1970 until 2009. As a justice of the peace from 1976 to 2003, she performed 207 marriages, including at least one same-sex marriage.

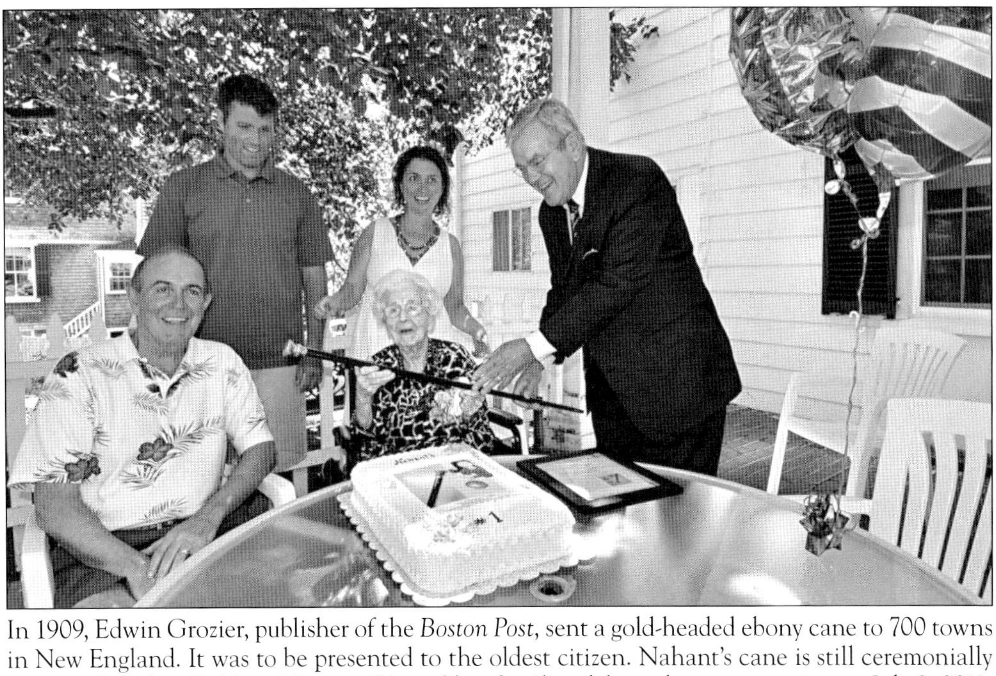

In 1909, Edwin Grozier, publisher of the *Boston Post*, sent a gold-headed ebony cane to 700 towns in New England. It was to be presented to the oldest citizen. Nahant's cane is still ceremonially presented. Helen Golding Niosi, at 96, and her family celebrate her presentation on July 2, 2011. Dave Conlin, town moderator, offers the cane on behalf of the town.

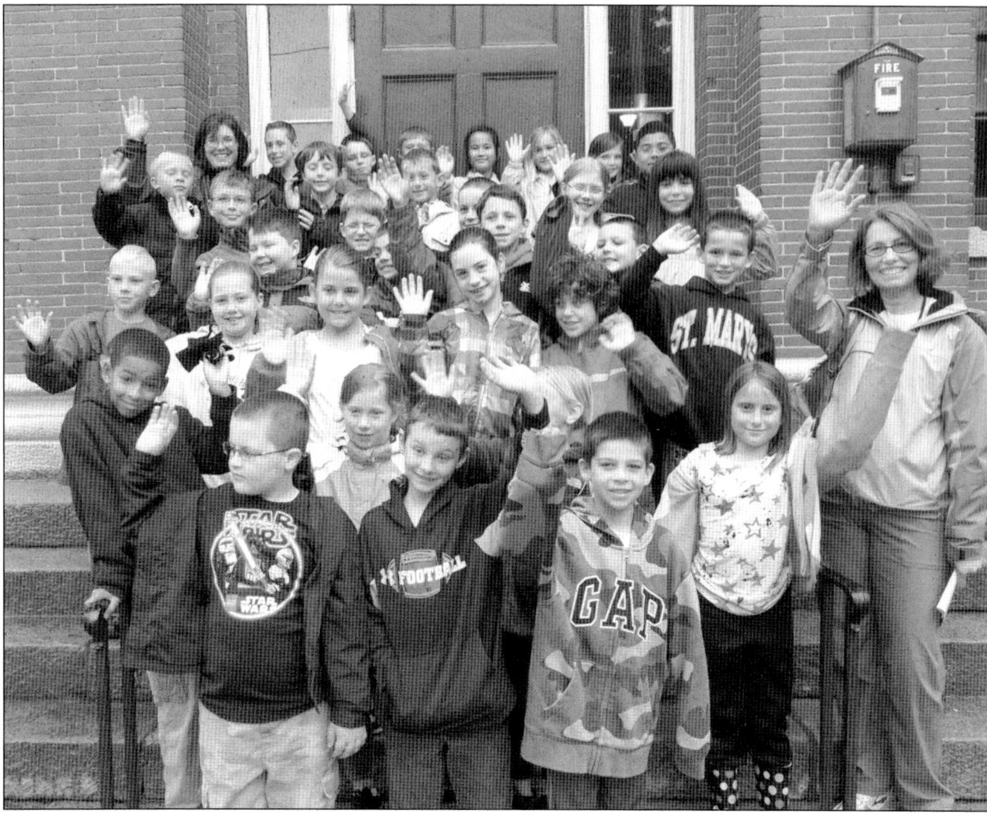

The Johnson School third-grade class makes yearly visits the Nahant Historical Society, where the students research a local historical or town landmark. The Massachusetts Curriculum Project mandates a finished report to complete the history course requirements. Pictured here on the steps of the Nahant Community Center are the 2012 students.

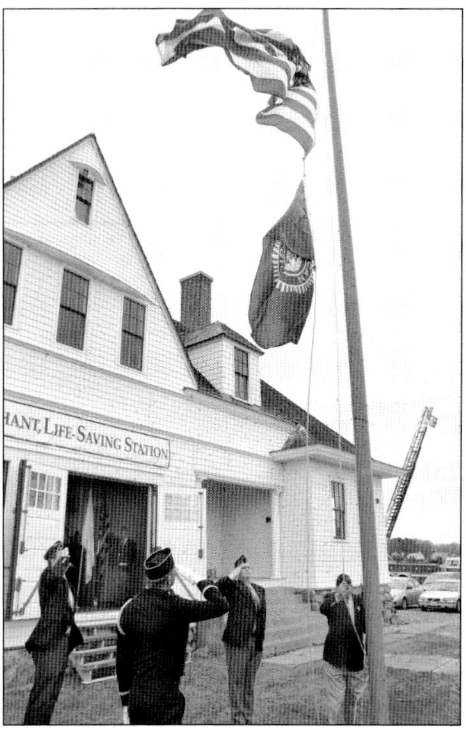

The Mortimer G. Robbins Post No. 215 of the American Legion celebrates its move to new quarters on April 16, 2011. The post gave up its former home to move into the newly restored Nahant Life Saving Station at Short Beach. There it continues its mission of support for veterans. The lifesaving station is managed by the Nahant Preservation Trust, a volunteer charitable nonprofit corporation.

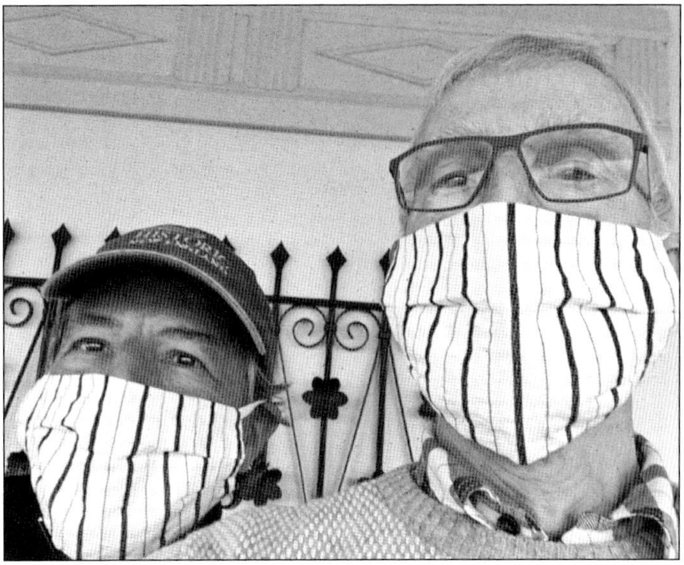

In 2020, the Covid 19 pandemic struck, and safety protocols were announced. On April 8, 2020, Ken Turino (left) and Chris Mathias tried on their hand-made masks. The shock of lockdown and subsequent isolation was somewhat mitigated by the visitation of North Atlantic right whales to Nahant's waters. Nahanters enjoyed watching them from the rocky coastline for three weeks, an unusually long stopover on their spring migration.

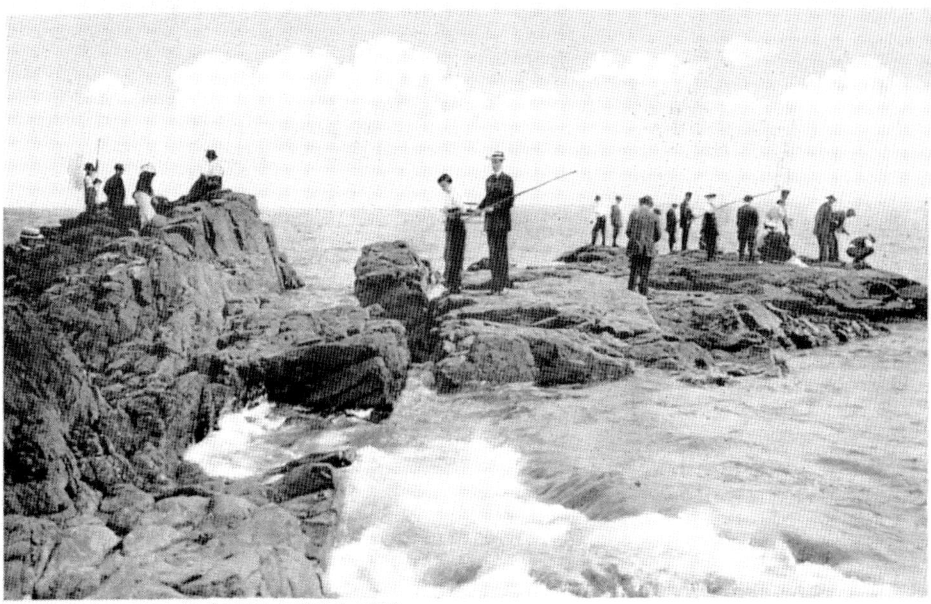

ROCKS AND SURF, BASS POINT, NAHANT, MASS.

The message on this summery postcard, dated October 3, 1918, to someone in New Brunswick carries a concern just as relevant today: "Dear Friend, I hear you are sick with Influenza. I hope you will soon be well. Write or have someone write and tell me how you are. Gus."

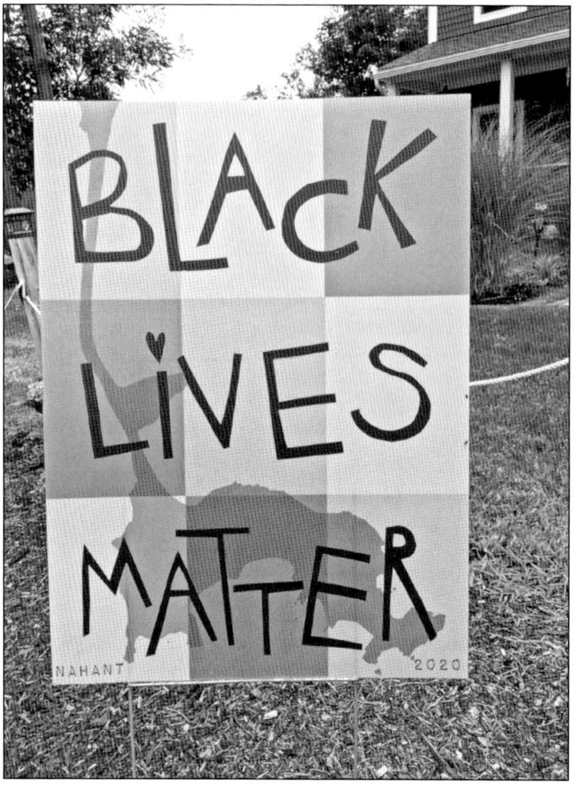

The Black Lives Matter movement began in 2013, following the death of Trayvon Martin in Florida. It gathered steam and went global after the death of George Floyd in May 2020. The outrage of systemic racism is felt worldwide. Nahant, the smallest town in Massachusetts, is no exception. These signs appeared throughout town.

Local resident Jim Walsh organized the June 4, 2020, rally in support of the Black Lives Matter movement. It took place on Pleasant Street near Nahant Road. Police chief Robert Dwyer, a 30-year veteran of the department, spoke movingly on the rights of all people and against racism, realized or unrealized.

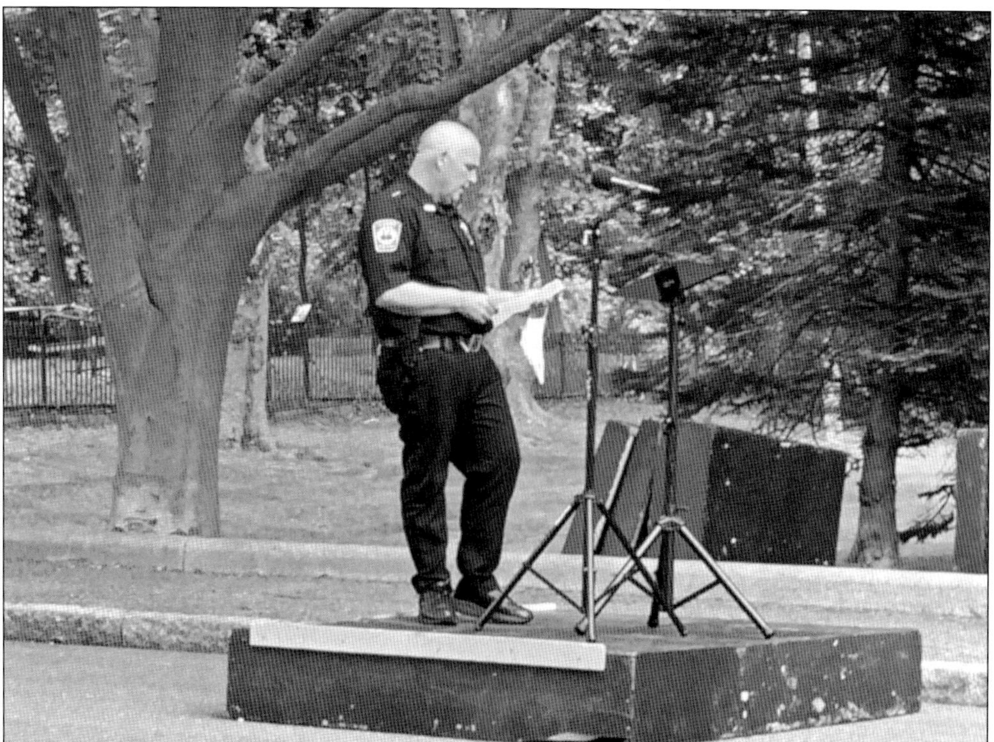

The audience for the Black Lives Matter rally in Nahant was small but attentive. Speakers reminded people of the need to be vigilant against all types of prejudice, including racial, ethnic, religious, and sexual orientation. The young Dolan family listens carefully. In front, from left to right, are Georgia (in the stroller), Jack, and Erin. Behind are James and baby Liberty.

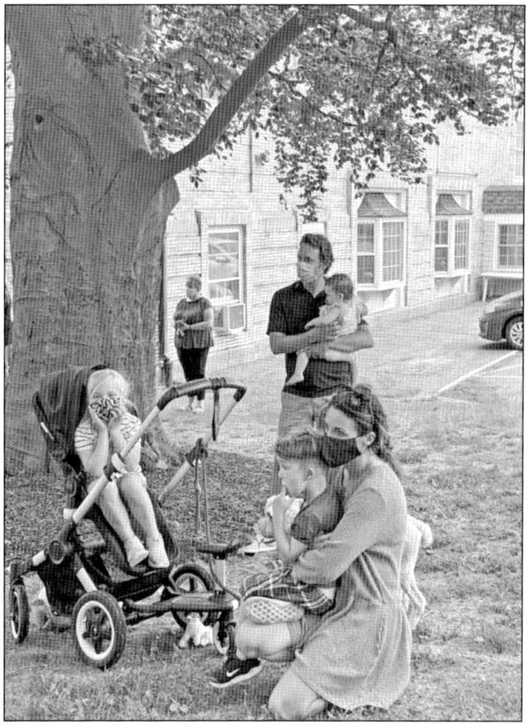

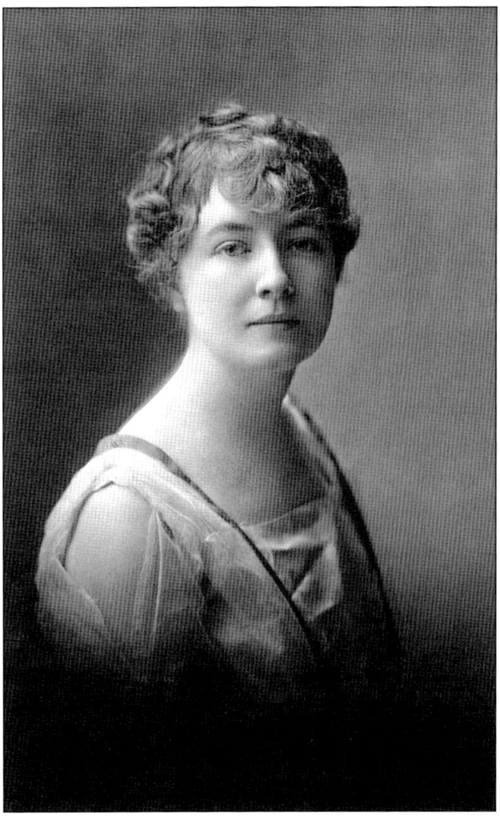

Abbie May Roland (1867–1945) was an ardent supporter of women's suffrage in New England and helped organize the Nahant Suffrage League, becoming its first president. She sponsored a rally at Marjoram Park on July 1, 1914, that drew 200 people. The league worked tirelessly until the final passage of the 19th Amendment in 1920. She was married to Thomas Roland, a successful commercial florist and gardener based in Nahant.

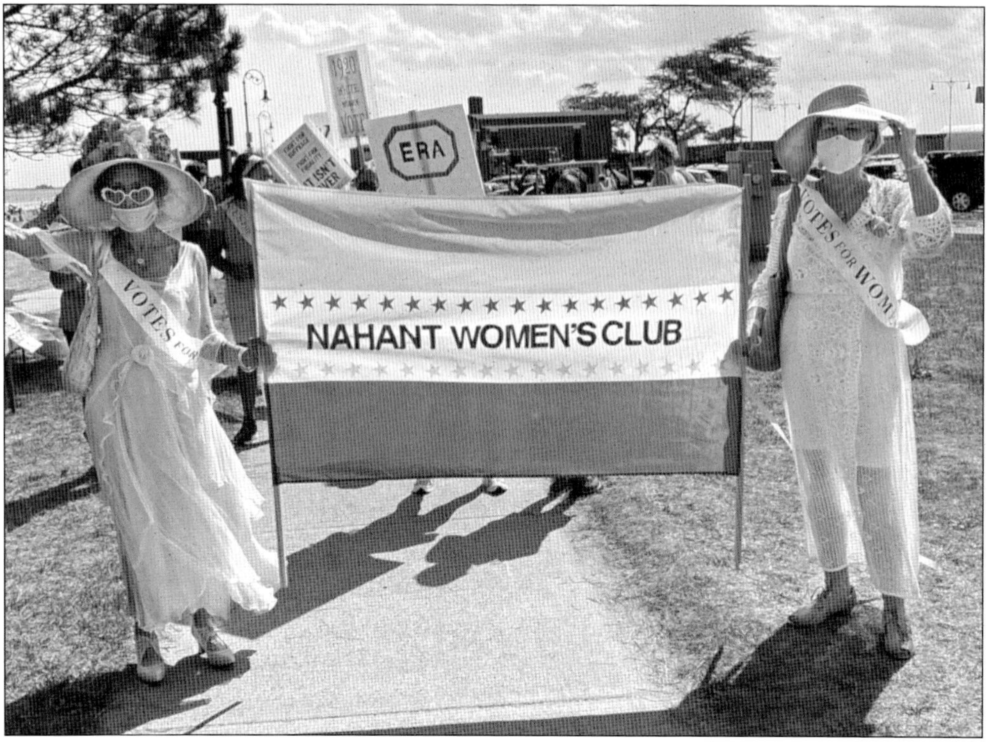

The Nahant Women's Club was formed on March 8, 1895, "to promote the . . . betterment of ladies of the village." The renamed Nahant Women's Club of the North Shore (seen here) celebrated the centennial of the ratification of the 19th Amendment on August 23, 2020, with a rally on Lynn Shore Drive. The club stressed equal rights for all people. (Courtesy Nahant Women's Club of the North Shore.)

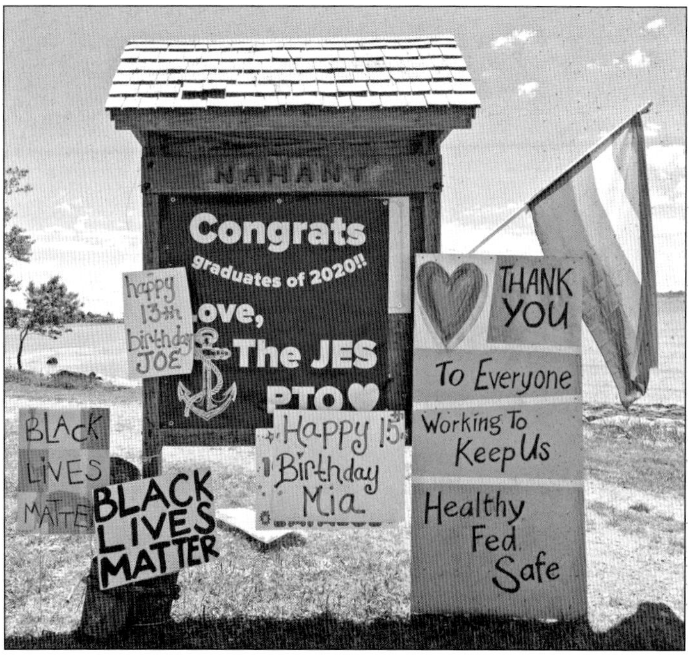

The community message board may be used by any town resident for short announcements. On June 13, 2020, there were seven notices. Visible were one congratulation to the graduates of the Johnson Elementary School, two birthday greetings, one thank-you to essential workers during the Covid pandemic, two in support of the Black Lives Matter movement, and one rainbow flag celebrating June as LGBTQ Pride Month. (Courtesy Chris Mathias.)

Eight

At Play

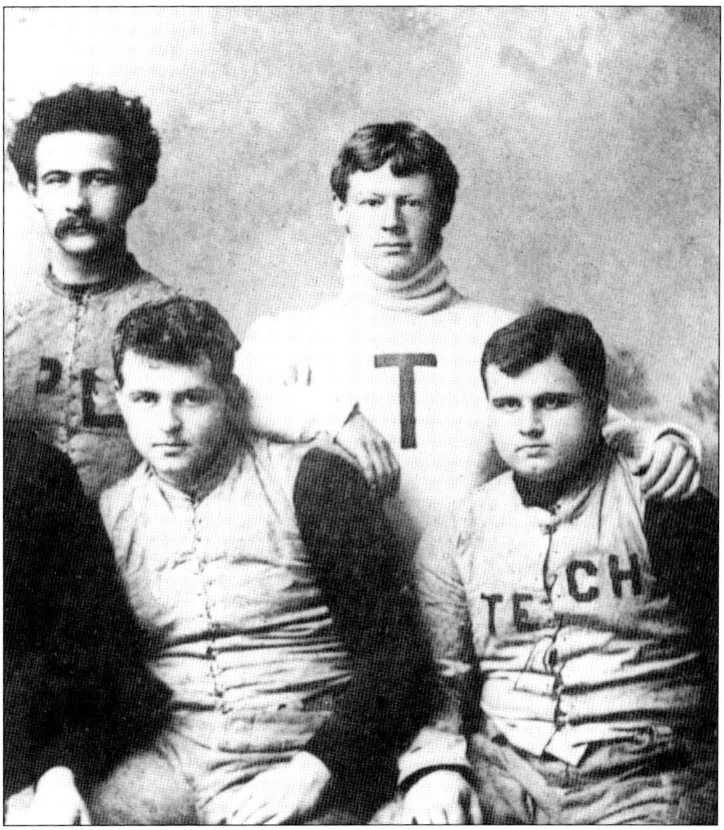

Thomas Pelham Curtis (1873–1944), seen in the second row on the right, graduated from the Massachusetts Institute of Technology (MIT) in 1894. While there, he was a star athlete. He competed in the first modern Olympic Games in Athens (1896), winning first place in the 110-meter hurdles. Also competing were two other Nahant summer residents, brothers John and Sumner Paine, not pictured here. Both placed first in shooting.

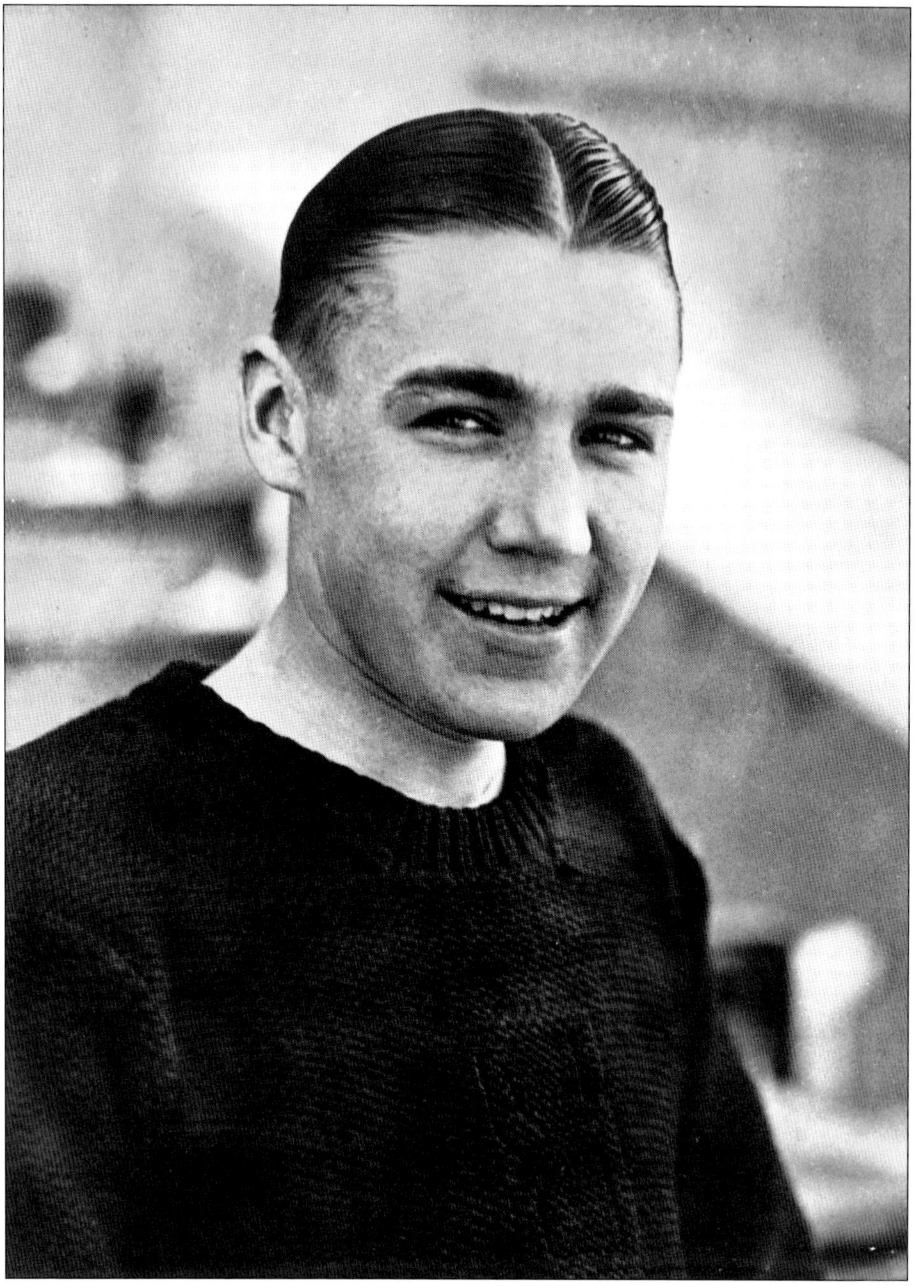

George Lermond (1904–1940) was a world-class runner who trained at Boston College, graduating in 1925. He competed in the 1924 Paris Olympics in the 5,000-meter race, coming in 24th. He coached American athletes in the pentathlon for the 1932 Olympic games in Los Angeles. George entered the US Military Academy at West Point in 1926 and had a distinguished career, including in the 15th Infantry Brigade defending Tientsin, China, during 1936. He also went to flight school and served in the United States. On leave with his family in 1940, he lost his life in a hotel fire in La Plata, Maryland. After rescuing his wife, Edith, four-year-old son Bill, and 15-month-old daughter Edith, he died attempting to rescue his son George, who also perished. Pres. Franklin Roosevelt accorded him and his son the honor of burial at Arlington National Cemetery.

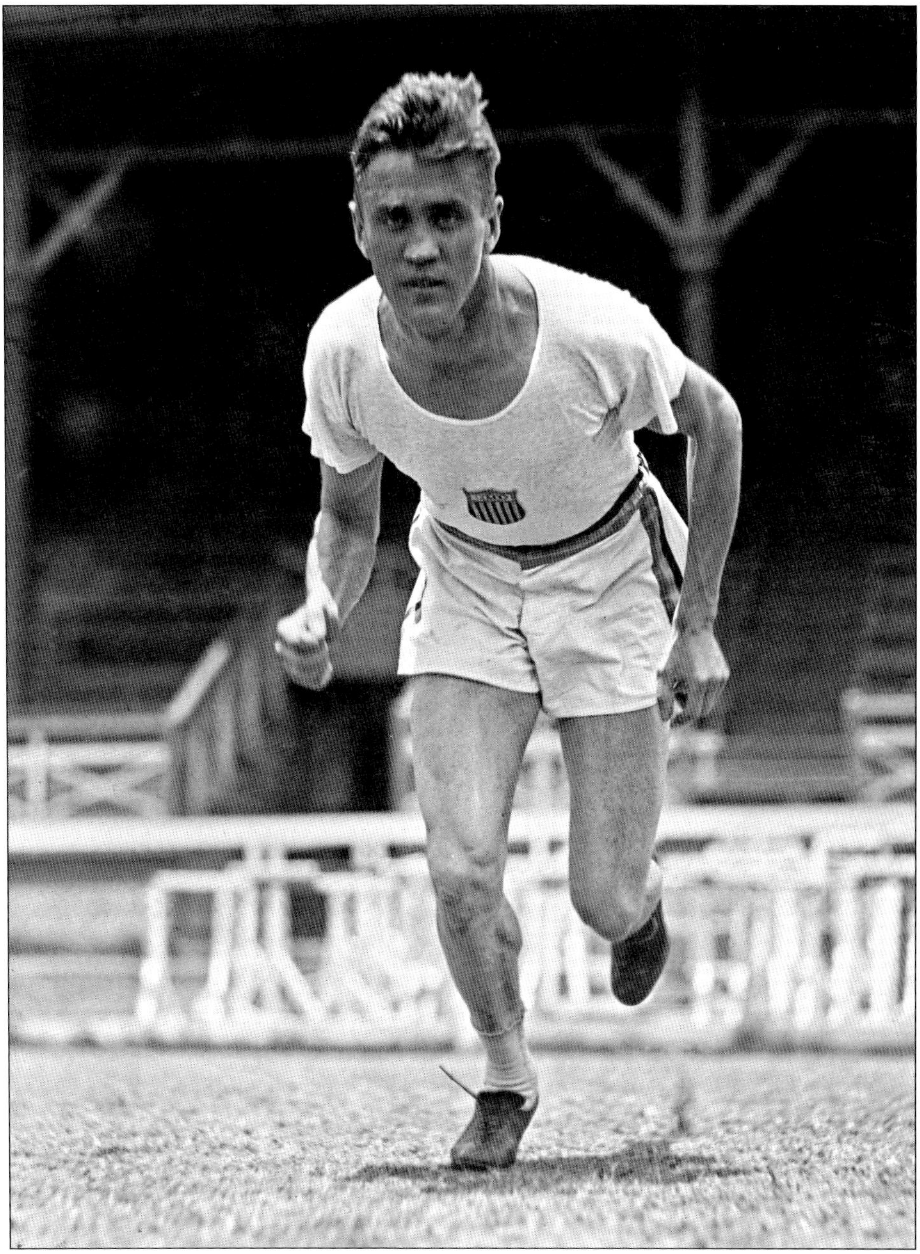

Francis Leo Lermond (1906–1986), his brothers George and Joseph, and their mother, Julia Lenehan Lermond, moved to Nahant around 1914 to be with her parents. Leo also was an Olympic competitor. After his brother George returned from the Paris Olympics, Leo became interested in competitive running. He trained with George along Short Beach on the bridle paths and sometimes down on the sand. Later, he trained at the Boston Athletic Association, which is the sponsor of the Boston Marathon. Leo ran the 5,000-meter event in the 1928 Olympics in Amsterdam, where he placed fourth. He is quoted as saying humbly, "I guess I just didn't have it that day." He served in the US Army during World War II and, afterward, was a long-serving employee of the town. He lived out his long life in the family house located above Short Beach at 1 Kennedy Court.

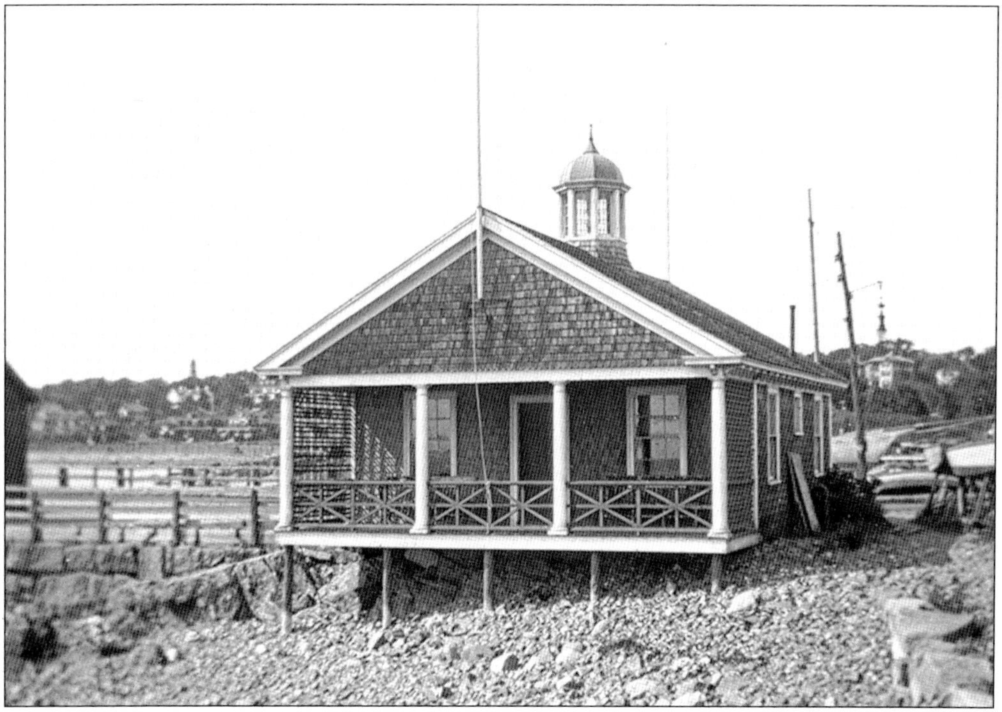

Established in 1894, the Nahant Dory Club predated its headquarters. This 1906 image shows the newly finished clubhouse built by the master builders J.T. Wilson and Son. It has been home to many classes of sailing vessels, including Dories, Bugs, Stars, Townies, and Monty Cats. (Courtesy Wilson family.)

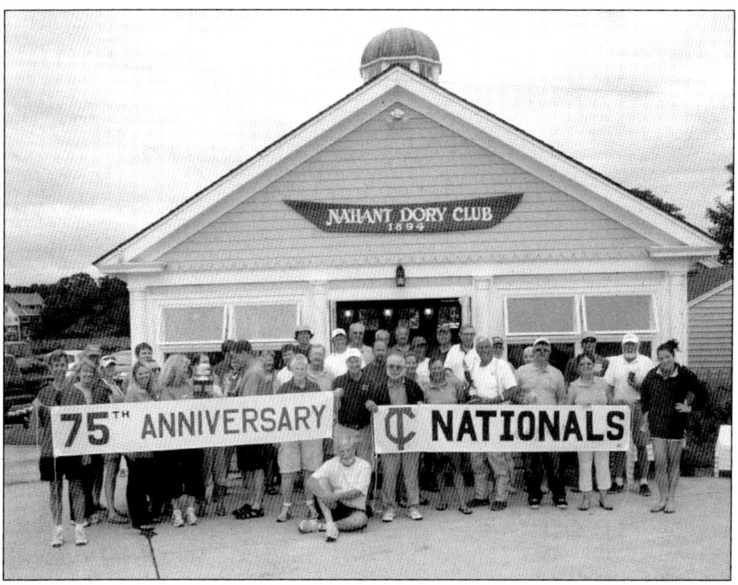

The Nahant Dory Club completed the construction of a small extension and patio on the water side of the clubhouse in 2005. A group gathers on the patio after the 2011 National Town Class Regatta to celebrate 75 years of Town-class racing in Nahant. Regatta champion Rex Antrim is seen with his family on the left, admiring his trophy.

Dining out has always been a popular activity. This elaborate menu cover from the Dutch Room at the Relay House hotel in Bass Point is from the early 20th century. The dishes served had little to do with the Holland theme, focusing on seafood, including clams, lobster, and fish, prepared in many styles.

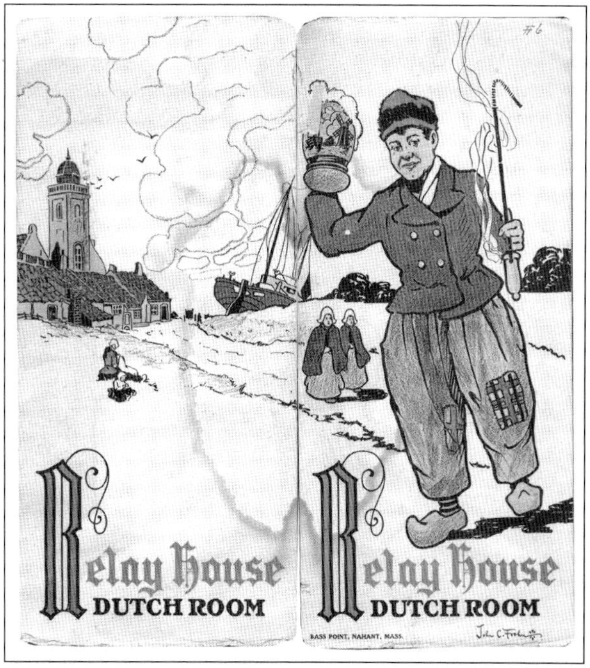

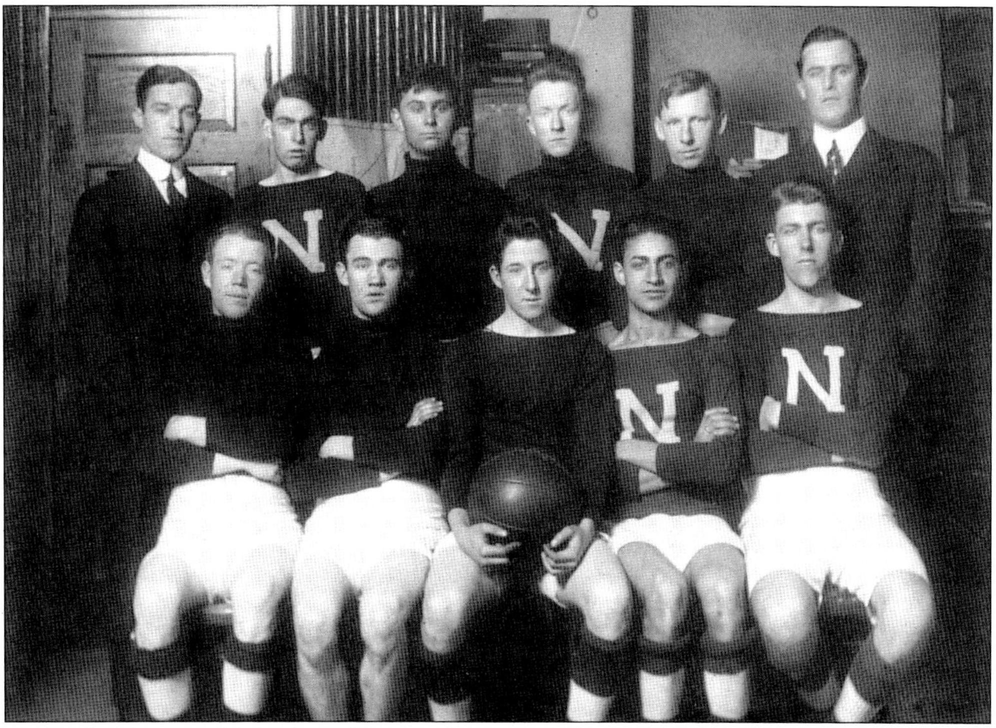

The Nahant Boy's Club basketball team of 1915 poses for a team portrait. From left to right are (first row) Frank Coakley, Francis O'Malley, Harry McLaughlin (captain), Leon Delano, and Joseph Hyde; (second row) Jack Deveney (manager), William McLaughlin, James Lane, Francis Coyne, Jack O'Connell, and Arthur Robertson (coach). On Monday, January 11, 1915, the *Lynn Evening Item* reported, "Nahant . . . played its usual snappy game."

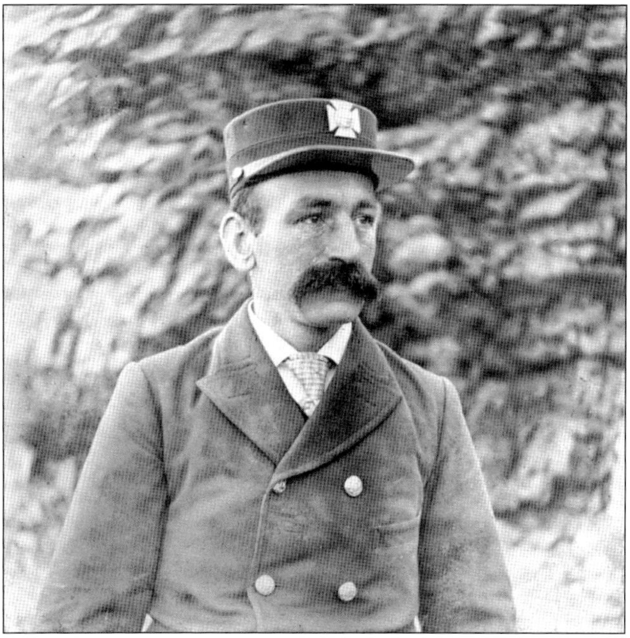

William F. Waters (1871–1935) was a fireman and the clerk of the Hook and Ladder Company in 1904 and was a well-respected town clerk from 1904 to 1935. During his tenure as town clerk, he ran unopposed, which demonstrates the great esteem Nahanters had for him. He was the grandfather of former police chief William Waters. Nahant has had a long tradition of creating its own entertainment, including plays, skits, and musicals. Although which role the image below represents is unknown, Waters certainly seems to have enjoyed creating it.

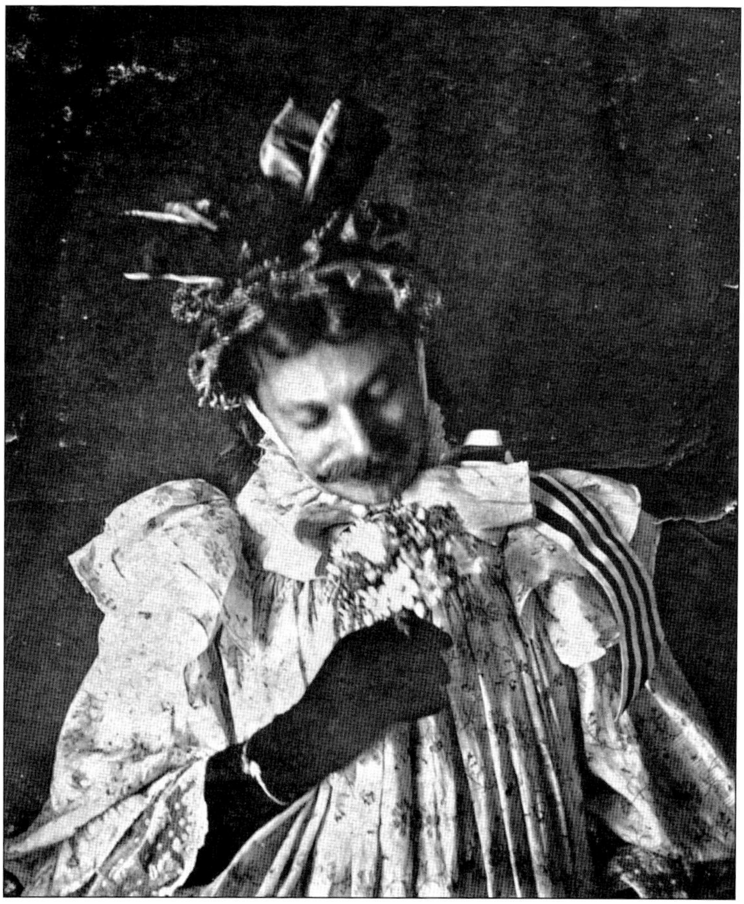

The Binney boys are enjoying playing firemen protecting their summer home around 1928. From left to right are William and Robert on the ladders, while Marshall mans the hose. The house at 240 Nahant Road, no longer standing, was built for Dr. Henry C. Haven in 1882 by J.T. Wilson. In 1916, it was purchased by Dr. George Hayward Binney and his wife, Susan Jeannette (Appleton) Binney.

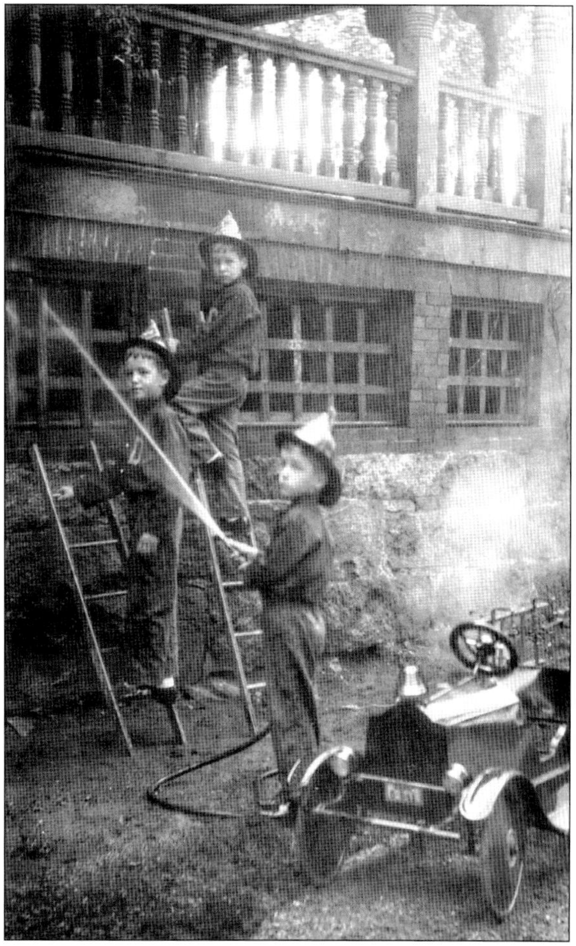

What Next, a musical comedy written and directed by Anne Tibbo, was presented on the town hall stage on July 23 and 24, 1947. This image is of the ballet waltz segment and features, from left to right, Virginia Gosselin, Erdine Howarth, unidentified, Jacqueline Roy, unidentified, Barbara Harvey, and unidentified. The costumes were always well done.

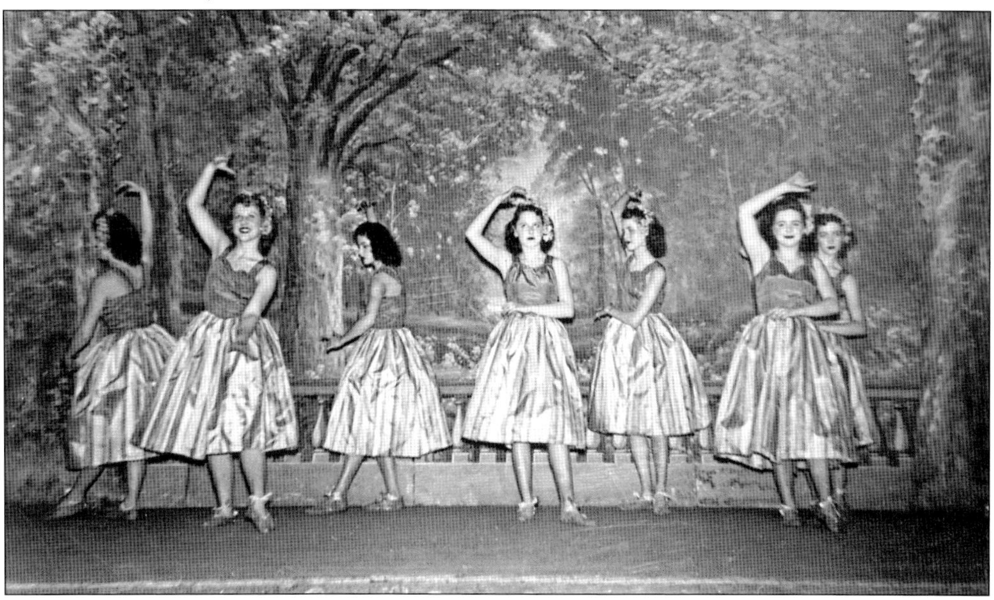

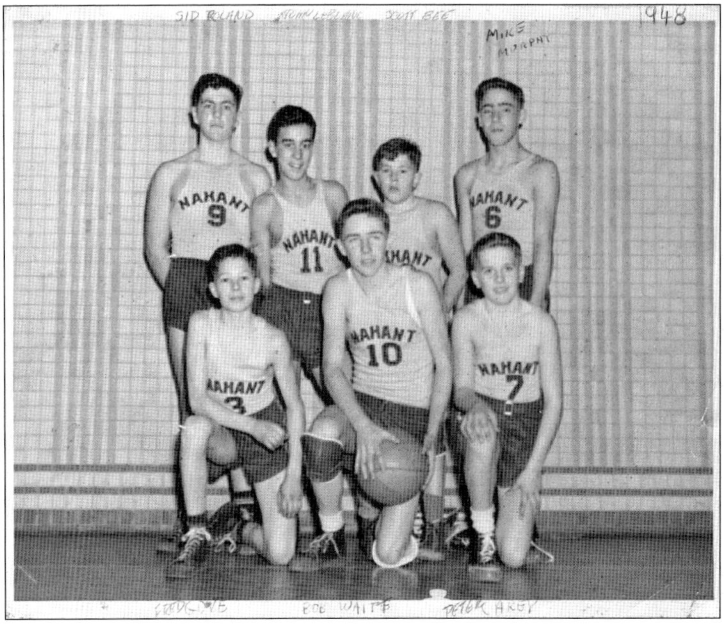

The 1948 Nahant Junior High School basketball team consisted of, from left to right, (first row) Fred Gove, Bob Waitt, and Peter Cary; (second row) Sid Roland, John LeBlanc, Scott Bee, and Mike Murphy. James Brown, not pictured, was an influential Nahant teacher and coach from September 1958 to May 1992 who donated many school sports photographs to the Nahant Historical Society.

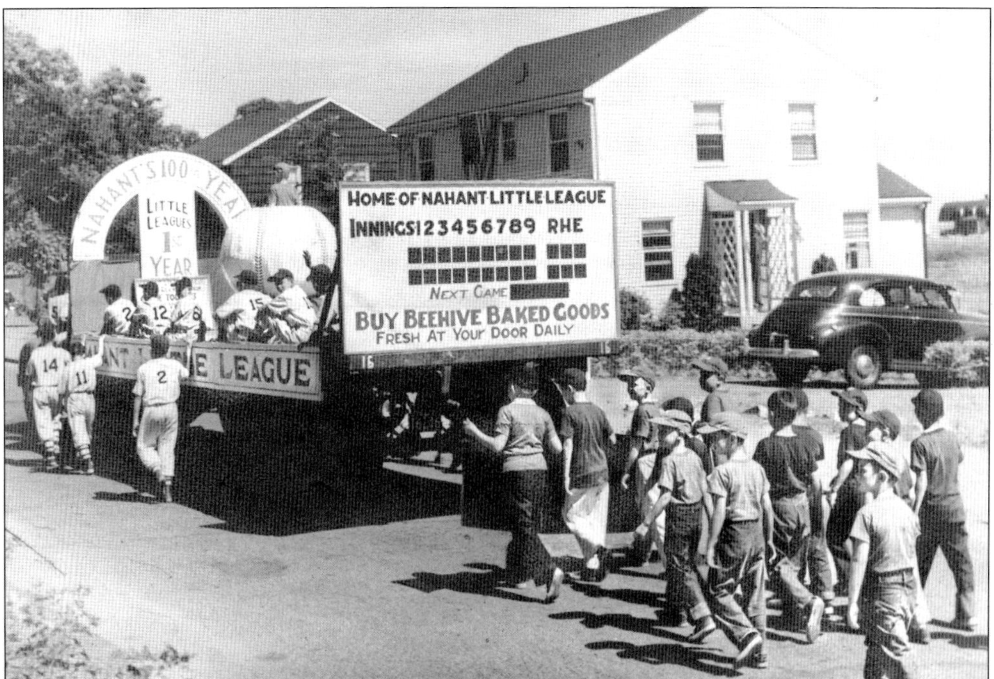

Little League baseball began in 1939 at Williamsport, Pennsylvania, and eventually spread worldwide. The team's float in the Nahant Centennial parade states that 1953 was the first year young Nahanters played in Little League. This image on Spring Road with non-uniformed boys following the float shows the interest was remarkably high.

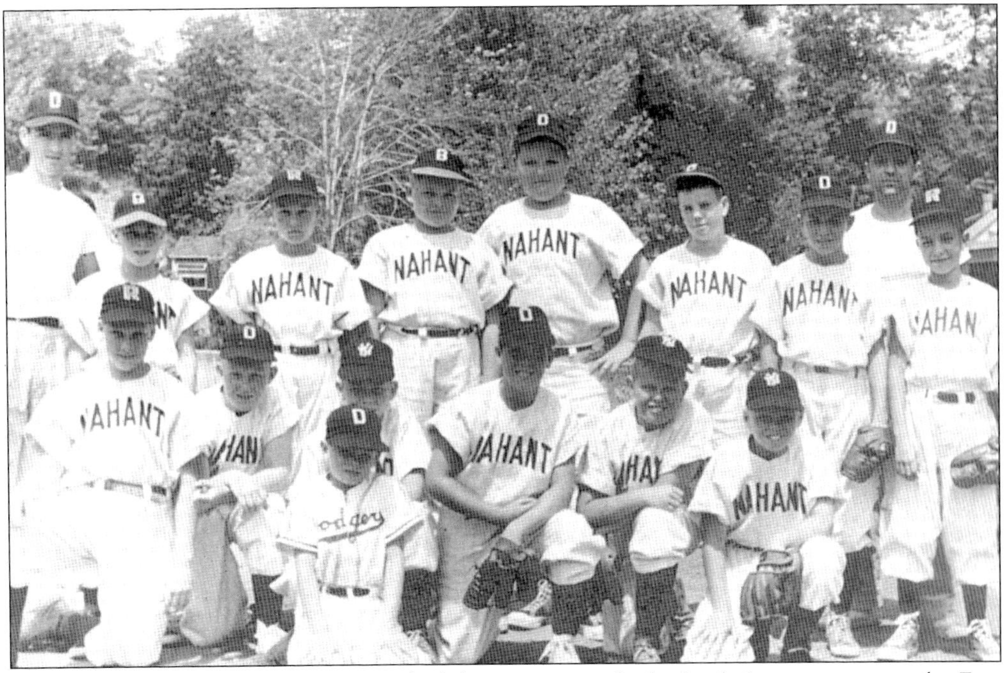

On August 15, 1955, the largest crowd of the season watched a Little League game at the Fort Ruckman field. The mothers of this team defeated their sons in the last inning of a special game, coming from behind to win. The boys demanded a rematch. It was granted, but the fathers stepped in to replace the mothers. No score or winning team was reported.

This 1960 photograph is an example of the American minstrel show that was widespread for over a hundred years. Actors would perform with black makeup in comedic skits, portraying African Americans in a demeaning manner. Many of these images reside in historical collections. It is important to acknowledge this past in order to examine the present and try to move into an egalitarian future.

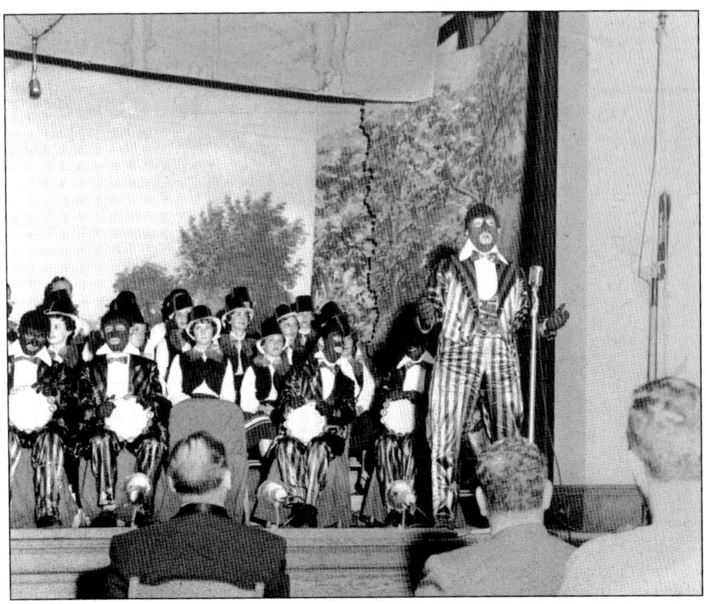

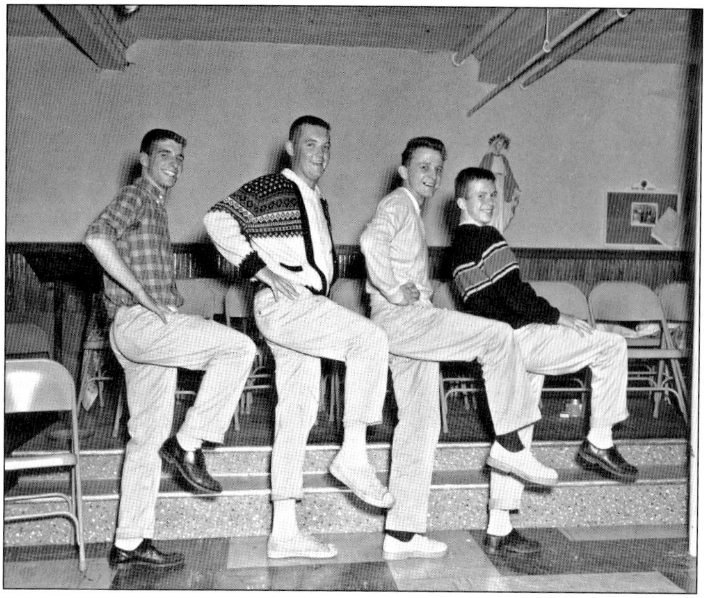

St. Thomas Aquinas Church organized a minstrel show that included vaudeville in 1960. This and the previous image are related to that show. Not all the skits were done in blackface or lampooned racial minorities. Some poked fun at local life or were silly amusements. Rehearsing in the church basement are, from left to right, Jim Cashman, Mike Morton, Jim Munroe (from Lynn), and Stephen Robinson. They performed in female attire.

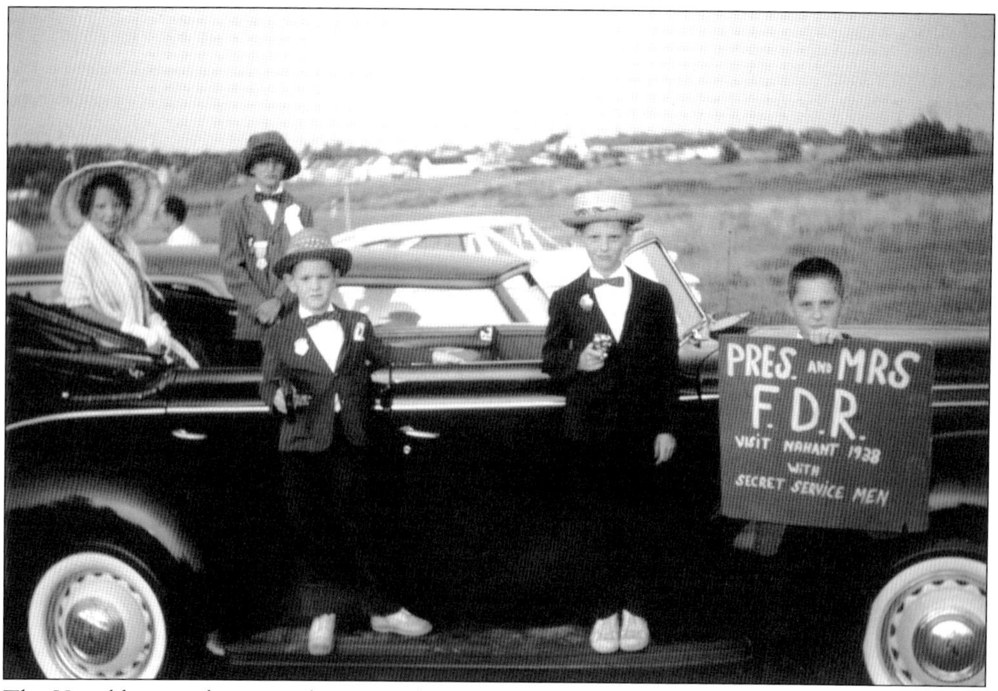

The Horribles parade is a tradition on the Fourth of July. This fun event for children, in 1963, featured a recreation of Pres. Franklin Roosevelt's visit to Nahant in June 1938. Portraying Eleanor in the back seat is Mary Jo Quinn Sanborn, and standing in the back is David Wilson as FDR. The Secret Service men in front are John P. Quinn (on the left) and Paul Wilson. Robert Wilson holds the sign.

In this 1960s image, a group of "soldier boys" takes a break on Pond Beach below the gun emplacement at Fort Ruckman. Steve McManus stands guard, Ken Oxton is assisted by Jason Angiulo, and in front, Dave Oxton watches for invaders from the sea. In the 50 years since this image was shot, the emplacement has been nearly obscured by the natural growth of vegetation.

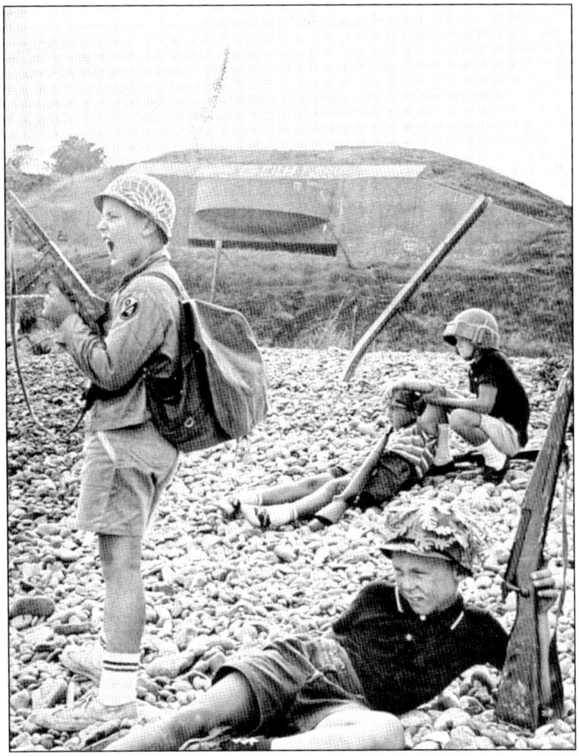

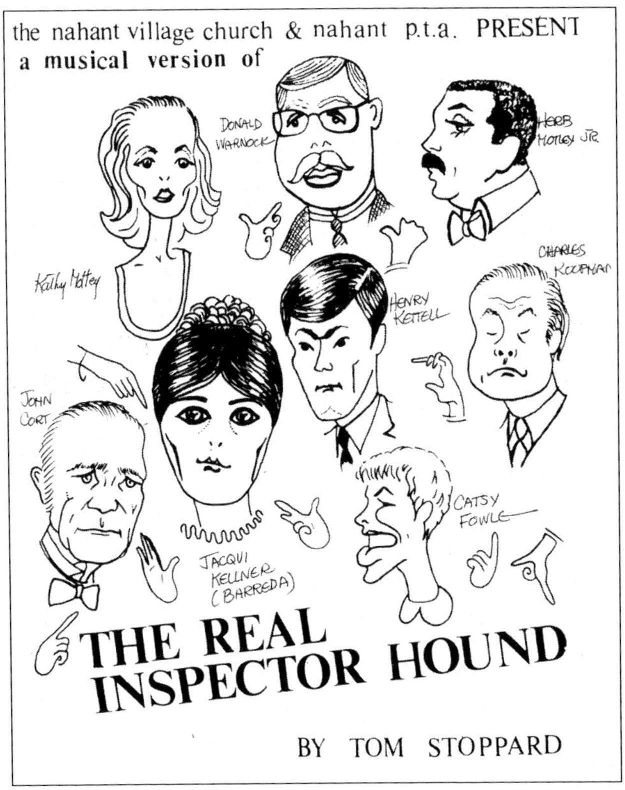

The Real Inspector Hound is a one-act play by Tom Stoppard that was first performed in 1968 and is a parody of Agatha Christie's *The Mousetrap.* This 1970s musical version was presented by the Nahant Village Church and the Nahant Parent Teacher Association. Many of these local performers participated in numerous entertainments that raised funds for various Nahant organizations. The artist of this announcement is unknown.

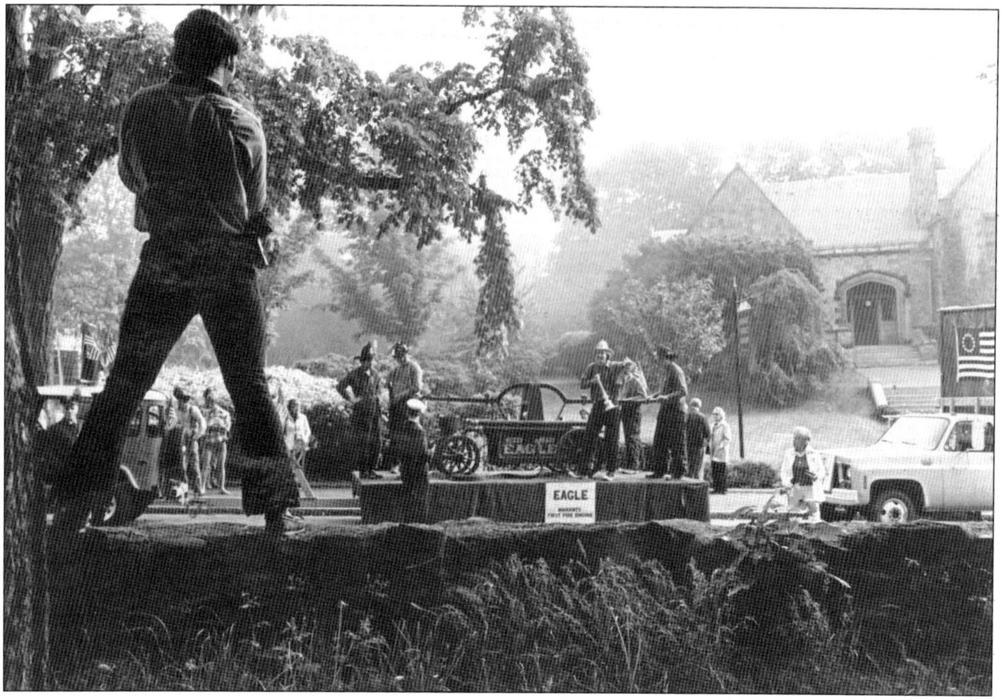

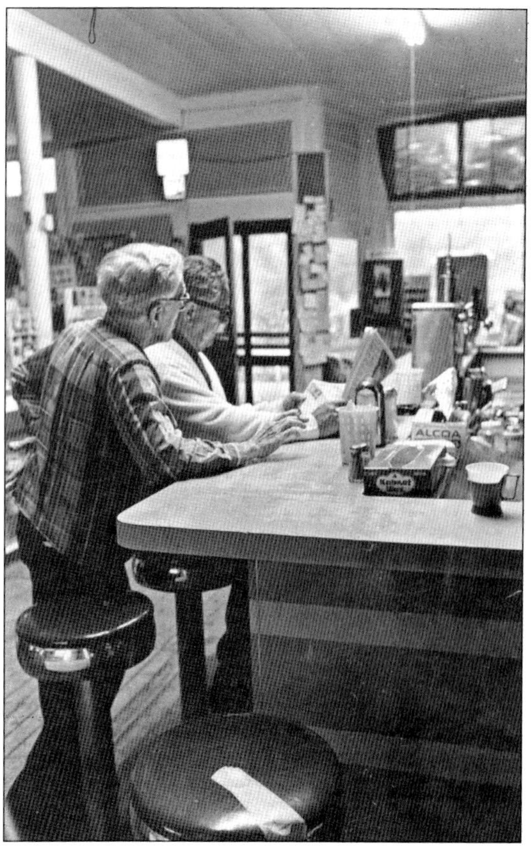

The 1976 Memorial Day parade is forming up, and the 1843 hand pumper has been loaded onto its float. Dennis Forbush is standing on the wall, and fire chief John Quinn (with the white cap) is instructing his men. The firemen accompanying the Eagle that day were Jack Hatfield, Paul Wilson, Bob Lehman, Tom Walsh, Brian Douilette, Richard Comeau, Dennis Forbush, John Dougherty, Chief John Quinn, and Assistant Chief Ray Robidoux.

Two men are taking a break at the counter of the Village Store on the morning of the bicentennial parade, May 31, 1976. This must have been a busy day at the store, where at that time one could get something to drink, an ice cream, or a snack while catching up on local news and of course some gossip. Thomas Hosker was the photographer.

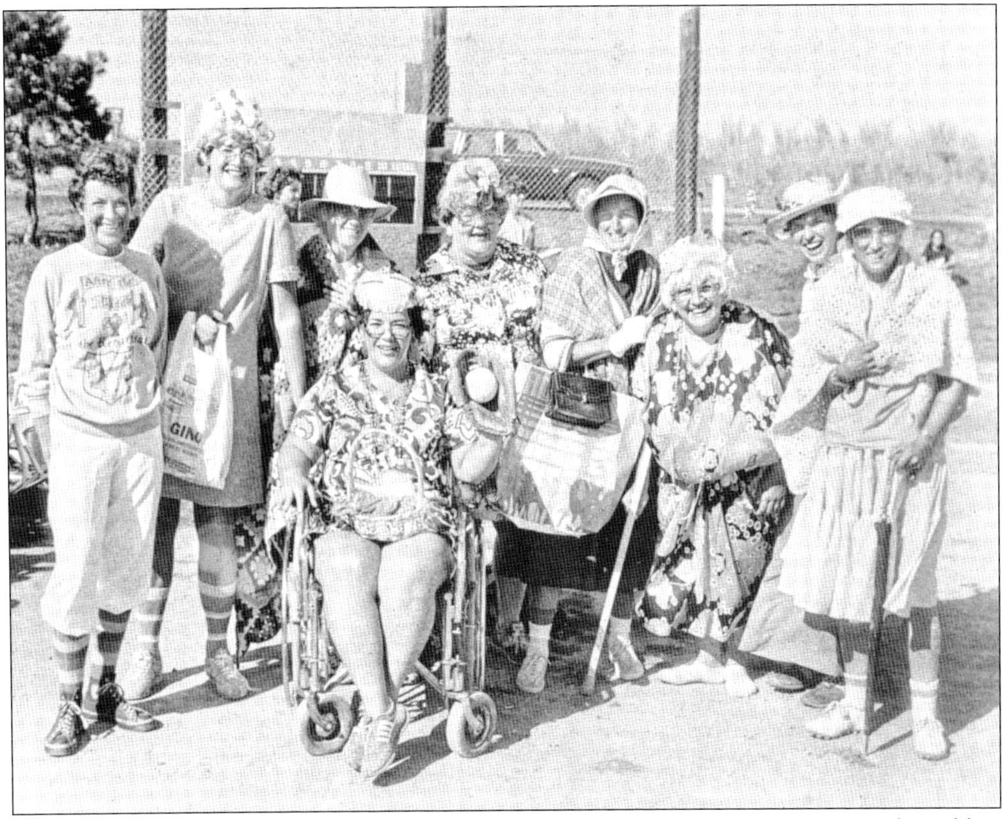

An "Over 30s" versus "Under 30s" women's softball game was played in August 1981. This "older" team, dressed to exaggerate their age, are, from left to right, Catsy Fowle, Pam Szostakowski, Dianne Urany, Penny Ross, Judy Kasper, Bonnie Lombard, Claire Collins, Molly Conlin, and Jeanne Scaglione. Some attempted to run the bases in the wheelchair.

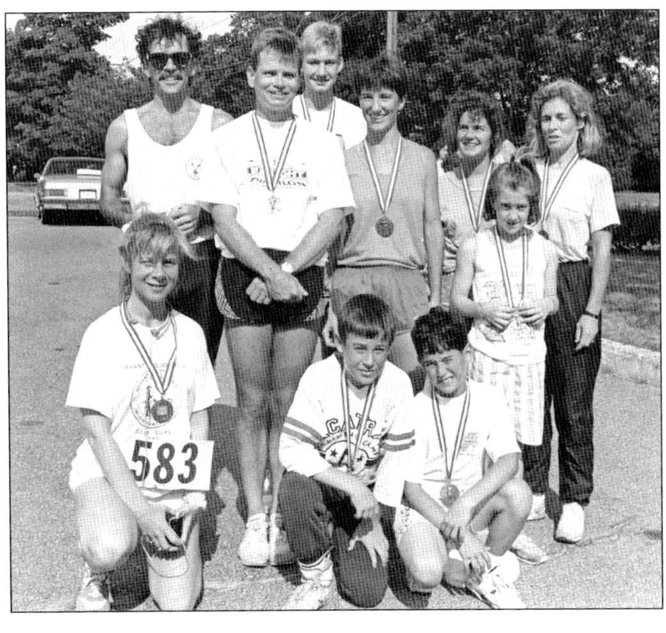

A tradition for the Fourth of July activities was road races. This 1990 photograph by Walter Hoey features some of the winners from various categories. From left to right are (first row, kneeling) Marie Di Lisio, Kevin Manning, and Jason Silva; (second row) Paul Hennessy, unidentified, Tom Flaherty, Trish Livingston, Mary Doyle, Kathy deStefano, and Barbara Devens.

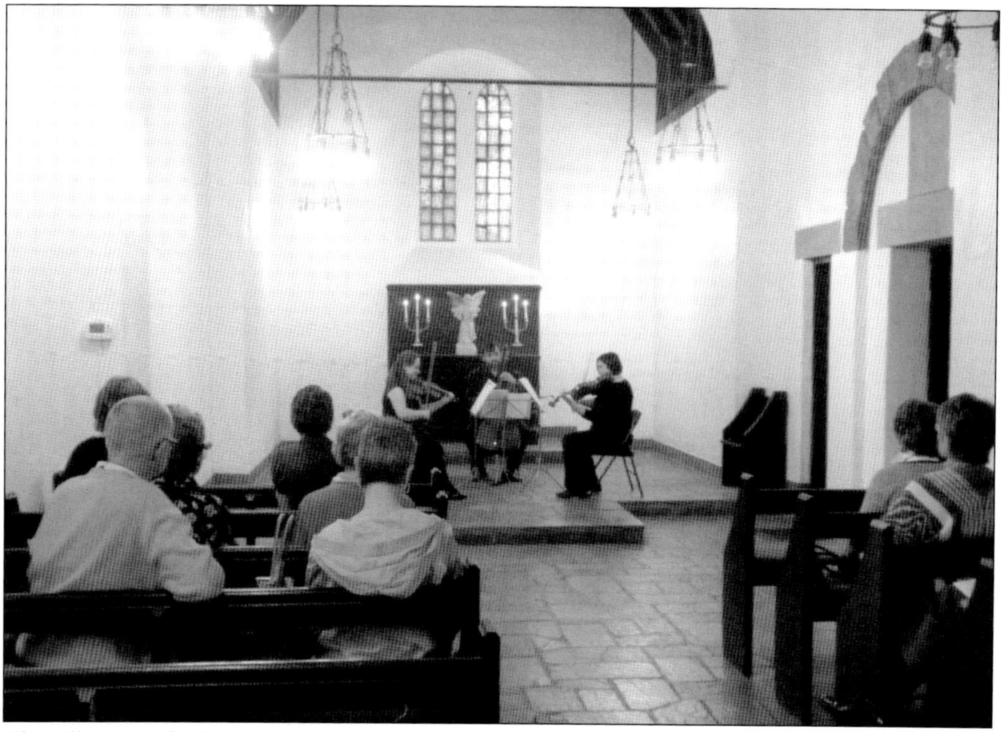

The Ellingwood Chapel Concert Series was started by Jim and Judy Walsh with the Nahant Historical Society in 2000. It brings professional musicians and aspiring students to perform at the chapel and other venues in town. This concert on October 12, 2014, was given by the Trio Kylix and featured, from left to right, violinist Katharina Radlberger (a Nahant resident), cellist Sassan Haghighi, and violinist Karen McConomy. (Courtesy Jim Walsh.)

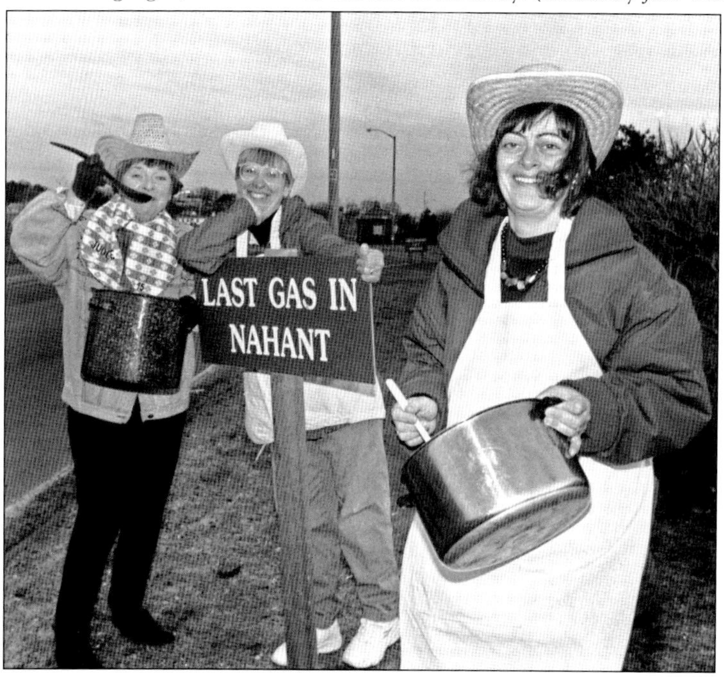

Grassroots fundraising has always been a need, especially in a small town. The 1996 Chili Challenge was an activity to support Nahant Youth Soccer. Out "beating the drum," from left to right, are some of the generous organizers: Molly Conlin, Anne Senk, and Janet Taylor. Everyone must have been well filled and enjoyed a good time.

Bibliography

Amory, Cleveland. *The Proper Bostonians*. New York: E.P. Dutton & Co. Inc, 1947.
Appleton, Thomas Gold. *A Sheaf of Papers*. Boston: Roberts Brothers, 1875.
Basbanes, Nicholas A. *Cross of Snow: A Life of Henry Wadsworth Longfellow*. New York: Alfred A. Knopf, 2020.
Garland, Joseph E. *Boston's North Shore*. Boston and Toronto: Little, Brown and Company, 1978.
Guth, Christine M.E. *Longfellow's Tattoos: Tourism, Collecting, and Japan*. Seattle and London: University of Washington Press, 2004.
Hale, Susan. *Life and Letters of Thomas Gold Appleton*. New York: D. Appleton and Company, 1885.
Hilen, Andrew, ed. *The Letters of Henry Wadsworth Longfellow*. Cambridge: The Belknap Press of Harvard University Press, 1982.
Morison, Samuel Eliot. *William Hickling Prescott*. Boston: Massachusetts Historical Society, 1958.
Paterson, Stanley C., and Carl G. Seaburg. *Nahant on the Rocks*. Nahant: Nahant Historical Society, 1991.
Seaburg, Carl, and Stanley Paterson. *Merchant Prince of Boston: Colonel T.H. Perkins, 1764–1854*. Cambridge: Harvard University Press, 1971.
Shand-Tucci, Douglas. *The Crimson Letter*. Gordonsville, VA: St. Martin's Press, 2003.
Wilson, Fred A. *Some Annals of Nahant*. Boston: Old Corner Book Store, 1928.

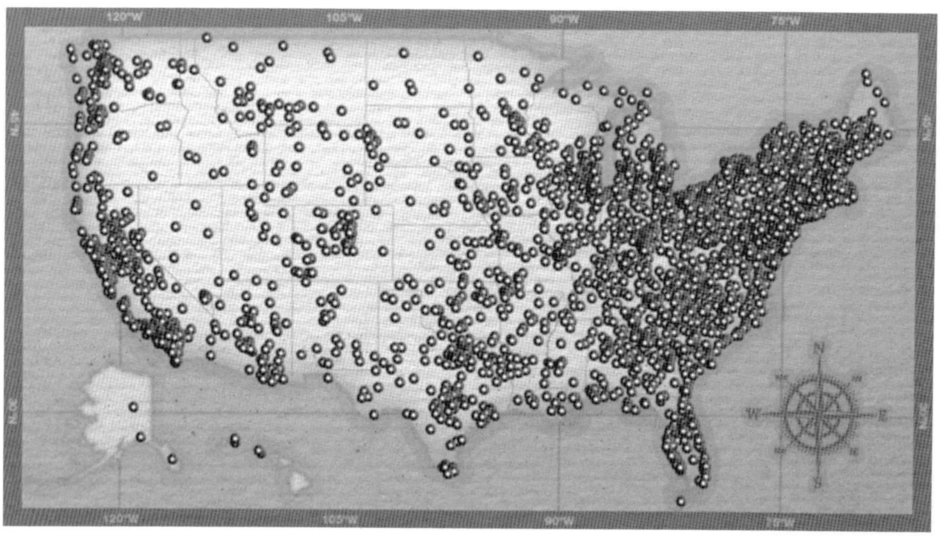